THE NEW ANDY CAPP COLLECTION
NUMBER 1

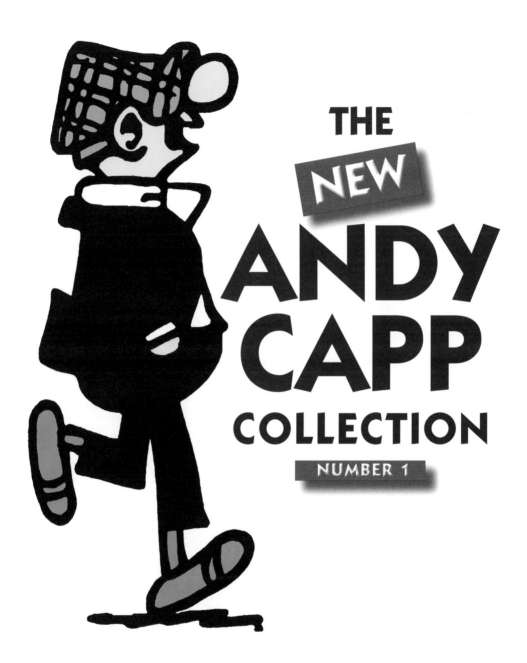

THE
NEW
ANDY
CAPP
COLLECTION
NUMBER 1

David & Charles

Edited by Duncan Ion

Visit Andy at www.andycapp.com

A DAVID & CHARLES BOOK

David & Charles is a subsidiary of F+W (UK) Ltd.,
an F+W Publications Inc. company

First published in the UK in 2004

Distributed in North America
by Adams Media
an F+W Publications Inc. Company
57 Littlefield Street
Avon, MA 02090
www.adamsmedia.com
1-800-872-5627

A catalogue record for this book is available from the British Library.

ISBN 0 7153 1995 7

Printed in Singapore by KHL Printing Co Pte Ltd
for David & Charles
Brunel House   Newton Abbot   Devon

Visit our website at **www.davidandcharles.co.uk**

David & Charles books are available from all good bookshops;
alternatively you can contact our Orderline on (0)1626 334555
or write to us at FREEPOST EX2110, David & Charles Direct,
Newton Abbot, TQ12 4ZZ (no stamp required UK mainland)

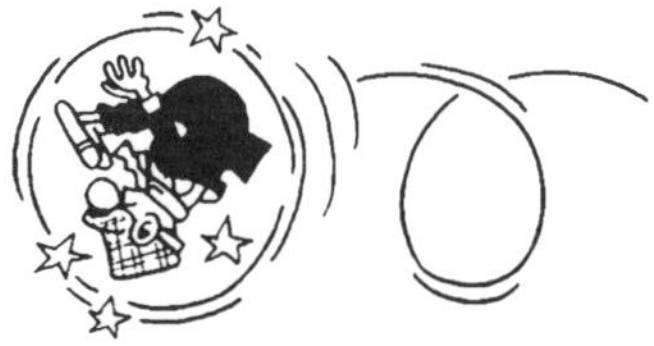

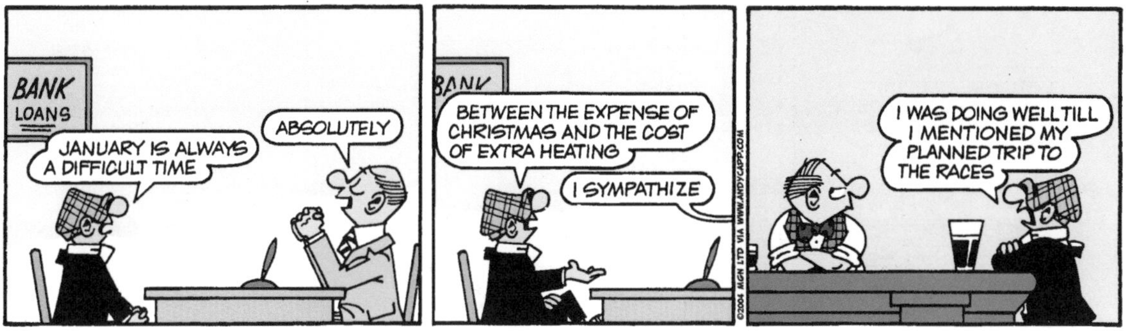

BANK
LOANS
JANUARY IS ALWAYS A DIFFICULT TIME
ABSOLUTELY
BANK
BETWEEN THE EXPENSE OF CHRISTMAS AND THE COST OF EXTRA HEATING
I SYMPATHIZE
©2004 MGN LTD VIA WWW.ANDYCAPP.COM
I WAS DOING WELL TILL I MENTIONED MY PLANNED TRIP TO THE RACES

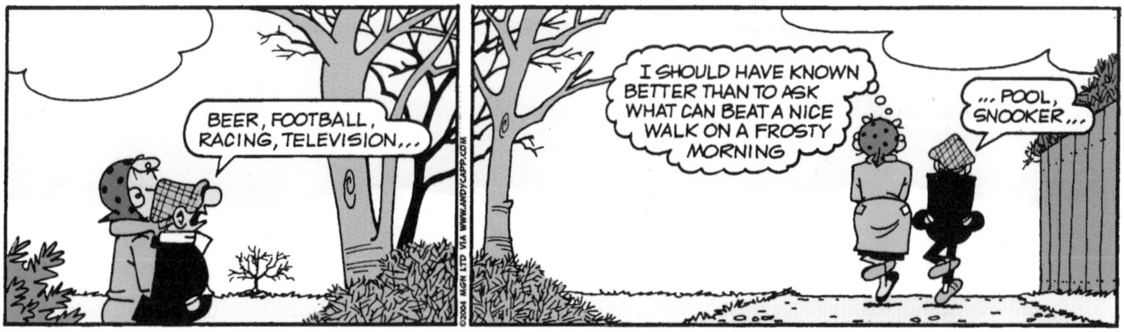

BEER, FOOTBALL, RACING, TELEVISION,..
©2004 MGN LTD VIA WWW.ANDYCAPP.COM
I SHOULD HAVE KNOWN BETTER THAN TO ASK WHAT CAN BEAT A NICE WALK ON A FROSTY MORNING
.., POOL, SNOOKER,..

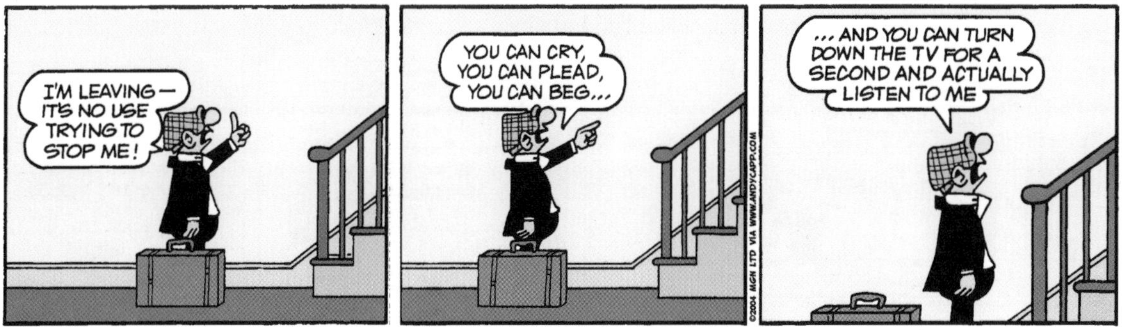

I'M LEAVING — IT'S NO USE TRYING TO STOP ME!
YOU CAN CRY, YOU CAN PLEAD, YOU CAN BEG,..
©2004 MGN LTD VIA WWW.ANDYCAPP.COM
... AND YOU CAN TURN DOWN THE TV FOR A SECOND AND ACTUALLY LISTEN TO ME

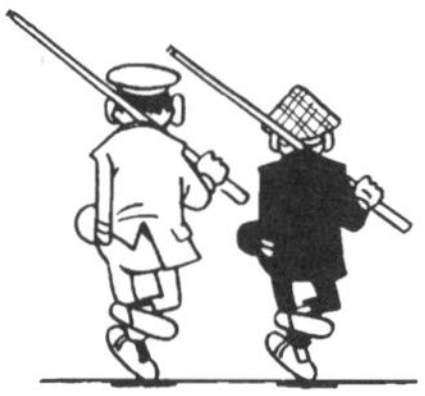

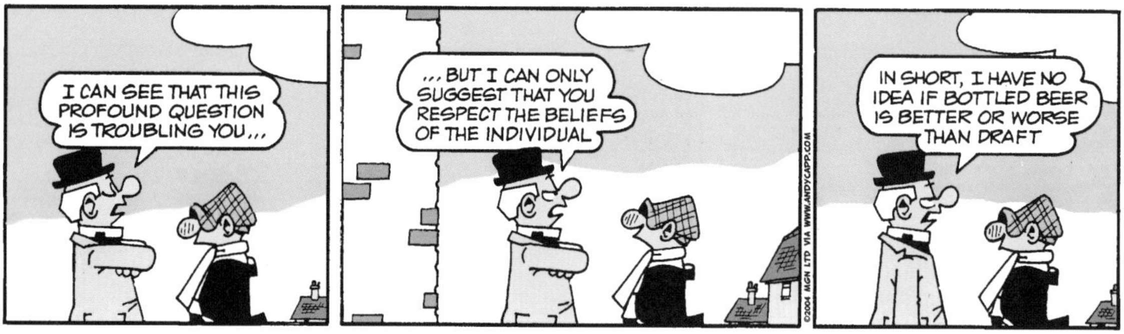

I CAN SEE THAT THIS PROFOUND QUESTION IS TROUBLING YOU,,,
,,, BUT I CAN ONLY SUGGEST THAT YOU RESPECT THE BELIEFS OF THE INDIVIDUAL
IN SHORT, I HAVE NO IDEA IF BOTTLED BEER IS BETTER OR WORSE THAN DRAFT
©2004 MGN LTD VIA WWW.ANDYCAPP.COM

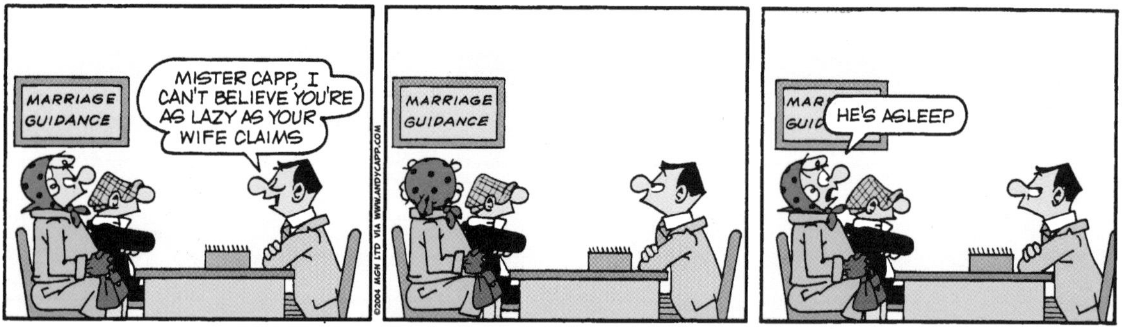

MARRIAGE GUIDANCE
MISTER CAPP, I CAN'T BELIEVE YOU'RE AS LAZY AS YOUR WIFE CLAIMS
©2004 MGN LTD VIA WWW.ANDYCAPP.COM
MARRIAGE GUIDANCE
HE'S ASLEEP

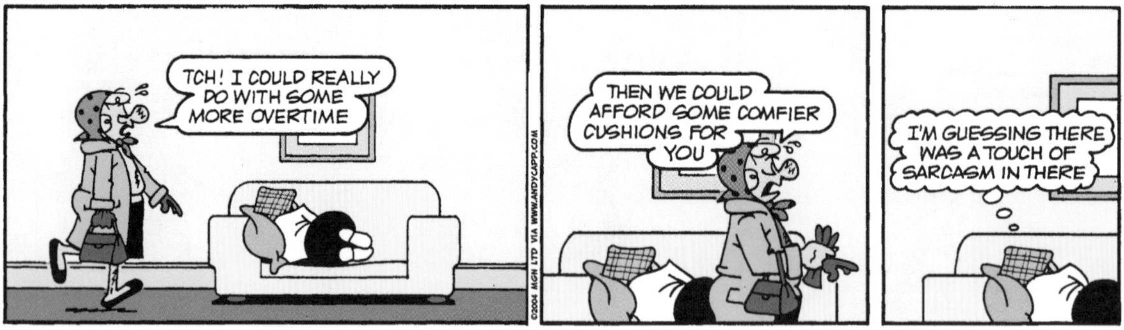

TCH! I COULD REALLY DO WITH SOME MORE OVERTIME
©2004 MGN LTD VIA WWW.ANDYCAPP.COM
THEN WE COULD AFFORD SOME COMFIER CUSHIONS FOR YOU
I'M GUESSING THERE WAS A TOUCH OF SARCASM IN THERE

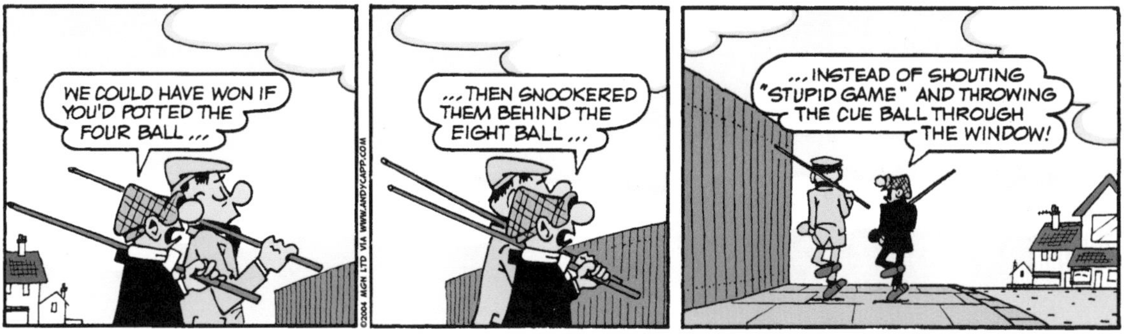
WE COULD HAVE WON IF YOU'D POTTED THE FOUR BALL ...
©2004 MGN LTD VIA WWW.ANDYCAPP.COM
... THEN SNOOKERED THEM BEHIND THE EIGHT BALL ...
... INSTEAD OF SHOUTING "STUPID GAME" AND THROWING THE CUE BALL THROUGH THE WINDOW!

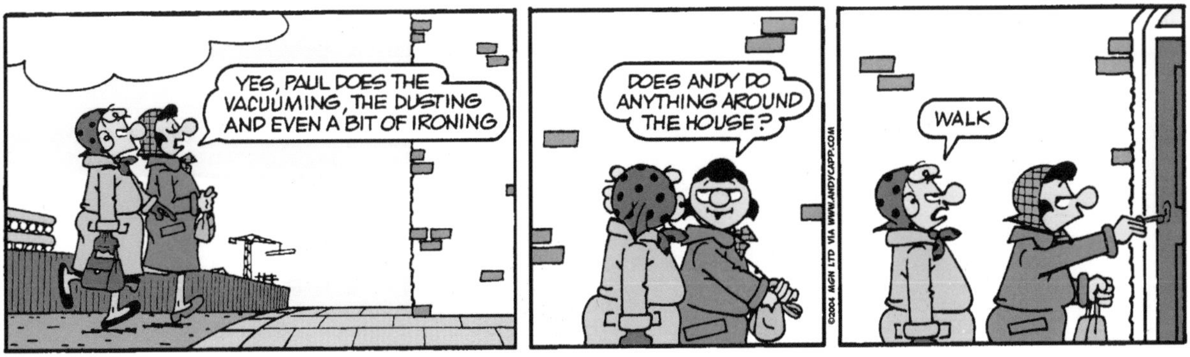
YES, PAUL DOES THE VACUUMING, THE DUSTING AND EVEN A BIT OF IRONING
DOES ANDY DO ANYTHING AROUND THE HOUSE?
©2004 MGN LTD VIA WWW.ANDYCAPP.COM
WALK

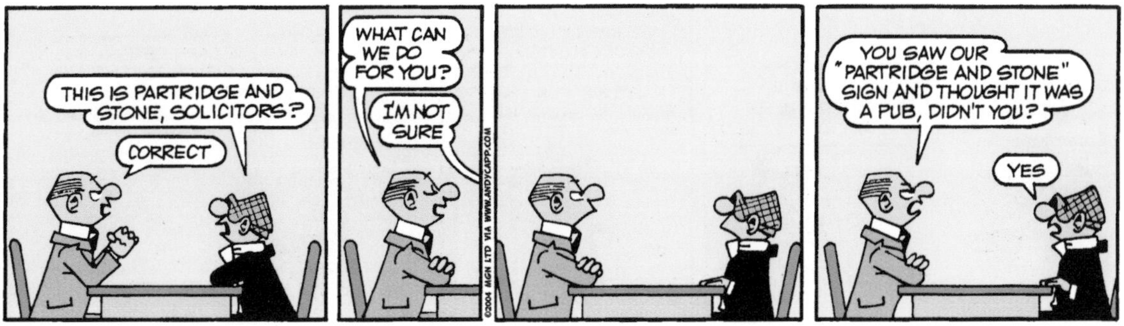
THIS IS PARTRIDGE AND STONE, SOLICITORS?
CORRECT
WHAT CAN WE DO FOR YOU?
I'M NOT SURE
©2004 MGN LTD VIA WWW.ANDYCAPP.COM
YOU SAW OUR "PARTRIDGE AND STONE" SIGN AND THOUGHT IT WAS A PUB, DIDN'T YOU?
YES

IT CERTAINLY TAUGHT *US* A LESSON, FLO
I HOPE *YOU'VE* GOT YOUR VALUABLES IN A SAFE PLACE
ABSOLUTELY
IT'S CALLED A PAWN SHOP
©2004 MGN LTD VIA WWW.ANDYCAPP.COM

I DON'T CARE *WHAT* RUBY AND FLO SAY— WE ARE *NOT* SEXIST
WHAT WE NEED IS A NEUTRAL OPINION—LET'S ASK THE BARMAID
HOI! BLONDIE!
©2004 MGN LTD VIA WWW.ANDYCAPP.COM

MARRIAGE GUIDANCE
IT'S IMPORTANT TO COMPROMISE WHERE IN-LAWS ARE CONCERNED
MRS. CAPP, PERHAPS YOU COULD VISIT YOUR MOTHER AT *HER* HOUSE RATHER THAN HER ALWAYS COMING TO YOU
AND, MR. CAPP, PERHAPS YOU COULD STOP REFERRING TO HER AS "THAT SATANIC HAG FROM HELL'S BOWELS"
©2004 MGN LTD VIA WWW.ANDYCAPP.COM

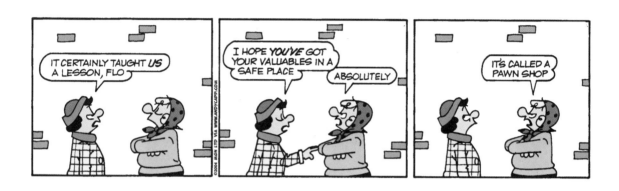

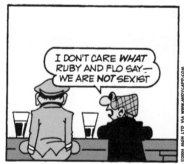

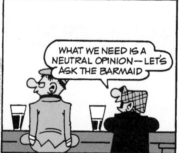

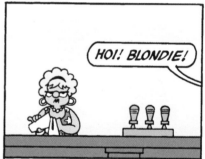

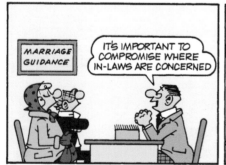

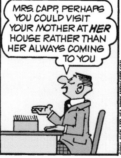

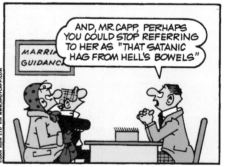

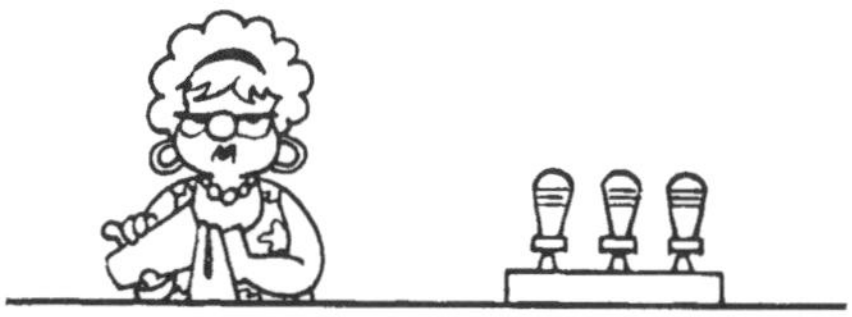

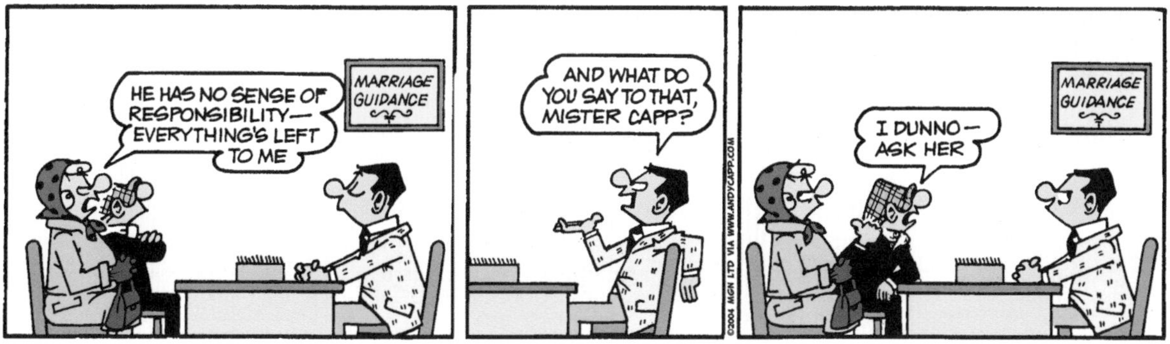

MARRIAGE GUIDANCE
HE HAS NO SENSE OF RESPONSIBILITY— EVERYTHING'S LEFT TO ME
AND WHAT DO YOU SAY TO THAT, MISTER CAPP?
©2004 MGN LTD VIA WWW.ANDYCAPP.COM
MARRIAGE GUIDANCE
I DUNNO — ASK HER

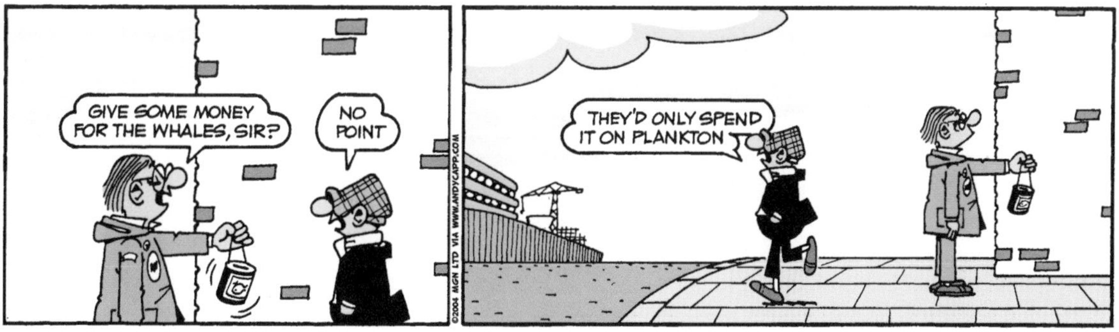

GIVE SOME MONEY FOR THE WHALES, SIR?
NO POINT
©2004 MGN LTD VIA WWW.ANDYCAPP.COM
THEY'D ONLY SPEND IT ON PLANKTON

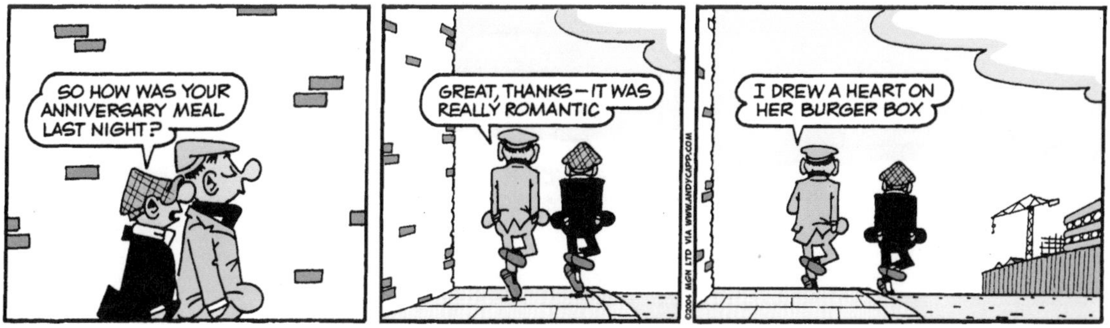

SO HOW WAS YOUR ANNIVERSARY MEAL LAST NIGHT?
GREAT, THANKS — IT WAS REALLY ROMANTIC
©2004 MGN LTD VIA WWW.ANDYCAPP.COM
I DREW A HEART ON HER BURGER BOX

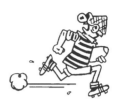

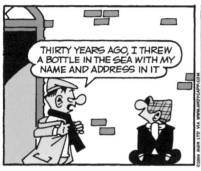

THIRTY YEARS AGO, I THREW A BOTTLE IN THE SEA WITH MY NAME AND ADDRESS IN IT
©2004 MGN LTD VIA WWW.ANDYCAPP.COM
IT'S BEEN FOUND – I GOT A LETTER FROM AUSTRALIA THIS MORNING
GREAT!
NOT REALLY — I'VE BEEN FINED FOR LITTERING A BEACH IN SYDNEY

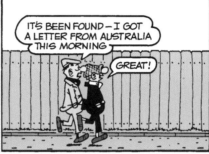

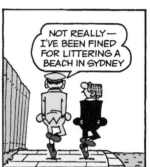

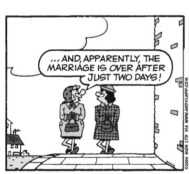

... AND, APPARENTLY, THE MARRIAGE IS OVER AFTER JUST TWO DAYS!
©2004 MGN LTD VIA WWW.ANDYCAPP.COM
WELL, I WAS AT THE WEDDING AND THE SIGNS WEREN'T GOOD...
... INSTEAD OF "I DO," HE SAID "I SUPPOSE SO"

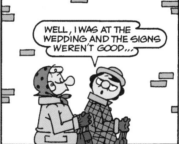

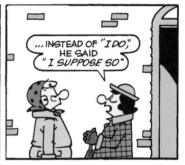

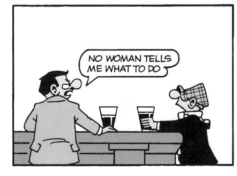

NO WOMAN TELLS ME WHAT TO DO
TAKE MY WIFE — FOR BREAKFAST, SHE LIKES A FOUR-MINUTE BOILED EGG ...
... WELL, SOMETIMES, I ONLY BOIL IT FOR THREE MINUTES FIFTY!
YOU REBEL
©2004 MGN LTD VIA WWW.ANDYCAPP.COM

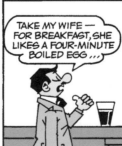

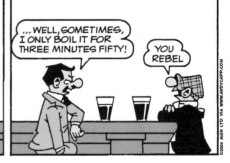

©2004 MGN LTD VIA WWW.ANDYCAPP.COM
I'M REALLY SORRY, FRANK. IT WAS AN ACCIDENT! ARE YOU OKAY? CAN I GET YOU SOMETHING? I'LL FETCH THE TRAINER!
WHO'S FRANK?
HE OWNS A PUB

SHE'S A GEM, MY WIFE
WHEN I GET HOME FROM WORK, SHE HAS MY DINNER ON THE TABLE, WAITING FOR ME
©2004 MGN LTD VIA WWW.ANDYCAPP.COM
WHEN I GET HOME FROM THE PUB, FLO HAS MY DINNER ON THE WALL, WAITING FOR ME

AND NOW HE'S ASKED ME TO SIGN A PRENUPTIAL AGREEMENT!
DID YOU AND ANDY DO THAT?
OH, YES,,,
,,,IF HE LEAVES ME, I GET HALF A POOL CUE

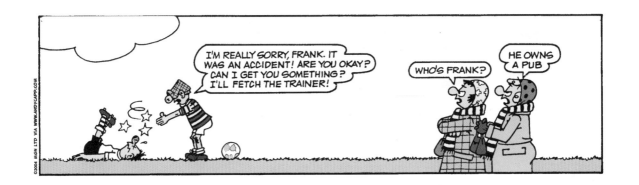

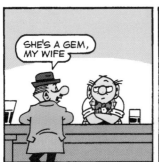

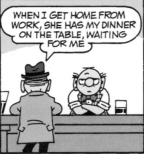

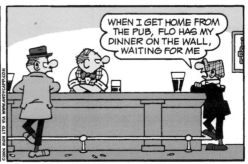

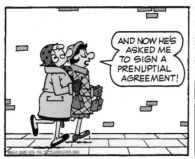

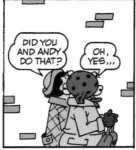

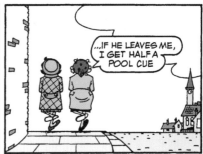

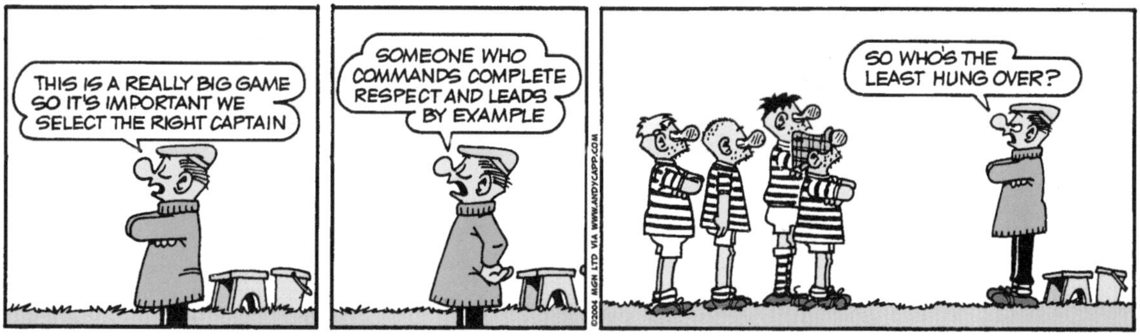
THIS IS A REALLY BIG GAME SO IT'S IMPORTANT WE SELECT THE RIGHT CAPTAIN
SOMEONE WHO COMMANDS COMPLETE RESPECT AND LEADS BY EXAMPLE
©2004 MGN LTD VIA WWW.ANDYCAPP.COM
SO WHO'S THE LEAST HUNG OVER?

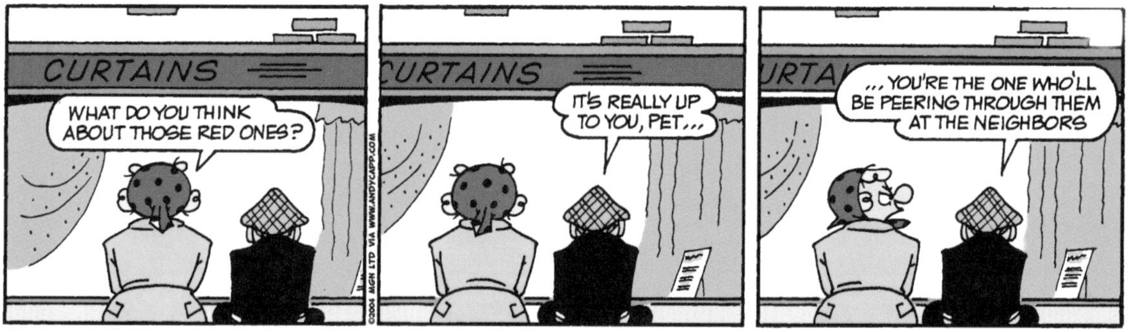
CURTAINS
WHAT DO YOU THINK ABOUT THOSE RED ONES?
©2004 MGN LTD VIA WWW.ANDYCAPP.COM
IT'S REALLY UP TO YOU, PET,,,
,,,YOU'RE THE ONE WHO'LL BE PEERING THROUGH THEM AT THE NEIGHBORS

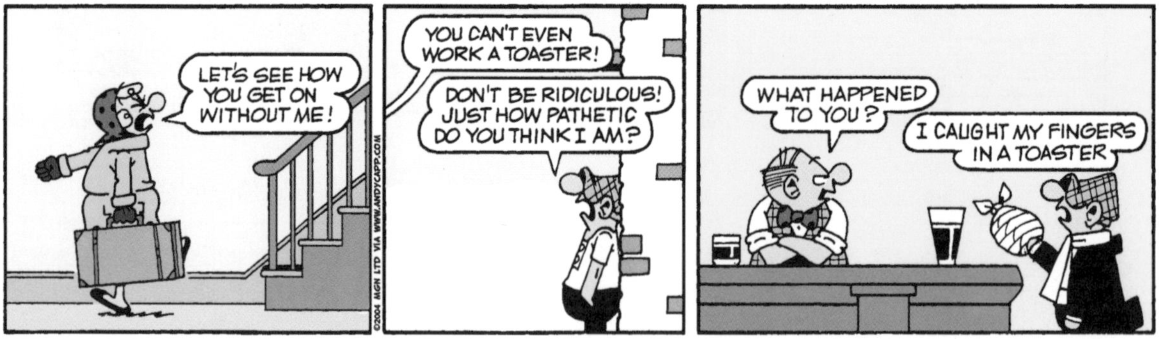
LET'S SEE HOW YOU GET ON WITHOUT ME!
©2004 MGN LTD VIA WWW.ANDYCAPP.COM
YOU CAN'T EVEN WORK A TOASTER!
DON'T BE RIDICULOUS! JUST HOW PATHETIC DO YOU THINK I AM?
WHAT HAPPENED TO YOU?
I CAUGHT MY FINGERS IN A TOASTER

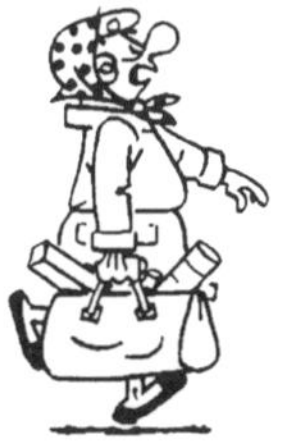

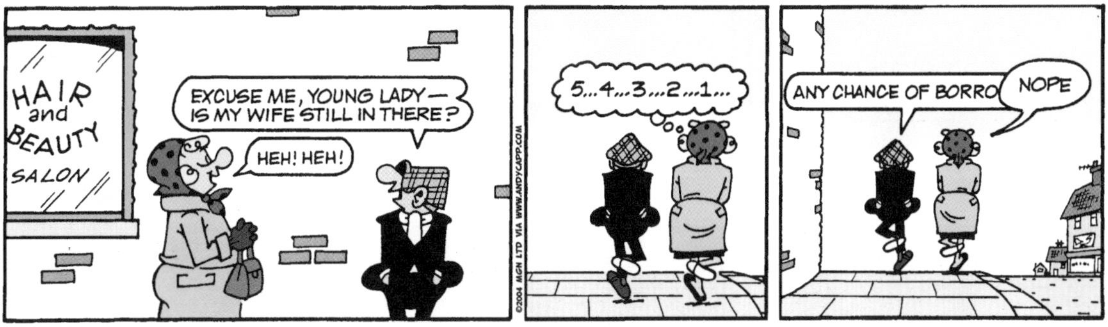
HAIR and BEAUTY SALON
EXCUSE ME, YOUNG LADY — IS MY WIFE STILL IN THERE?
HEH! HEH!
©2004 MGN LTD VIA WWW.ANDYCAPP.COM
5...4...3...2...1...
ANY CHANCE OF BORRO
NOPE

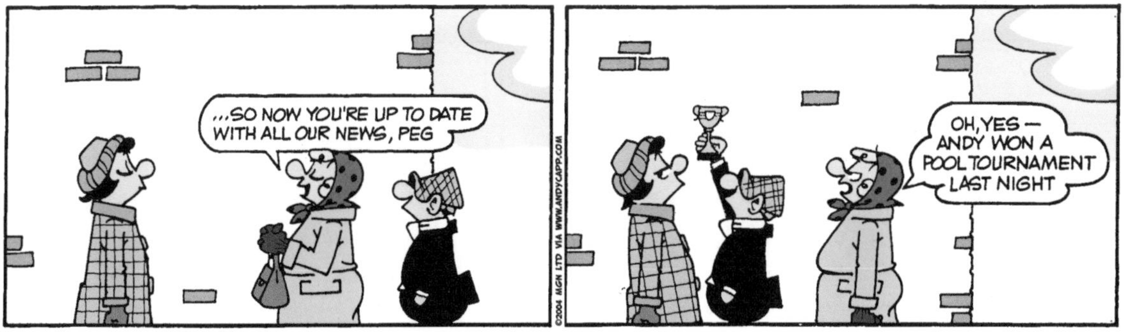
...SO NOW YOU'RE UP TO DATE WITH ALL OUR NEWS, PEG
©2004 MGN LTD VIA WWW.ANDYCAPP.COM
OH, YES — ANDY WON A POOL TOURNAMENT LAST NIGHT

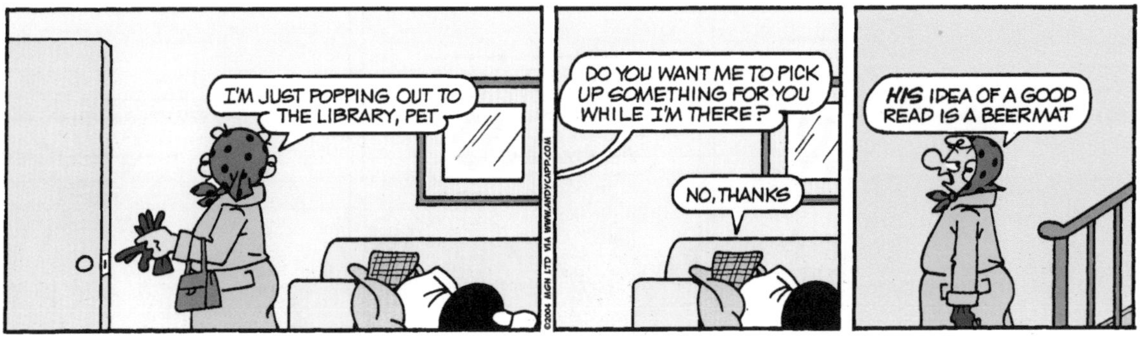
I'M JUST POPPING OUT TO THE LIBRARY, PET
©2004 MGN LTD VIA WWW.ANDYCAPP.COM
DO YOU WANT ME TO PICK UP SOMETHING FOR YOU WHILE I'M THERE?
NO, THANKS
HIS IDEA OF A GOOD READ IS A BEERMAT

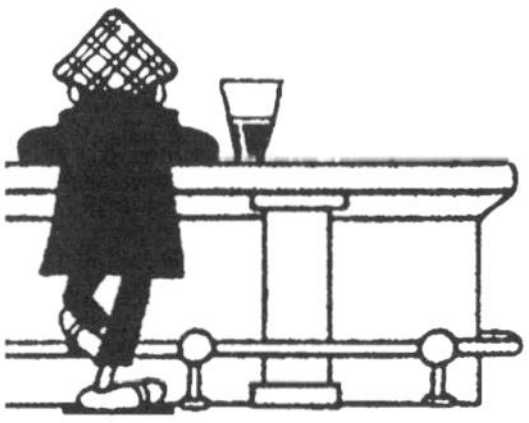

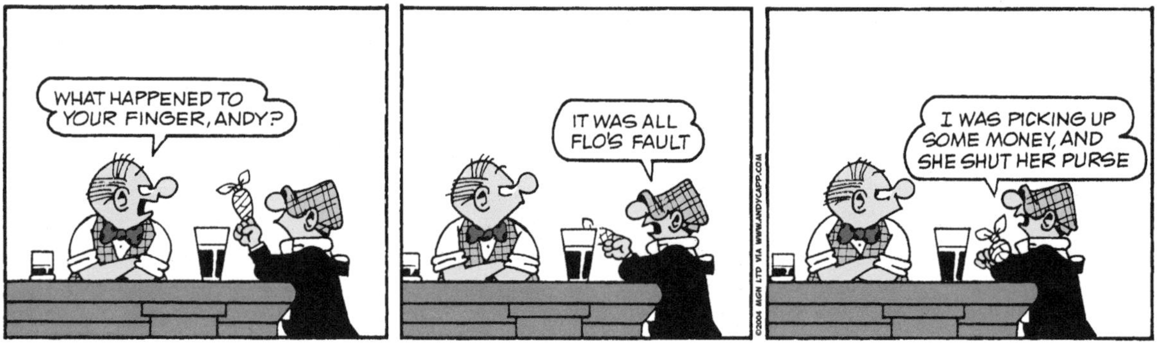
WHAT HAPPENED TO YOUR FINGER, ANDY?
IT WAS ALL FLO'S FAULT
©2004 MGN LTD VIA WWW.ANDYCAPP.COM
I WAS PICKING UP SOME MONEY, AND SHE SHUT HER PURSE

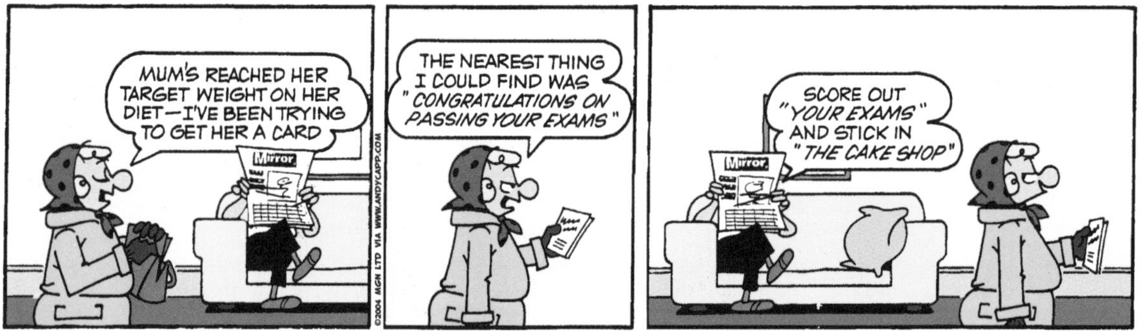
MUM'S REACHED HER TARGET WEIGHT ON HER DIET—I'VE BEEN TRYING TO GET HER A CARD
Mirror
©2004 MGN LTD VIA WWW.ANDYCAPP.COM
THE NEAREST THING I COULD FIND WAS "*CONGRATULATIONS ON PASSING YOUR EXAMS*"
Mirror
SCORE OUT "*YOUR EXAMS*" AND STICK IN "*THE CAKE SHOP*"

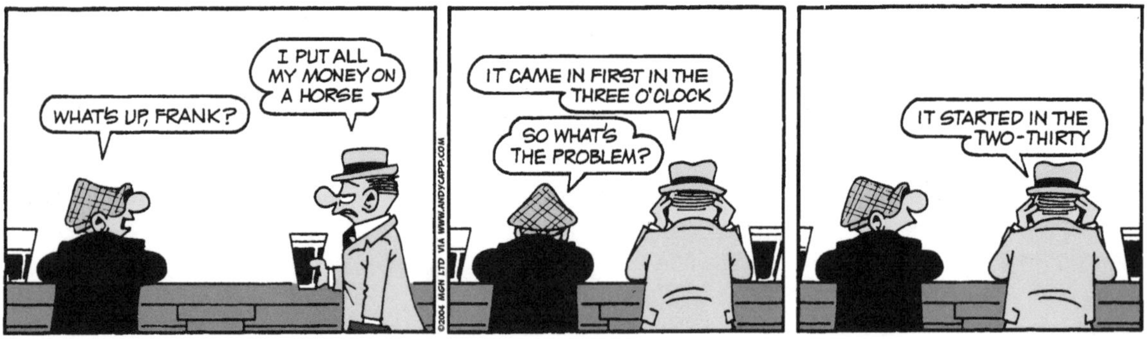
WHAT'S UP, FRANK?
I PUT ALL MY MONEY ON A HORSE
©2004 MGN LTD VIA WWW.ANDYCAPP.COM
IT CAME IN FIRST IN THE THREE O'CLOCK
SO WHAT'S THE PROBLEM?
IT STARTED IN THE TWO-THIRTY

I CAN'T WIN, CAN I? IF I COME HOME AT **FOUR** IN THE MORNING, YOU'RE ANNOYED... IF I COME HOME AT **FIVE** IN THE MORNING, YOU'RE ANNOYED...
©2004 MGN LTD VIA WWW.ANDYCAPP.COM

HE IS **SO** ROMANTIC! I'D BEEN AT MY MUM'S FOR TWO DAYS...
...AND WHEN I GOT HOME, HE'D LEFT ROSES ALL OVER THE BEDROOM!
JUST LIKE ANDY!
©2004 MGN LTD VIA WWW.ANDYCAPP.COM
WELL, EMPTY BEER CANS... ROSES... SIMILAR

ONE HOUR— THAT'S ALL I ASKED FOR!
©2004 MGN LTD VIA WWW.ANDYCAPP.COM
BE CIVIL TO MY MUM FOR **ONE** HOUR WHILE WE'RE VISITING!
I TRIED, PET
YOU **TRIED**? SHE HADN'T ANSWERED THE DOOR AND YOU INSULTED HER THROUGH THE LETTER BOX!

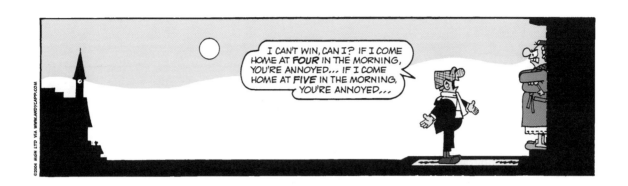

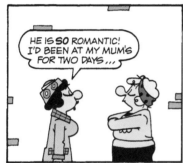

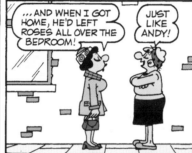

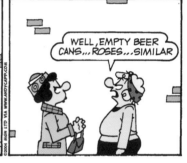

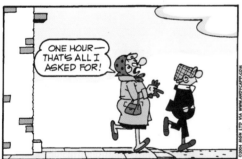

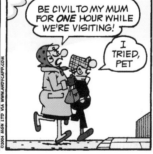

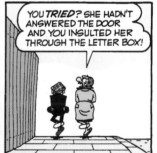

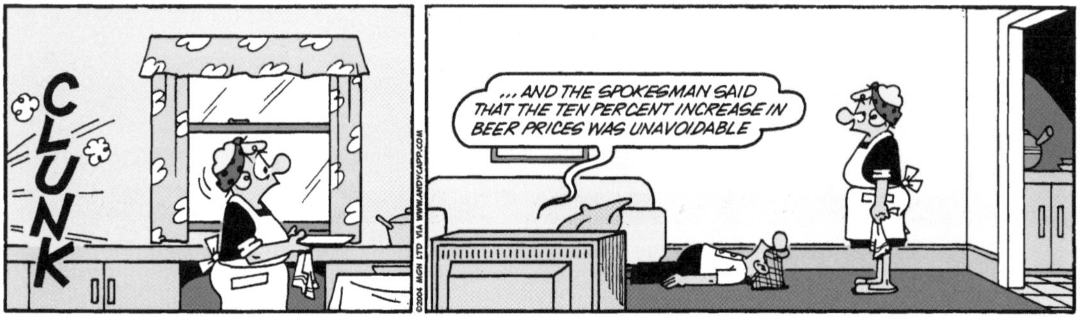
CLUNK
©2004 MGN LTD VIA WWW.ANDYCAPP.COM
... AND THE SPOKESMAN SAID THAT THE TEN PERCENT INCREASE IN BEER PRICES WAS UNAVOIDABLE

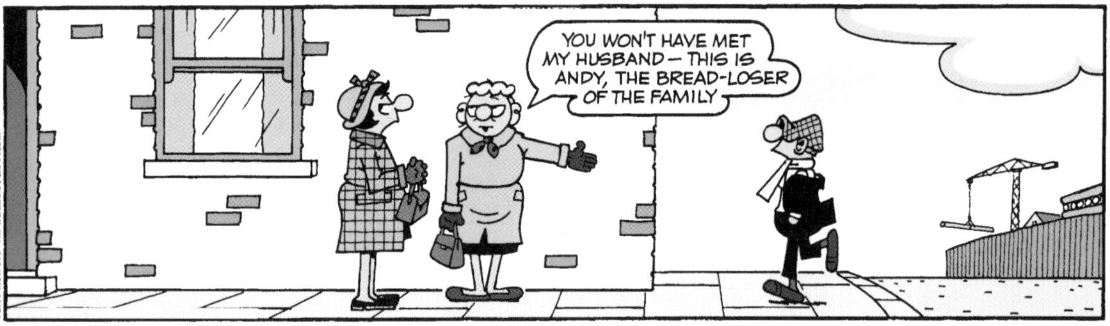
©2004 MGN LTD VIA WWW.ANDYCAPP.COM
YOU WON'T HAVE MET MY HUSBAND – THIS IS ANDY, THE BREAD-LOSER OF THE FAMILY

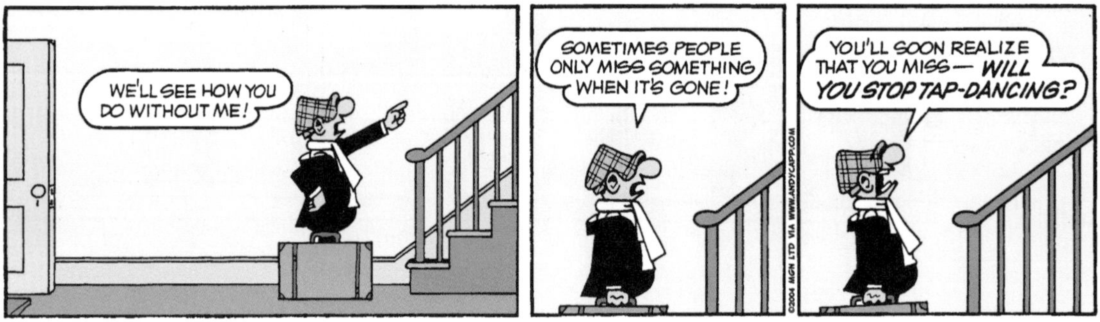
WE'LL SEE HOW YOU DO WITHOUT ME!
SOMETIMES PEOPLE ONLY MISS SOMETHING WHEN IT'S GONE!
©2004 MGN LTD VIA WWW.ANDYCAPP.COM
YOU'LL SOON REALIZE THAT YOU MISS— WILL YOU STOP TAP-DANCING?

...AND SHE'S ACTUALLY TRYING TO SAY SHE HASN'T HAD A FACE-LIFT!
©2004 MGN LTD VIA WWW.ANDYCAPP.COM
WELL, YOU DON'T KNOW FOR SURE, AGNES — MAYBE SHE HASN'T
PUT IT THIS WAY — WHEN SHE WINKS WITH HER RIGHT EYE, HER LEFT EAR GOES UP FOUR INCHES!

MY MOTHER HAS JUST BEEN ON THE PHONE!
©2004 MGN LTD VIA WWW.ANDYCAPP.COM
SHE WAS BENDING DOWN, PET, TYING HER SHOELACE...
...THESE KIDS HAD A GIANT WATER PISTOL — I'M ONLY HUMAN, PET! FLESH AND BLOOD!

I HONESTLY FEEL I COME ABOUT FOURTH IN HIS LIST OF PRIORITIES
MARRIAGE GUIDANCE
THAT'S AFTER FOOTBALL, BEER AND SNOOKER
©2004 MGN LTD VIA WWW.ANDYCAPP.COM
WITH HINDSIGHT, I PROBABLY SHOULDN'T HAVE SAID, "WHAT ABOUT HORSE RACING?"

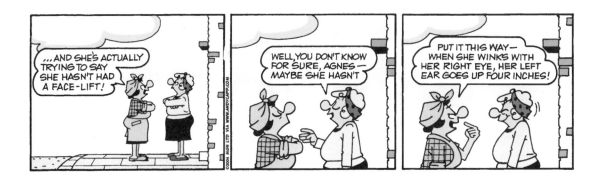

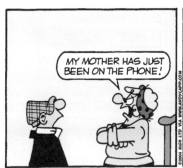

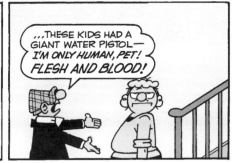

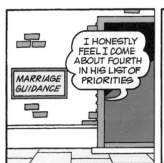

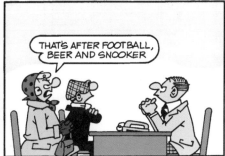

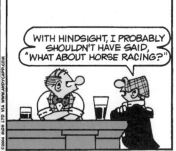

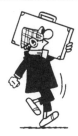

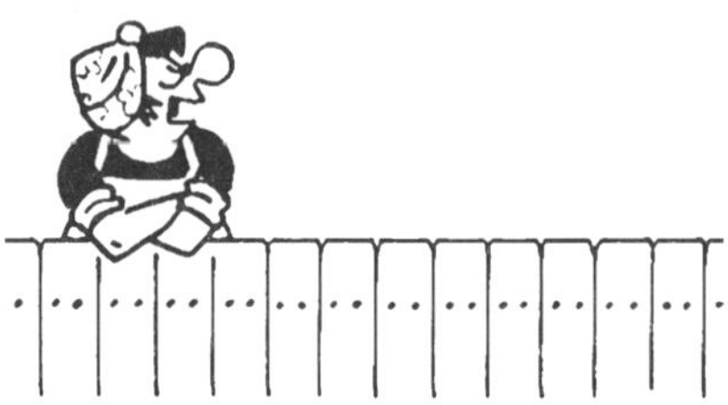

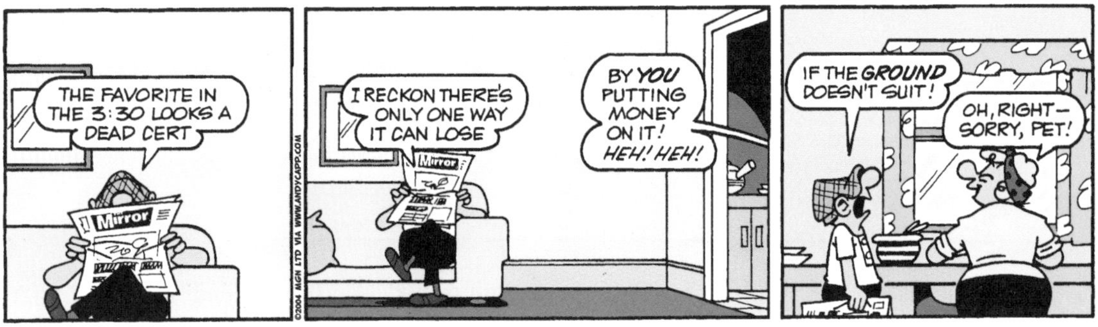
THE FAVORITE IN THE 3:30 LOOKS A DEAD CERT
Mirror
©2004 MGN LTD VIA WWW.ANDYCAPP.COM
I RECKON THERE'S ONLY ONE WAY IT CAN LOSE
Mirror
BY YOU PUTTING MONEY ON IT! HEH! HEH!
IF THE GROUND DOESN'T SUIT!
OH, RIGHT— SORRY, PET!

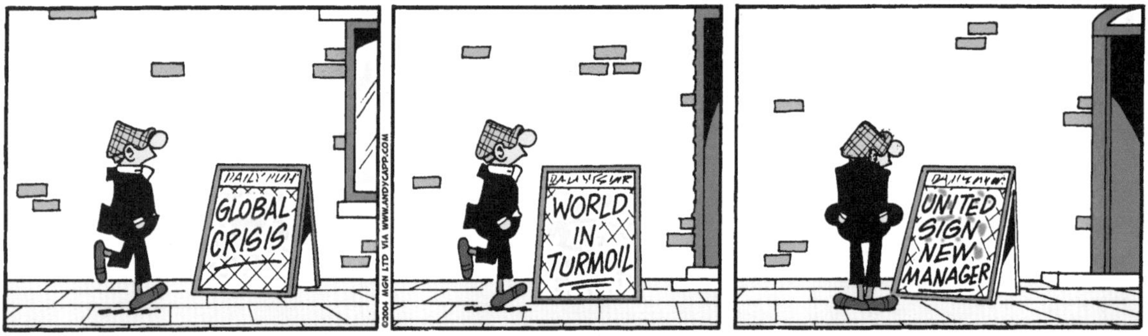
GLOBAL CRISIS
©2004 MGN LTD VIA WWW.ANDYCAPP.COM
WORLD IN TURMOIL
UNITED SIGN NEW MANAGER

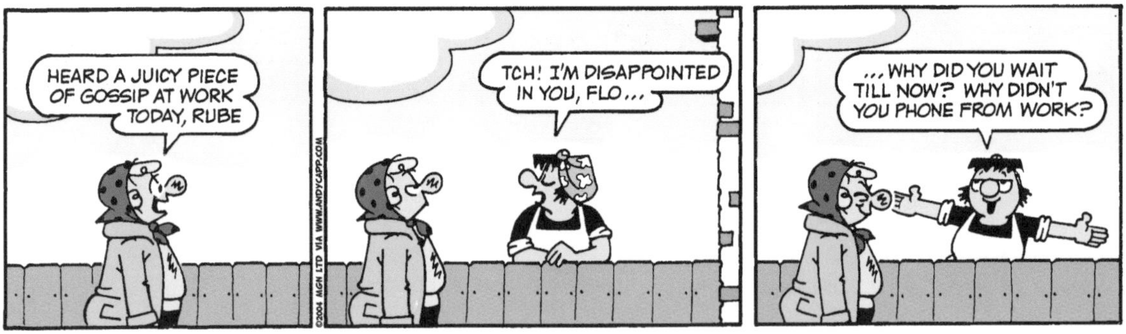
HEARD A JUICY PIECE OF GOSSIP AT WORK TODAY, RUBE
©2004 MGN LTD VIA WWW.ANDYCAPP.COM
TCH! I'M DISAPPOINTED IN YOU, FLO...
...WHY DID YOU WAIT TILL NOW? WHY DIDN'T YOU PHONE FROM WORK?

I'M REALLY LOOKING FORWARD TO OUR LITTLE SESSION TODAY — THEY'RE SO HELPFUL
MARRIAGE GUIDANCE
©2004 MGN LTD VIA WWW.ANDYCAPP.COM
AFTER YOU, MY PRECIOUS!
WHY, THANK YOU!
I STILL CAN'T BELIEVE SHE FELL FOR IT!

NOW ISN'T THIS BETTER THAN SITTING AT HOME, WATCHING RACING ON TV?
FRESH AIR AND A HEALTHY WALK! WHAT TIME IS IT NOW?
©2004 MGN LTD VIA WWW.ANDYCAPP.COM
JUST AFTER THE 3:30 AT ASCOT AND JUST BEFORE THE 3:40 AT YORK

HOW'S THE PATIENT?
NOT TOO GOOD, MUM...
...THE DOCTOR SAYS HE'S TO HAVE COMPLETE REST FOR A WEEK
©2004 MGN LTD VIA WWW.ANDYCAPP.COM
WOO! BIG LIFESTYLE CHANGE THERE!
IT'S MY BACK THAT'S GONE, NOT MY HEARING!

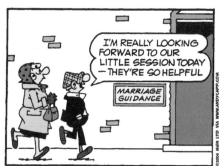

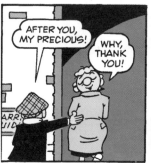

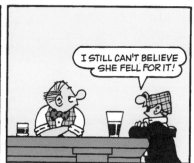

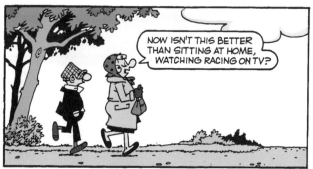

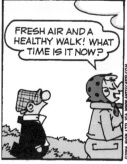

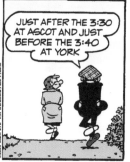

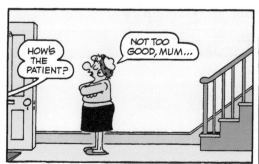

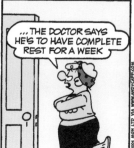

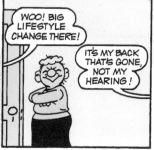

THAT'S THE TROUBLE WITH WORKING FOR A MULTINATIONAL COMPANY
I MAKE ALL THESE BUSINESS CALLS TO PLACES LIKE JAPAN AND AUSTRALIA SO I HAVE TO WORK OUT THE LOCAL TIME
©2004 MGN LTD VIA WWW.ANDYCAPP.COM
YEAH — IT WOULDN'T BE FAIR TO BORE SOME GUY IN TOKYO AT THREE IN THE MORNING

HE'S ALWAYS THE SAME AT THE START OF A NEW FOOTBALL SEASON
IT TAKES HIM A FEW GAMES TO GET HIS TIMING RIGHT
©2004 MGN LTD VIA WWW.ANDYCAPP.COM
HE MISSED THAT PUNCH BY MILES

TCH! LOOK AT THE PRICE OF THOSE COMPUTERS!
YEAH BUT THEY'RE AMAZING — YOU CAN CONTACT PEOPLE ALL OVER THE WORLD WITH THOSE!
©2004 MGN LTD VIA WWW.ANDYCAPP.COM
AT THAT PRICE YOU COULD VISIT THEM

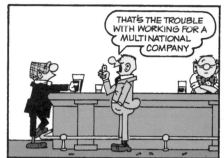

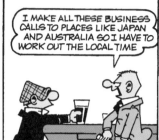

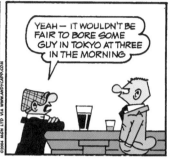

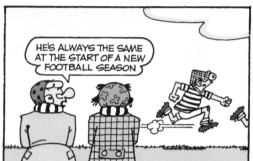

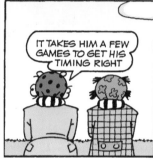

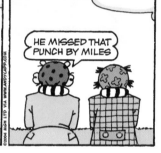

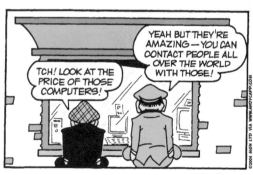

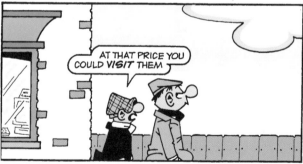

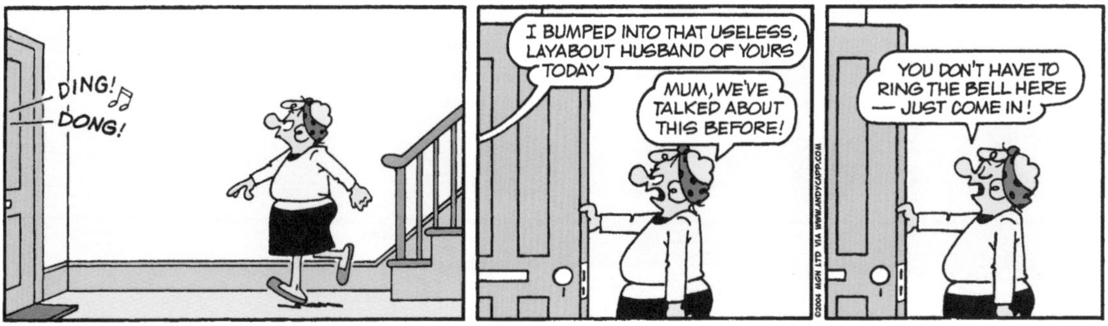
DING!
DONG!
I BUMPED INTO THAT USELESS, LAYABOUT HUSBAND OF YOURS TODAY
MUM, WE'VE TALKED ABOUT THIS BEFORE!
YOU DON'T HAVE TO RING THE BELL HERE — JUST COME IN!
©2004 MGN LTD VIA WWW.ANDYCAPP.COM

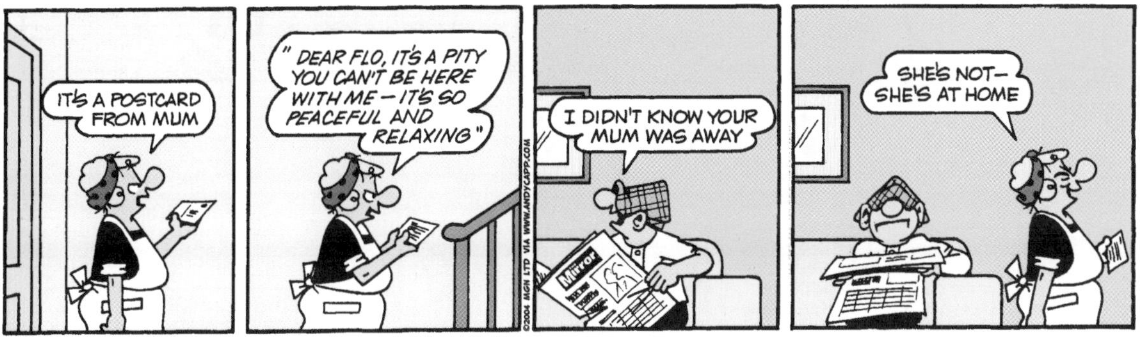
IT'S A POSTCARD FROM MUM
" DEAR FLO, IT'S A PITY YOU CAN'T BE HERE WITH ME – IT'S SO PEACEFUL AND RELAXING "
©2004 MGN LTD VIA WWW.ANDYCAPP.COM
I DIDN'T KNOW YOUR MUM WAS AWAY
SHE'S NOT– SHE'S AT HOME

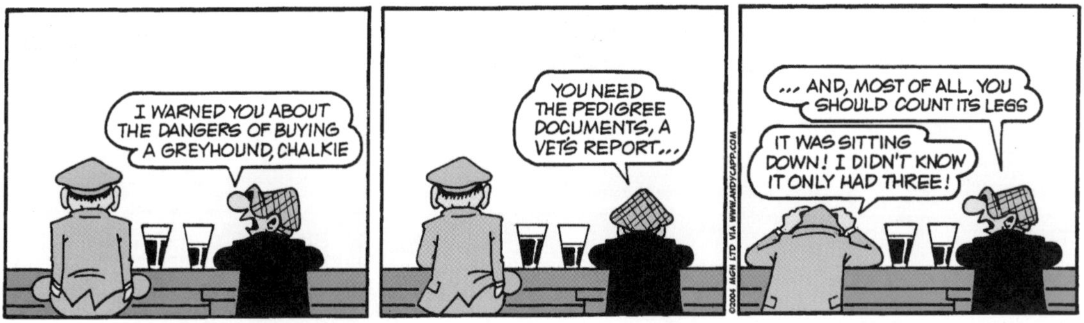
I WARNED YOU ABOUT THE DANGERS OF BUYING A GREYHOUND, CHALKIE
YOU NEED THE PEDIGREE DOCUMENTS, A VET'S REPORT...
©2004 MGN LTD VIA WWW.ANDYCAPP.COM
... AND, MOST OF ALL, YOU SHOULD COUNT ITS LEGS
IT WAS SITTING DOWN! I DIDN'T KNOW IT ONLY HAD THREE!

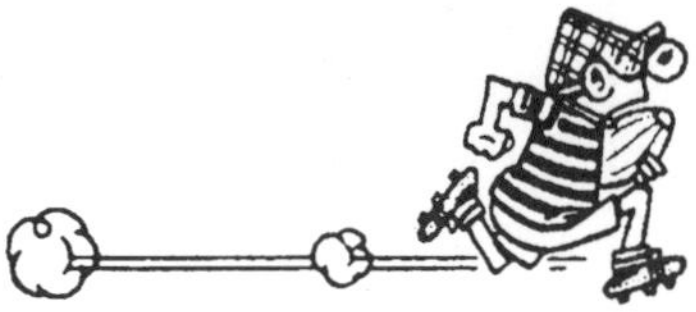

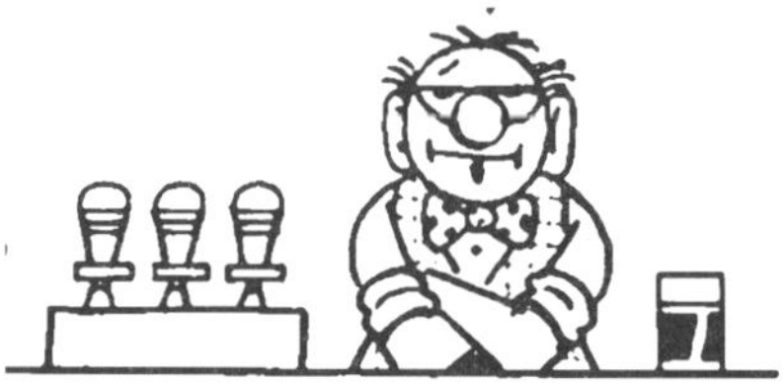

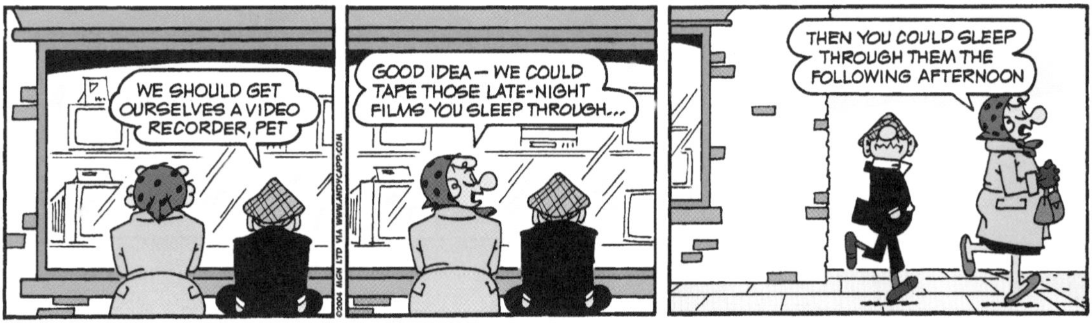
WE SHOULD GET OURSELVES A VIDEO RECORDER, PET
©2004 MGN LTD VIA WWW.ANDYCAPP.COM
GOOD IDEA — WE COULD TAPE THOSE LATE-NIGHT FILMS YOU SLEEP THROUGH...
THEN YOU COULD SLEEP THROUGH THEM THE FOLLOWING AFTERNOON

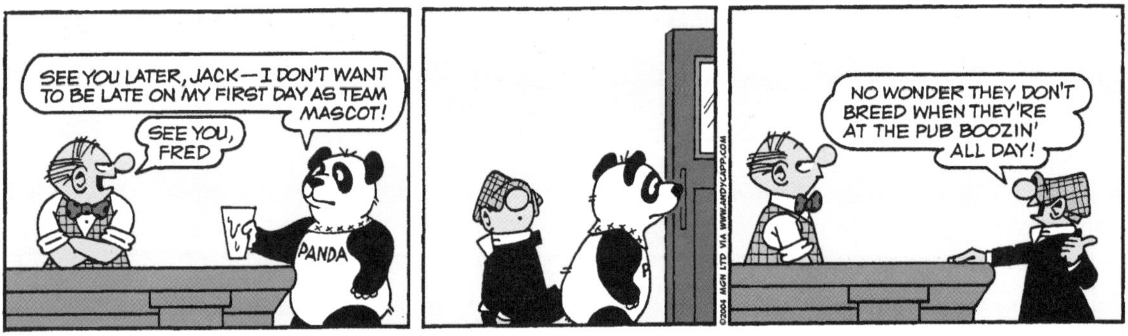
SEE YOU LATER, JACK — I DON'T WANT TO BE LATE ON MY FIRST DAY AS TEAM MASCOT!
SEE YOU, FRED
PANDA
©2004 MGN LTD VIA WWW.ANDYCAPP.COM
NO WONDER THEY DON'T BREED WHEN THEY'RE AT THE PUB BOOZIN' ALL DAY!

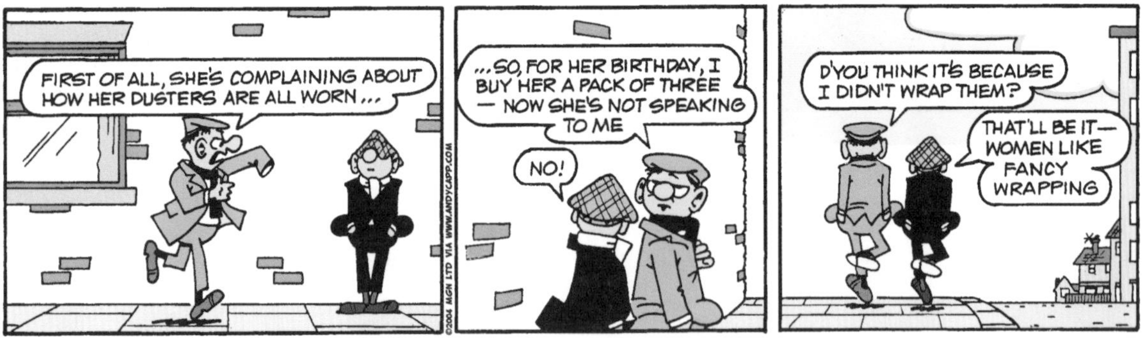
FIRST OF ALL, SHE'S COMPLAINING ABOUT HOW HER DUSTERS ARE ALL WORN...
©2004 MGN LTD VIA WWW.ANDYCAPP.COM
...SO, FOR HER BIRTHDAY, I BUY HER A PACK OF THREE — NOW SHE'S NOT SPEAKING TO ME
NO!
D'YOU THINK IT'S BECAUSE I DIDN'T WRAP THEM?
THAT'LL BE IT — WOMEN LIKE FANCY WRAPPING

©2004 MGN LTD VIA WWW.ANDYCAPP.COM
SPECIAL OFFER ALL MINERAL WATER 1/2 PRICE!
OH, GOODY

REMEMBER THE FUN WE USED TO HAVE IN THIS PARK, CHALKIE?
LEAPFROG, HIDE 'N' SEEK...
©2004 MGN LTD VIA WWW.ANDYCAPP.COM
YEP—WE DID SOME DAFT THINGS LAST YEAR!

SIGH
WHAT'S UP, JACK?
©2004 MGN LTD VIA WWW.ANDYCAPP.COM
I'VE JUST REALIZED THAT THERE ARE CERTAIN THINGS I'LL NEVER SAY AGAIN IN MY LIFE
LIKE "JUST A TRIM AND TIDY-UP—LEAVE THE FRINGE AS IT IS"

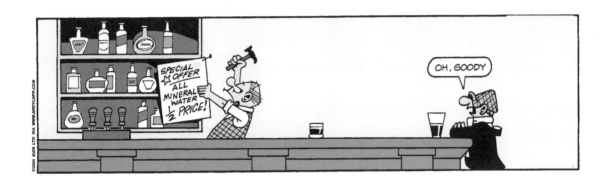

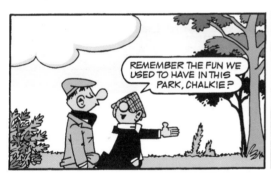

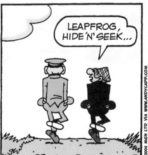

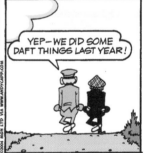

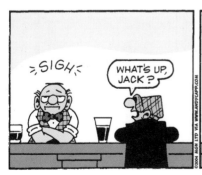

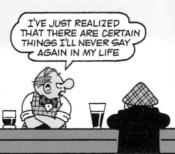

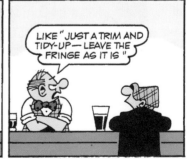

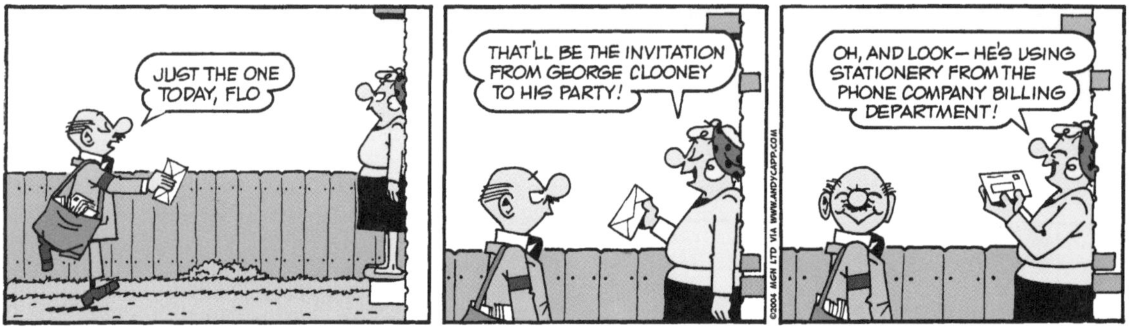
JUST THE ONE TODAY, FLO
THAT'LL BE THE INVITATION FROM GEORGE CLOONEY TO HIS PARTY!
OH, AND LOOK— HE'S USING STATIONERY FROM THE PHONE COMPANY BILLING DEPARTMENT!
©2004 MGN LTD VIA WWW.ANDYCAPP.COM

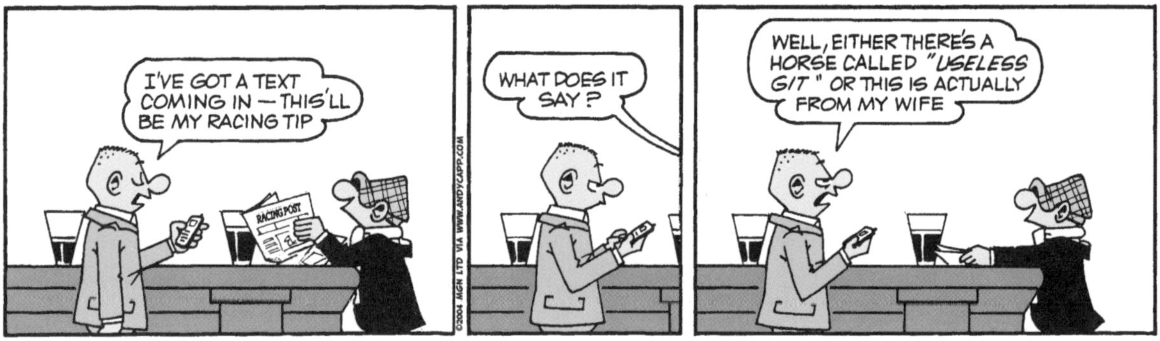
I'VE GOT A TEXT COMING IN — THIS'LL BE MY RACING TIP
RACING POST
WHAT DOES IT SAY ?
WELL, EITHER THERE'S A HORSE CALLED "USELESS GIT" OR THIS IS ACTUALLY FROM MY WIFE
©2004 MGN LTD VIA WWW.ANDYCAPP.COM

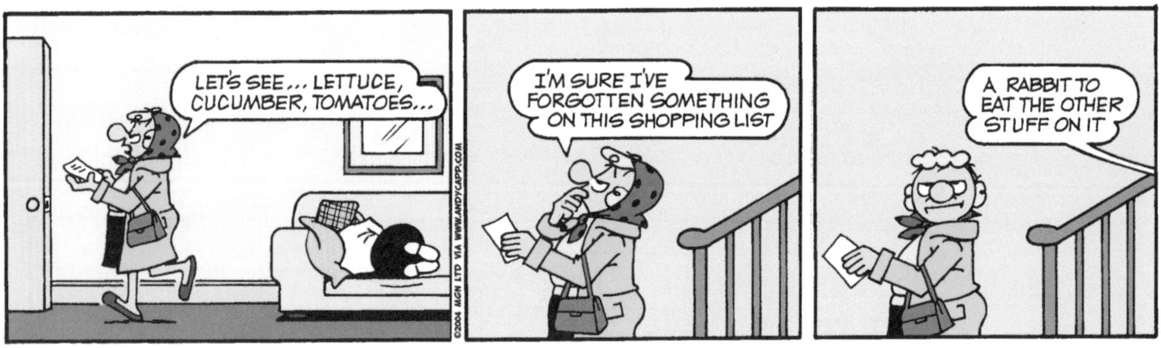
LET'S SEE... LETTUCE, CUCUMBER, TOMATOES...
I'M SURE I'VE FORGOTTEN SOMETHING ON THIS SHOPPING LIST
A RABBIT TO EAT THE OTHER STUFF ON IT
©2004 MGN LTD VIA WWW.ANDYCAPP.COM

...SO I SAID, "I EXPECT A DECENT MEAL AFTER A HARD DAY'S WORK"
I TOLD HER STRAIGHT — "TAKE THIS MUCK AWAY!"
©2004 MGN LTD VIA WWW.ANDYCAPP.COM
BY THE WAY, YOU'VE STILL GOT SOME OF IT IN YOUR HAIR AND BEHIND YOUR EAR

I'VE DECIDED TO GO ON A DIET, FLO
GOOD FOR YOU, MUM
THIS SHOULD BE INTERESTING...
©2004 MGN LTD VIA WWW.ANDYCAPP.COM
...HER IDEA OF A DIET IS TO TAKE THE WRAPPER OFF THE CHOCOLATE BEFORE SHE EATS IT

MARRIAGE GUIDANCE
I ENCOURAGE MY COUPLES TO SPEAK OUT...
©2004 MGN LTD VIA WWW.ANDYCAPP.COM
HE'S A LAZY PIG
SHE'S A NAGGING COW
MARRIAGE GUIDANCE
YOU KIND OF JUMPED IN BEFORE I GOT TO THE "IN A POSITIVE WAY" BIT

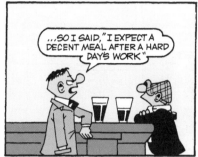

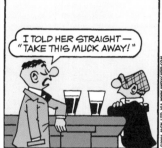

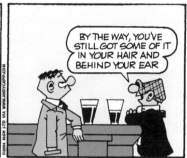

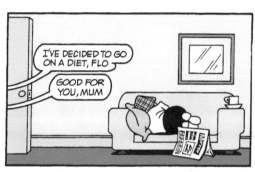

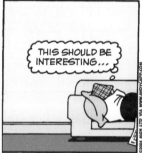

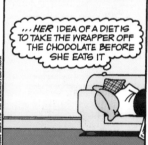

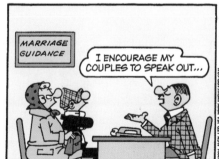

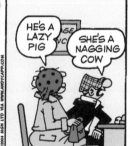

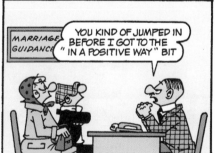

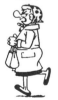

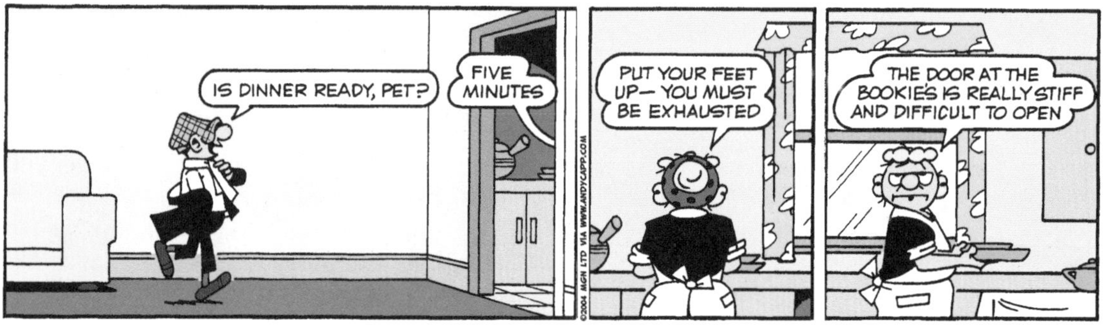
IS DINNER READY, PET?
FIVE MINUTES
PUT YOUR FEET UP— YOU MUST BE EXHAUSTED
THE DOOR AT THE BOOKIE'S IS REALLY STIFF AND DIFFICULT TO OPEN
©2004 MGN LTD VIA WWW.ANDYCAPP.COM

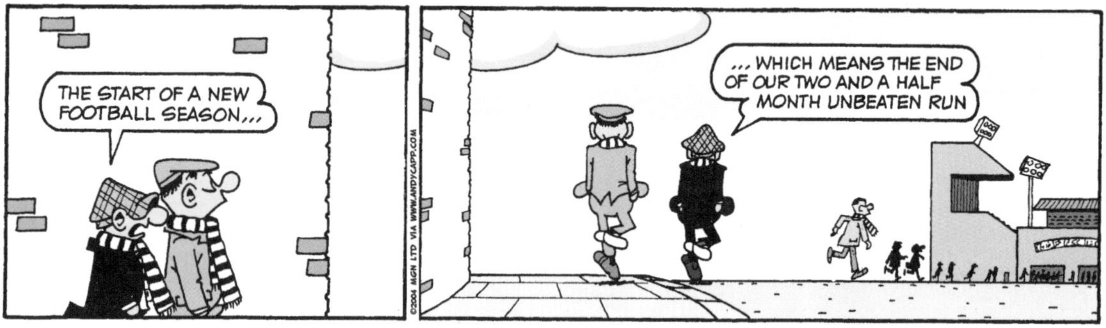
THE START OF A NEW FOOTBALL SEASON,,,
,,, WHICH MEANS THE END OF OUR TWO AND A HALF MONTH UNBEATEN RUN
©2004 MGN LTD VIA WWW.ANDYCAPP.COM

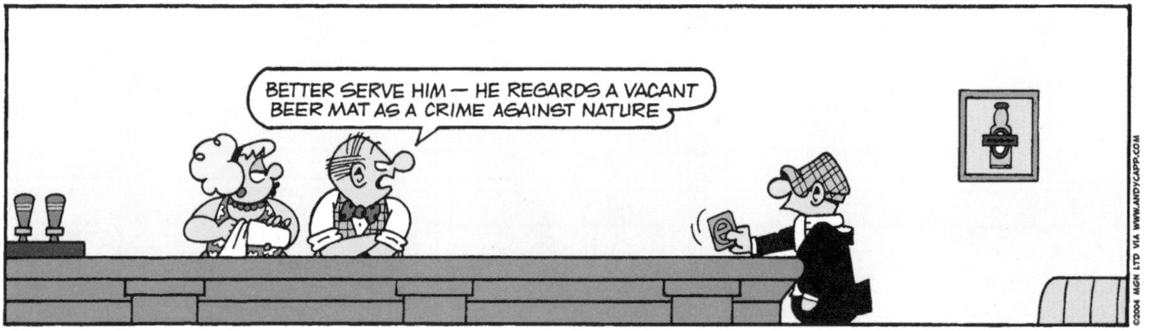
BETTER SERVE HIM — HE REGARDS A VACANT BEER MAT AS A CRIME AGAINST NATURE
©2004 MGN LTD VIA WWW.ANDYCAPP.COM

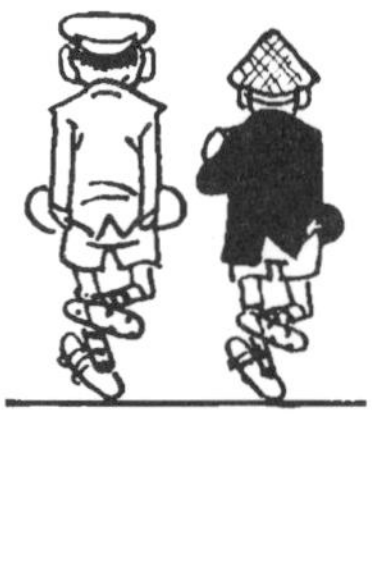

RIGHT, PET, I'M OFF TO BINGO WITH RUBE
YOUR DINNER'S IN THE OVEN — IT'LL BE READY IN AN HOUR
OKAY
©2004 MGN LTD VIA WWW.ANDYCAPP.COM
SO WHEN YOU WAKE UP IN THREE HOURS, PUT THE FIRE OUT AND GET YOURSELF SOME FISH AND CHIPS

I ENJOYED THE HOLIDAY BUT I'M GLAD TO BE HOME
©2004 MGN LTD VIA WWW.ANDYCAPP.COM
IT'S NICE TO BE IN YOUR OWN HOUSE, SURROUNDED BY YOUR OWN BITS AND PIECES
IF I WANTED TO DO THAT, I'D HAVE TO SIT IN THE PAWN SHOP

THIS'LL INTEREST YOU, JACK
©2004 MGN LTD VIA WWW.ANDYCAPP.COM
THERE'S A REPORT HERE ABOUT A SURVEY THAT—
LATER, ANDY. I'M BUSY
—SAYS BARMEN ARE THE BEST LISTENERS

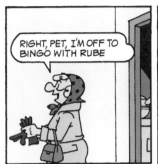

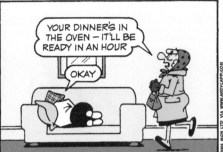

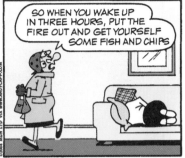

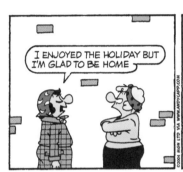

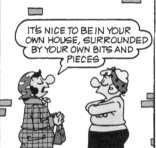

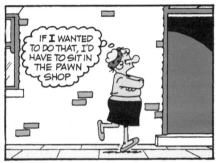

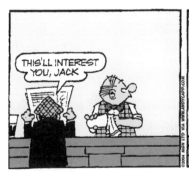

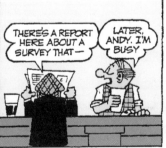

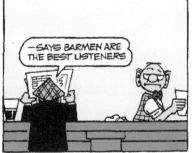

I WISH I COULD STAND AROUND CHATTING ALL DAY!
©2004 MGN LTD VIA WWW.ANDYCAPP.COM
SORRY ABOUT THAT, FLO — HE'S NOT HIMSELF TODAY
DON'T WORRY...
...I HAVE TO APOLOGIZE FOR ANDY WHEN HE IS HIMSELF!

THOSE WOMEN OVER THERE SAID I WAS GOOD LOOKING
GREAT!
©2004 MGN LTD VIA WWW.ANDYCAPP.COM
THEN THEY ADDED THE THREE DREADED WORDS
THAT'S THEM
"FOR HIS AGE"

GARDEN CENTRE
OO, JUST WHAT I NEED — ANOTHER LITTLE MAN WITH A HAT ON WHO SITS IN THE GARDEN DOING NOTHING
©2004 MGN LTD VIA WWW.ANDYCAPP.COM

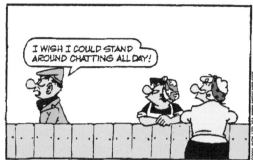

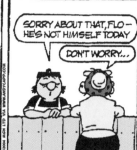

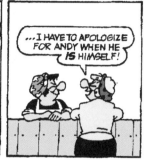

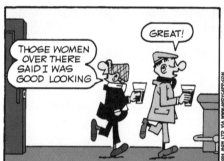

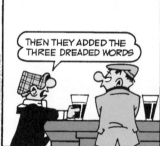

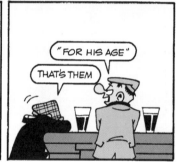

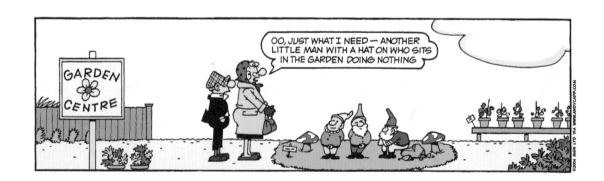

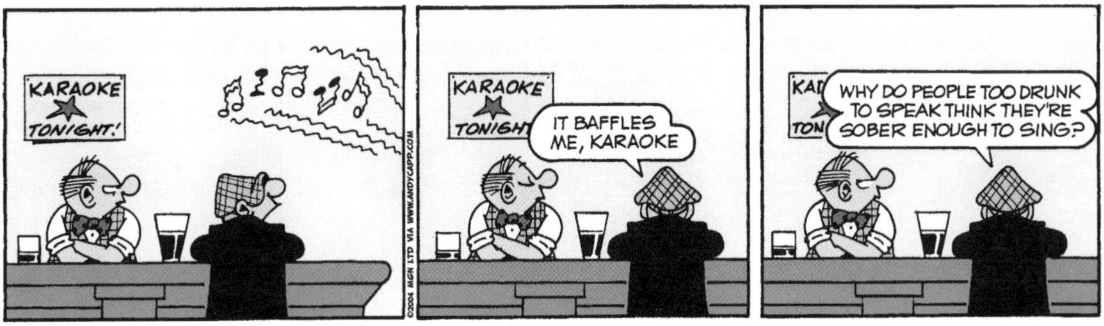
KARAOKE TONIGHT!
IT BAFFLES ME, KARAOKE
WHY DO PEOPLE TOO DRUNK TO SPEAK THINK THEY'RE SOBER ENOUGH TO SING?
©2004 MGN LTD VIA WWW.ANDYCAPP.COM

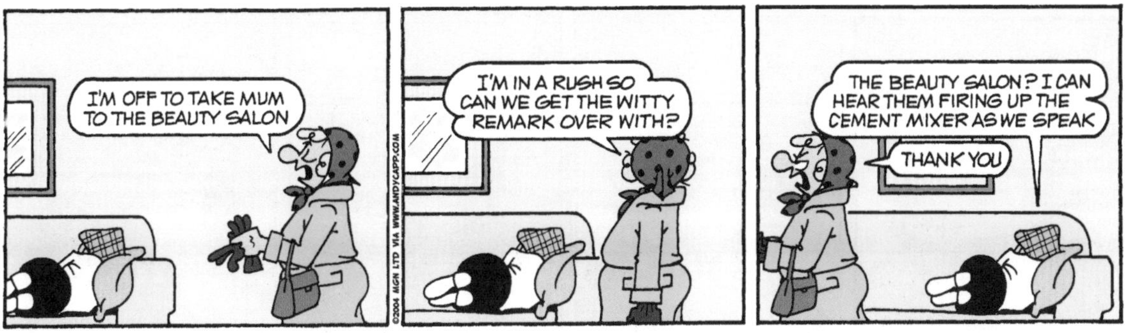
I'M OFF TO TAKE MUM TO THE BEAUTY SALON
I'M IN A RUSH SO CAN WE GET THE WITTY REMARK OVER WITH?
THE BEAUTY SALON? I CAN HEAR THEM FIRING UP THE CEMENT MIXER AS WE SPEAK
THANK YOU
©2004 MGN LTD VIA WWW.ANDYCAPP.COM

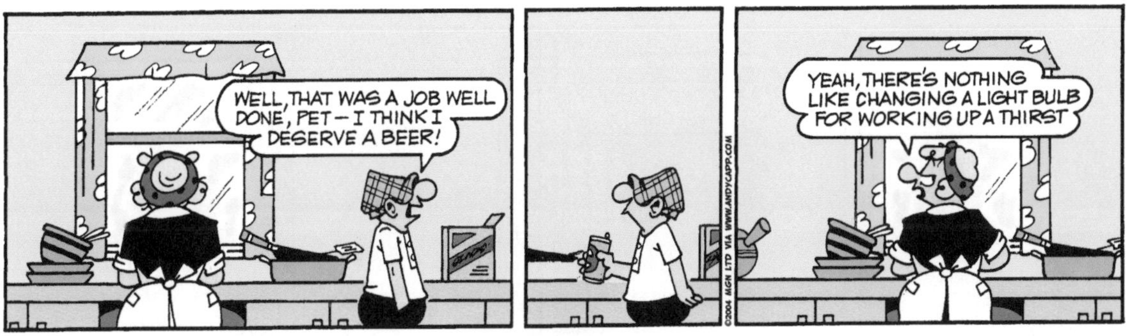
WELL, THAT WAS A JOB WELL DONE, PET — I THINK I DESERVE A BEER!
YEAH, THERE'S NOTHING LIKE CHANGING A LIGHT BULB FOR WORKING UP A THIRST
©2004 MGN LTD VIA WWW.ANDYCAPP.COM

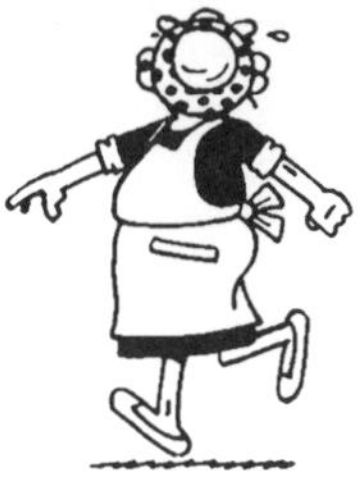

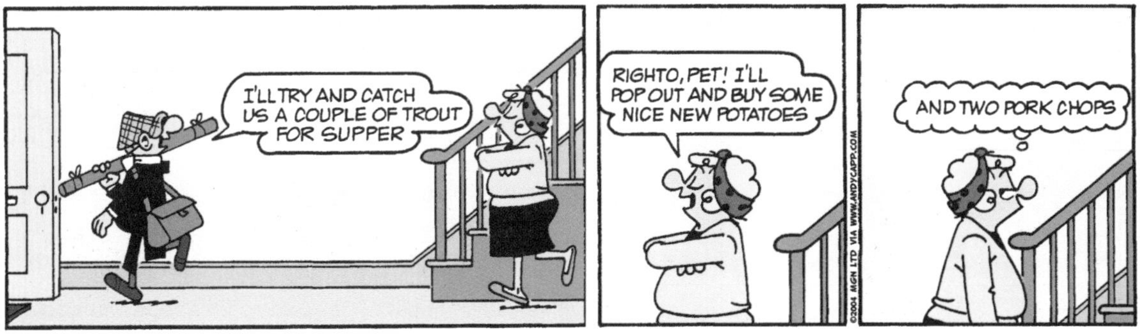
I'LL TRY AND CATCH US A COUPLE OF TROUT FOR SUPPER
RIGHTO, PET! I'LL POP OUT AND BUY SOME NICE NEW POTATOES
©2004 MGN LTD VIA WWW.ANDYCAPP.COM
AND TWO PORK CHOPS

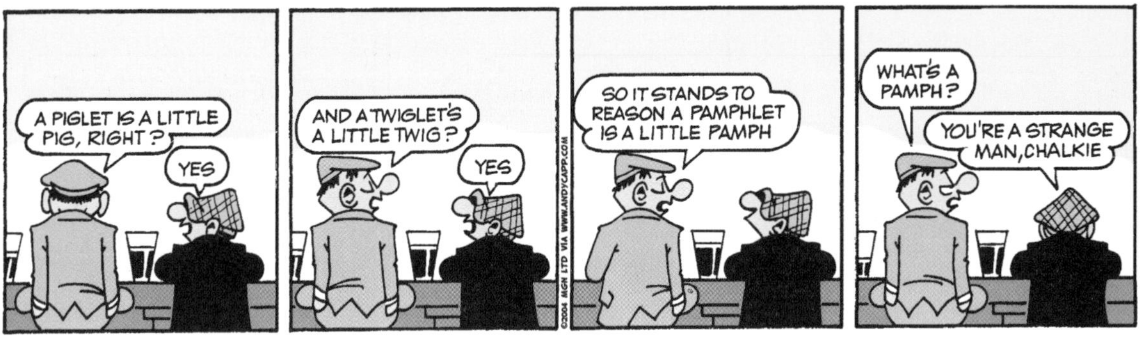
A PIGLET IS A LITTLE PIG, RIGHT?
YES
AND A TWIGLET'S A LITTLE TWIG?
YES
©2004 MGN LTD VIA WWW.ANDYCAPP.COM
SO IT STANDS TO REASON A PAMPHLET IS A LITTLE PAMPH
WHAT'S A PAMPH?
YOU'RE A STRANGE MAN, CHALKIE

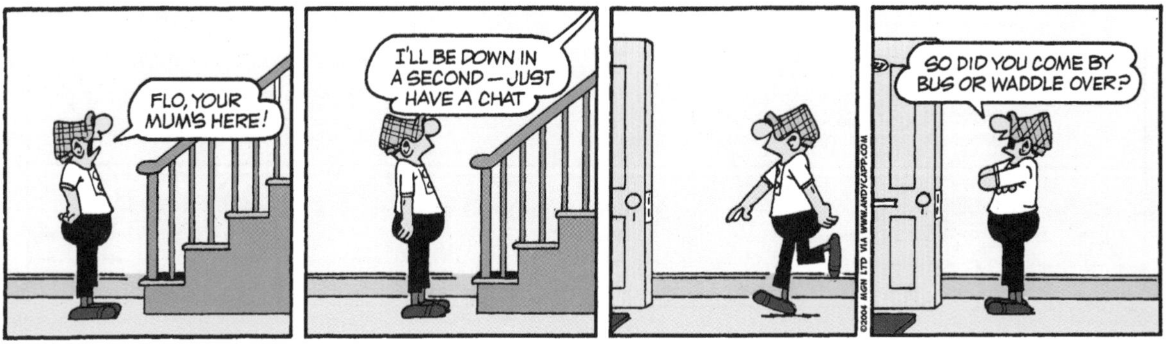
FLO, YOUR MUM'S HERE!
I'LL BE DOWN IN A SECOND — JUST HAVE A CHAT
©2004 MGN LTD VIA WWW.ANDYCAPP.COM
SO DID YOU COME BY BUS OR WADDLE OVER?

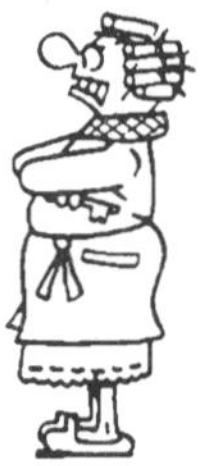

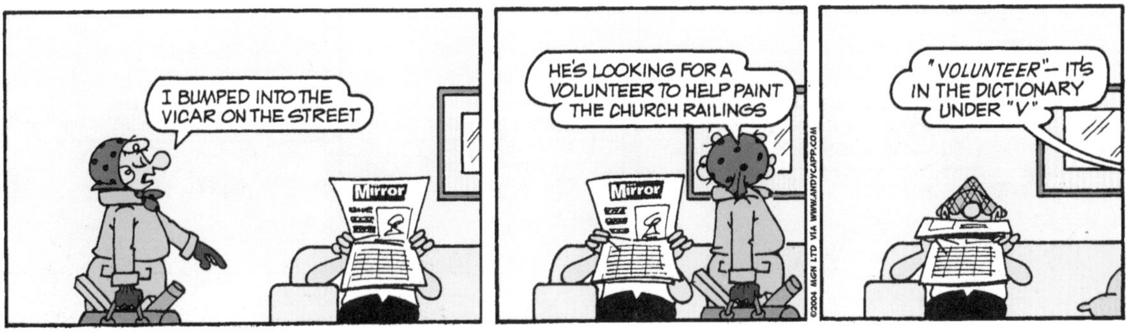
I BUMPED INTO THE VICAR ON THE STREET
Mirror
HE'S LOOKING FOR A VOLUNTEER TO HELP PAINT THE CHURCH RAILINGS
©2004 MGN LTD VIA WWW.ANDYCAPP.COM
"VOLUNTEER"– IT'S IN THE DICTIONARY UNDER "V"

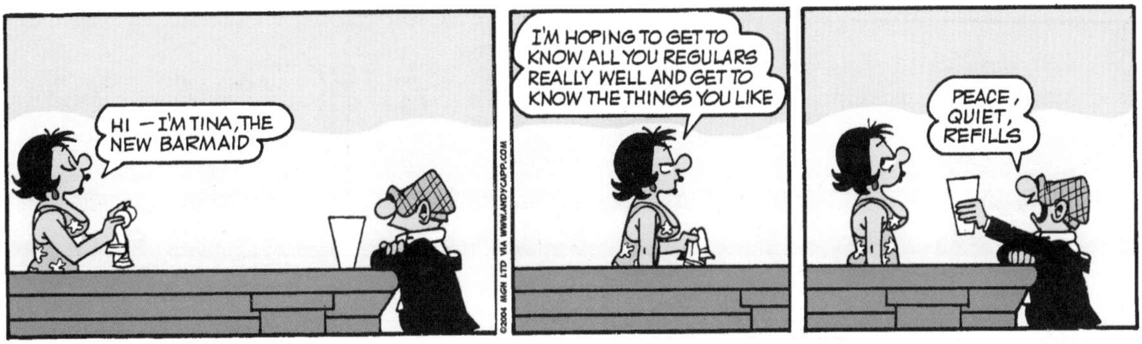
HI – I'M TINA, THE NEW BARMAID
©2004 MGN LTD VIA WWW.ANDYCAPP.COM
I'M HOPING TO GET TO KNOW ALL YOU REGULARS REALLY WELL AND GET TO KNOW THE THINGS YOU LIKE
PEACE, QUIET, REFILLS

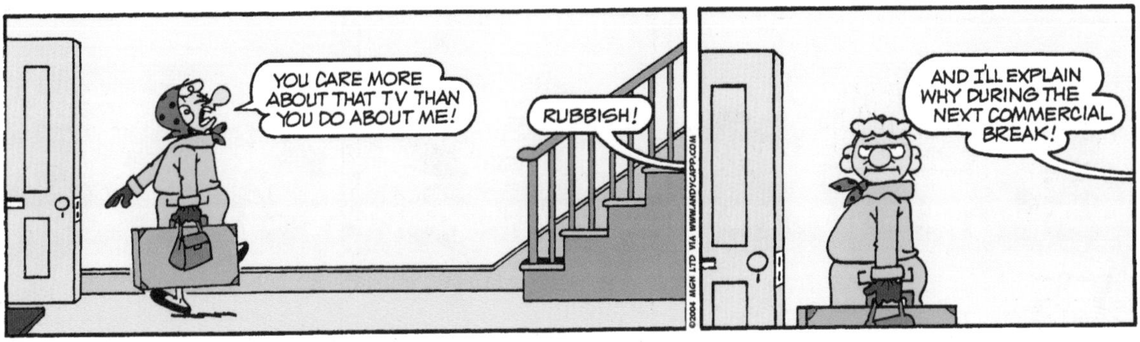
YOU CARE MORE ABOUT THAT TV THAN YOU DO ABOUT ME!
RUBBISH!
©2004 MGN LTD VIA WWW.ANDYCAPP.COM
AND I'LL EXPLAIN WHY DURING THE NEXT COMMERCIAL BREAK!

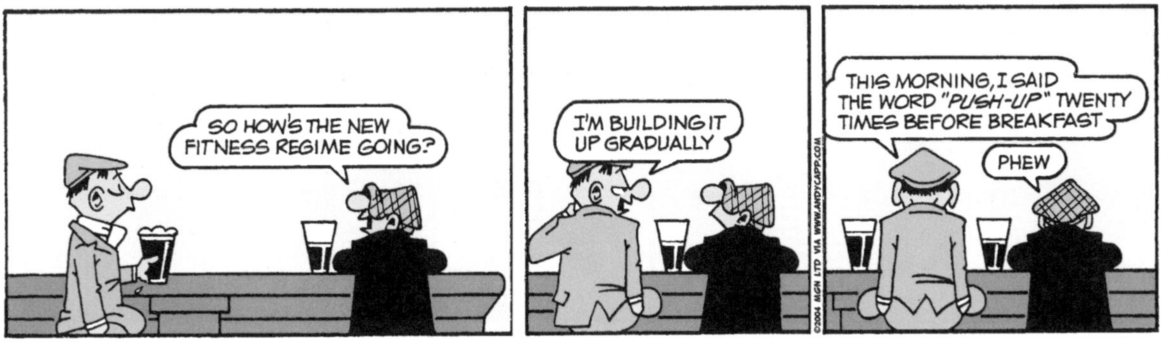
SO HOW'S THE NEW FITNESS REGIME GOING?
I'M BUILDING IT UP GRADUALLY
©2004 MGN LTD VIA WWW.ANDYCAPP.COM
THIS MORNING, I SAID THE WORD "PUSH-UP" TWENTY TIMES BEFORE BREAKFAST
PHEW

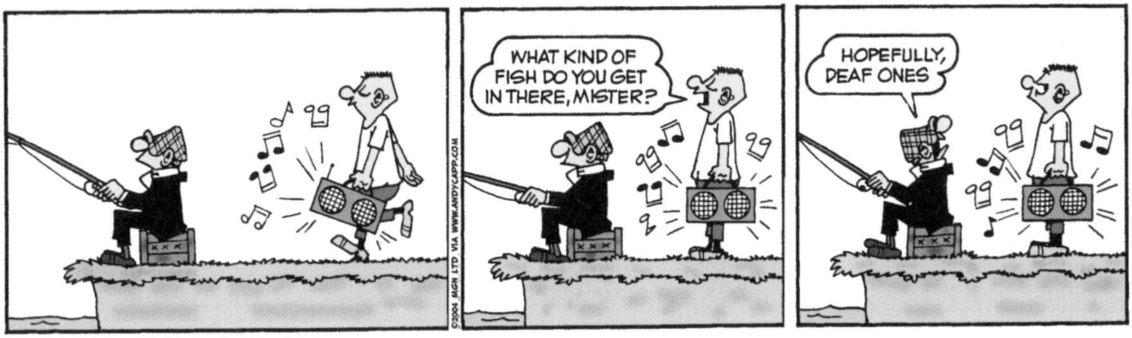
©2004 MGN LTD VIA WWW.ANDYCAPP.COM
WHAT KIND OF FISH DO YOU GET IN THERE, MISTER?
HOPEFULLY, DEAF ONES

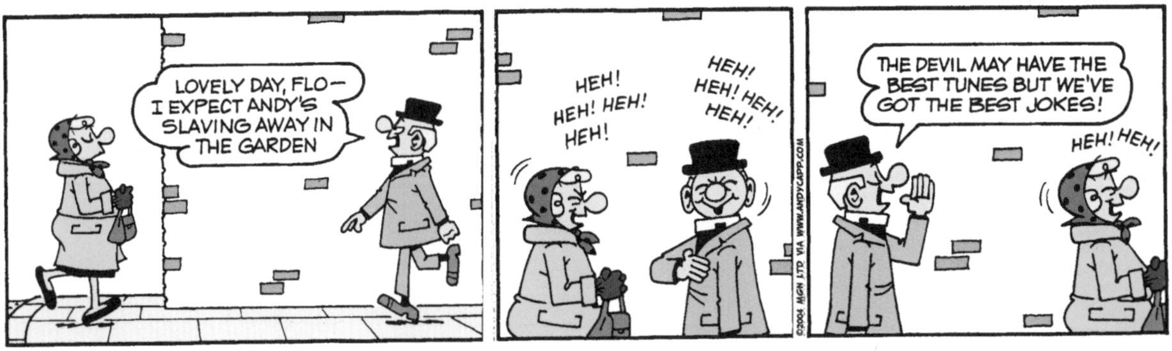
LOVELY DAY, FLO— I EXPECT ANDY'S SLAVING AWAY IN THE GARDEN
HEH! HEH! HEH! HEH!
HEH! HEH! HEH! HEH!
©2004 MGN LTD VIA WWW.ANDYCAPP.COM
THE DEVIL MAY HAVE THE BEST TUNES BUT WE'VE GOT THE BEST JOKES!
HEH! HEH!

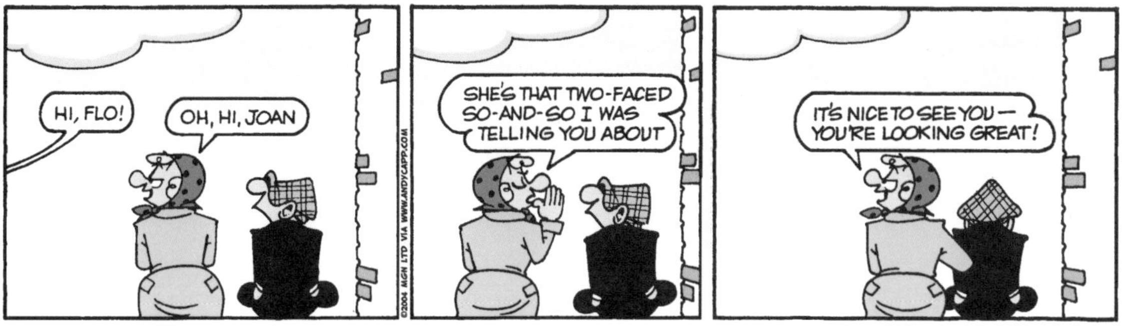

HI, FLO!
OH, HI, JOAN
©2004 MGN LTD VIA WWW.ANDYCAPP.COM
SHE'S THAT TWO-FACED SO-AND-SO I WAS TELLING YOU ABOUT
IT'S NICE TO SEE YOU — YOU'RE LOOKING GREAT!

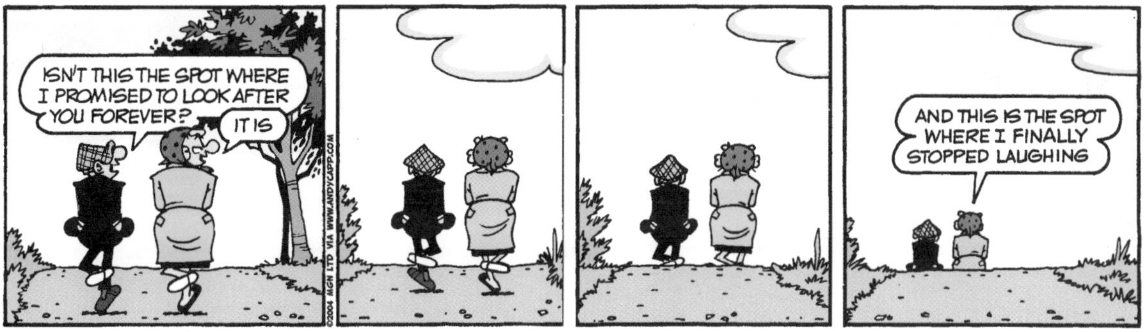

ISN'T THIS THE SPOT WHERE I PROMISED TO LOOK AFTER YOU FOREVER?
IT IS
©2004 MGN LTD VIA WWW.ANDYCAPP.COM
AND THIS IS THE SPOT WHERE I FINALLY STOPPED LAUGHING

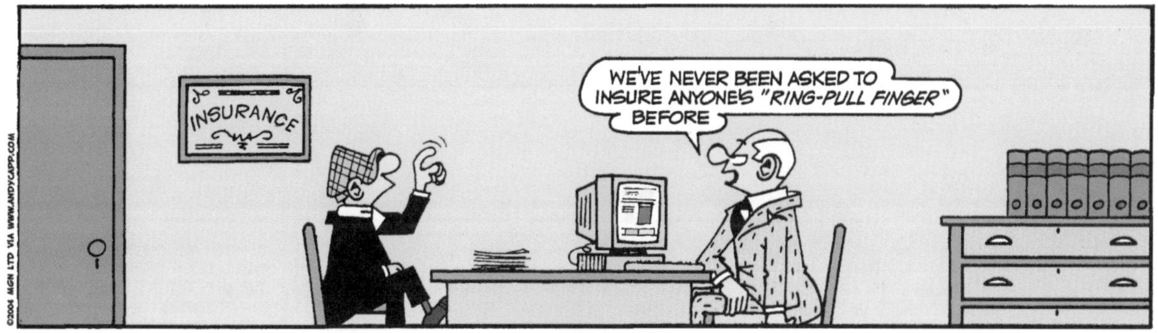

©2004 MGN LTD VIA WWW.ANDYCAPP.COM
INSURANCE
WE'VE NEVER BEEN ASKED TO INSURE ANYONE'S "RING-PULL FINGER" BEFORE

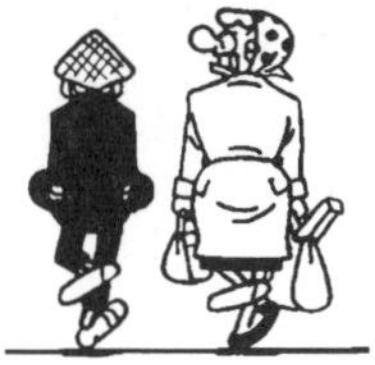

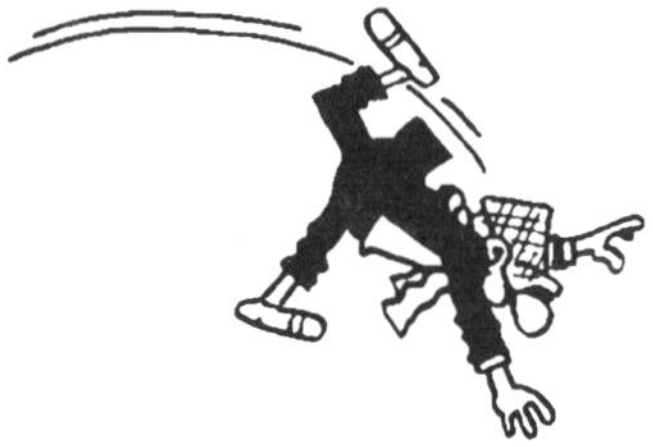

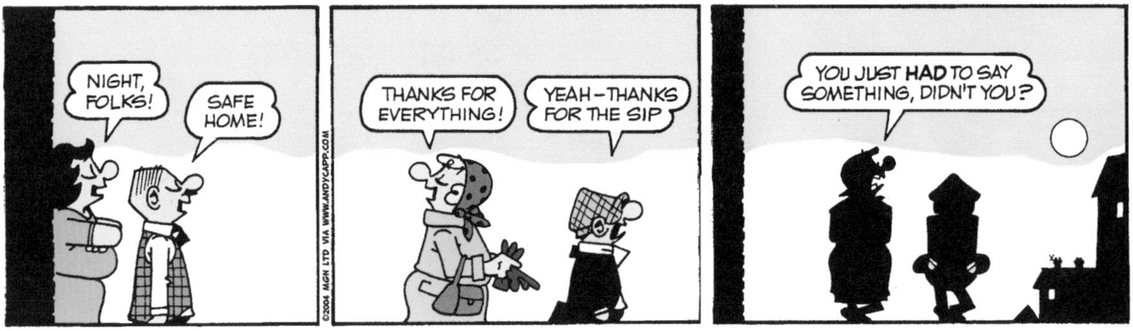
NIGHT, FOLKS!
SAFE HOME!
THANKS FOR EVERYTHING!
YEAH – THANKS FOR THE SIP
YOU JUST **HAD** TO SAY SOMETHING, DIDN'T YOU?
©2004 MGN LTD VIA WWW.ANDYCAPP.COM

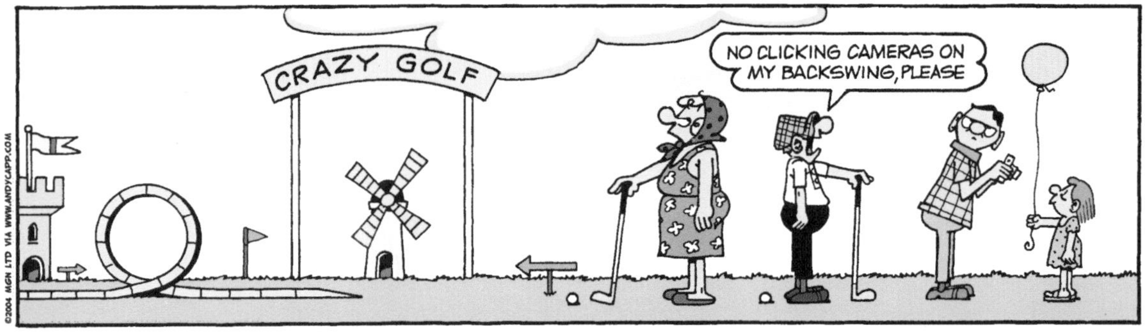
CRAZY GOLF
NO CLICKING CAMERAS ON MY BACKSWING, PLEASE
©2004 MGN LTD VIA WWW.ANDYCAPP.COM

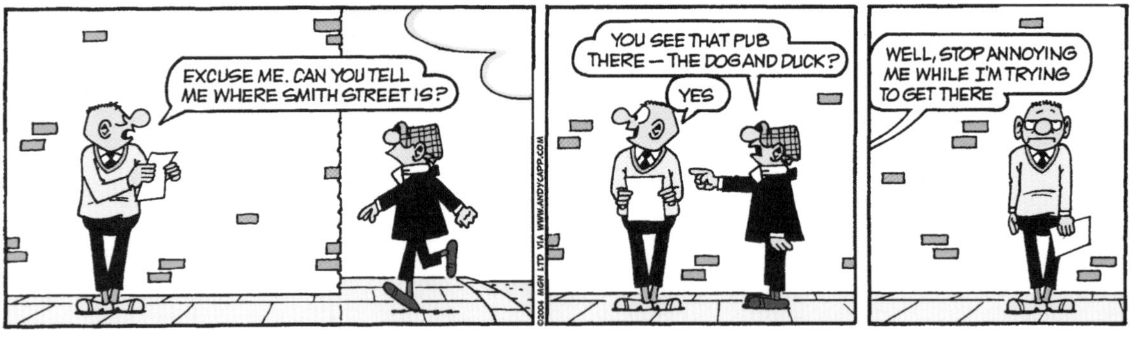
EXCUSE ME. CAN YOU TELL ME WHERE SMITH STREET IS?
YOU SEE THAT PUB THERE – THE DOG AND DUCK?
YES
WELL, STOP ANNOYING ME WHILE I'M TRYING TO GET THERE
©2004 MGN LTD VIA WWW.ANDYCAPP.COM

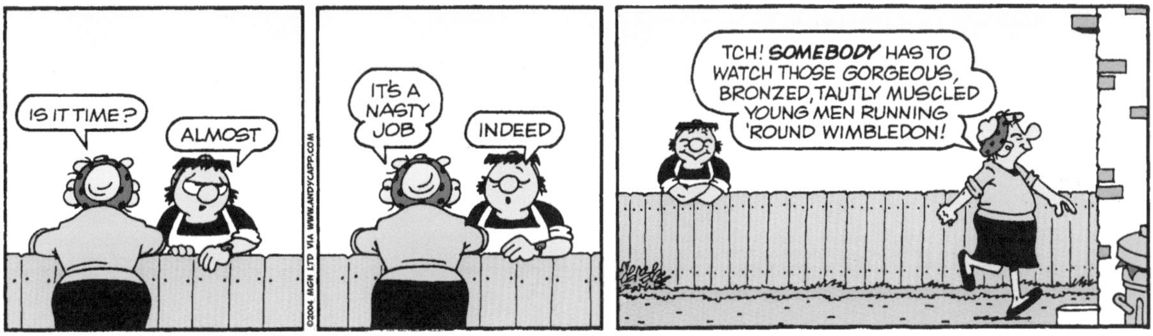
IS IT TIME?
ALMOST
©2004 MGN LTD VIA WWW.ANDYCAPP.COM
IT'S A NASTY JOB
INDEED
TCH! SOMEBODY HAS TO WATCH THOSE GORGEOUS, BRONZED, TAUTLY MUSCLED YOUNG MEN RUNNING 'ROUND WIMBLEDON!

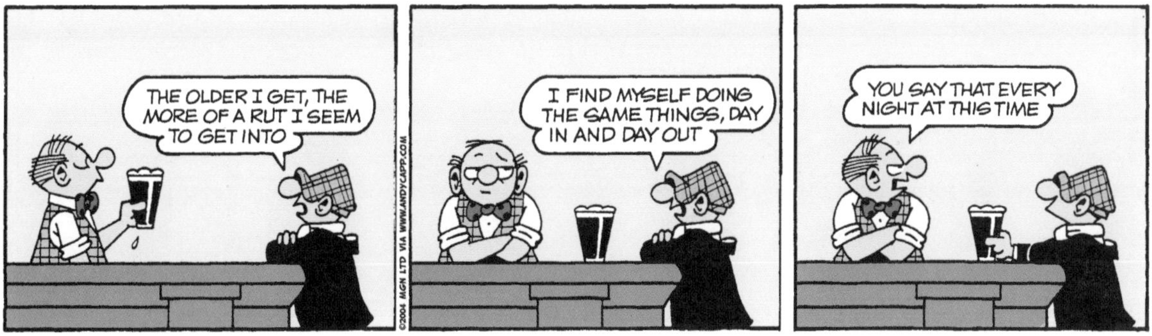
THE OLDER I GET, THE MORE OF A RUT I SEEM TO GET INTO
©2004 MGN LTD VIA WWW.ANDYCAPP.COM
I FIND MYSELF DOING THE SAME THINGS, DAY IN AND DAY OUT
YOU SAY THAT EVERY NIGHT AT THIS TIME

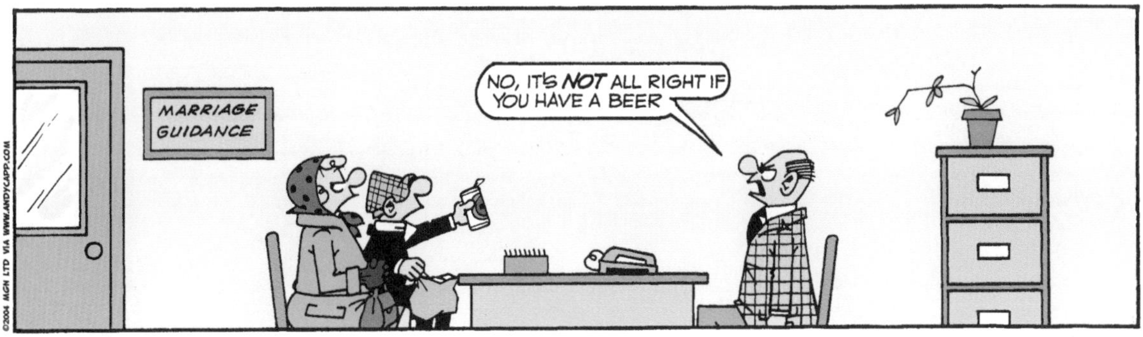
©2004 MGN LTD VIA WWW.ANDYCAPP.COM
MARRIAGE GUIDANCE
NO, IT'S NOT ALL RIGHT IF YOU HAVE A BEER

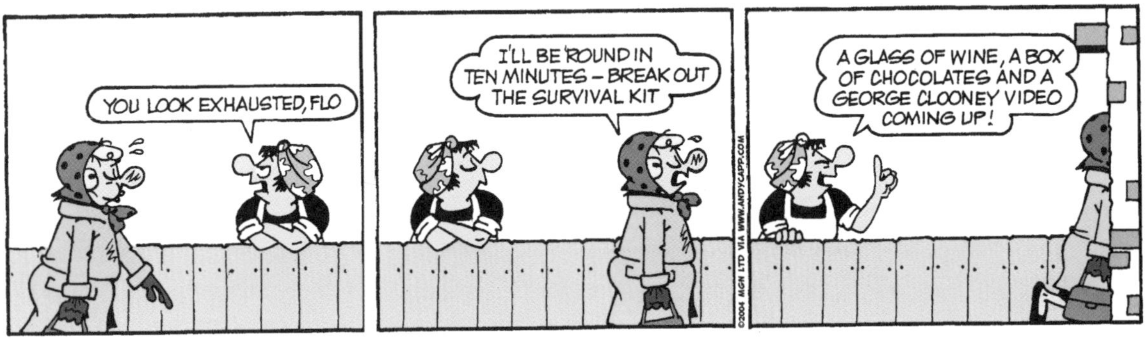
YOU LOOK EXHAUSTED, FLO
I'LL BE 'ROUND IN TEN MINUTES – BREAK OUT THE SURVIVAL KIT
©2004 MGN LTD VIA WWW.ANDYCAPP.COM
A GLASS OF WINE, A BOX OF CHOCOLATES AND A GEORGE CLOONEY VIDEO COMING UP!

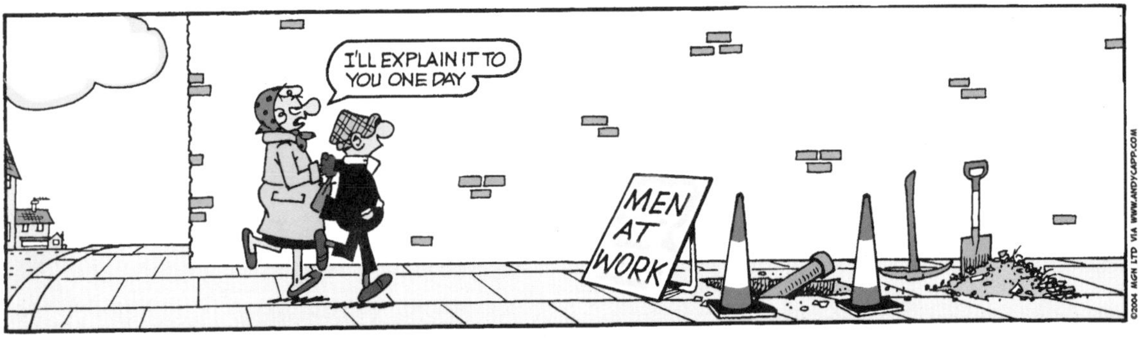
I'LL EXPLAIN IT TO YOU ONE DAY
MEN AT WORK
©2004 MGN LTD VIA WWW.ANDYCAPP.COM

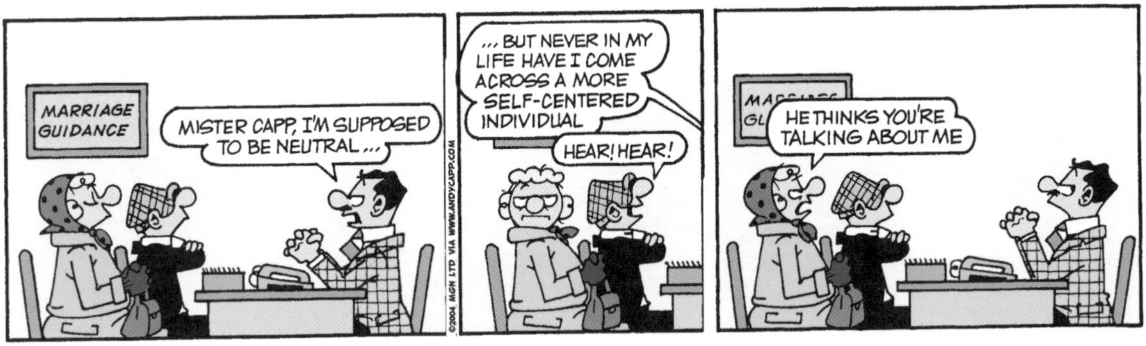
MARRIAGE GUIDANCE
MISTER CAPP, I'M SUPPOSED TO BE NEUTRAL...
©2004 MGN LTD VIA WWW.ANDYCAPP.COM
...BUT NEVER IN MY LIFE HAVE I COME ACROSS A MORE SELF-CENTERED INDIVIDUAL
HEAR! HEAR!
HE THINKS YOU'RE TALKING ABOUT ME

GOSH, WHAT A COMMOTION IN THE STREET – POLICE CARS AND EVERYTHING!
THAT'S INTERESTING, PET
DIVERSIONARY TACTICS —THE PUB'S OPEN AND MY PURSE IS IN HERE
©2004 MGN LTD VIA WWW.ANDYCAPP.COM

AH, THE OLD SCHOOL!
REMEMBER THOSE GRAINY, OLD, WOODEN DESKS WE USED TO SIT AT?
THEY'D LEAVE MARKS ON YOUR FACE WHERE YOU'D BEEN SLEEPING
©2004 MGN LTD VIA WWW.ANDYCAPP.COM

RATTLE!
THAT'S FLO HOME
OH, HELLO, PET – I'VE JUST BEEN SCOURING THE PAPER FOR A JOB
GOOD FOR YOU...
...THOUGH A GOOD TIP IS TO HAVE THE PAPER THE RIGHT WAY UP
DAMN
©2004 MGN LTD VIA WWW.ANDYCAPP.COM

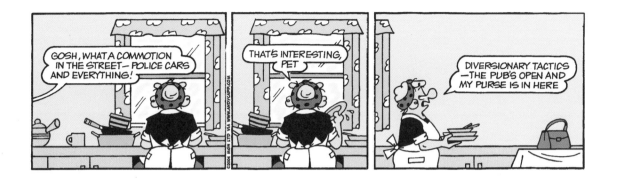

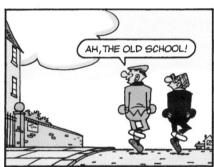

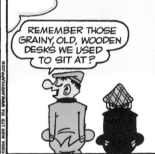

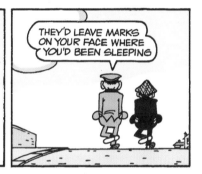

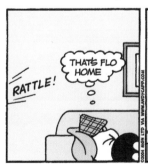

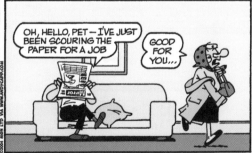

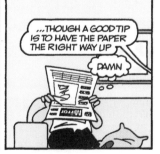

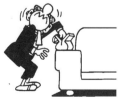

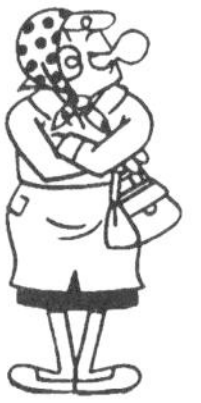

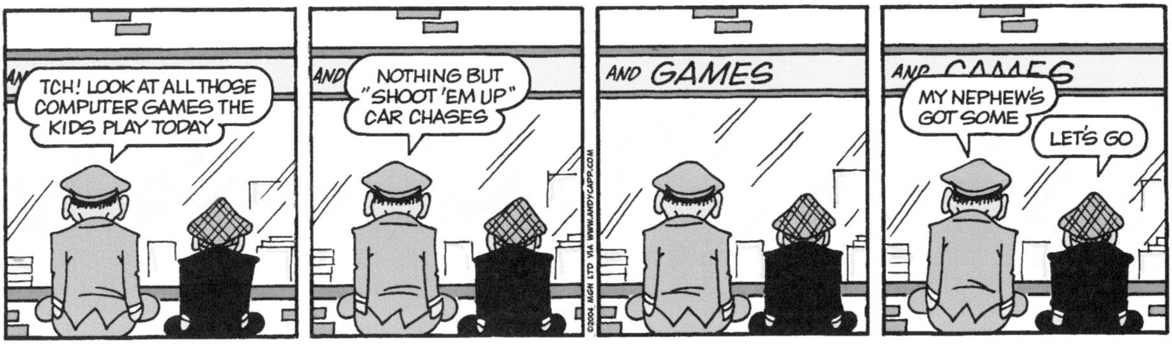

TCH! LOOK AT ALL THOSE COMPUTER GAMES THE KIDS PLAY TODAY
NOTHING BUT "SHOOT 'EM UP" CAR CHASES
AND GAMES
©2004 MGN LTD VIA WWW.ANDYCAPP.COM
MY NEPHEW'S GOT SOME
LET'S GO

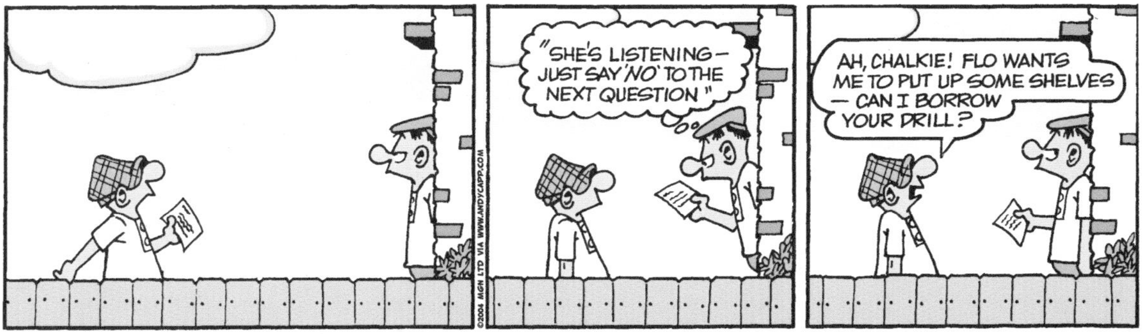

©2004 MGN LTD VIA WWW.ANDYCAPP.COM
"SHE'S LISTENING – JUST SAY 'NO' TO THE NEXT QUESTION"
AH, CHALKIE! FLO WANTS ME TO PUT UP SOME SHELVES – CAN I BORROW YOUR DRILL?

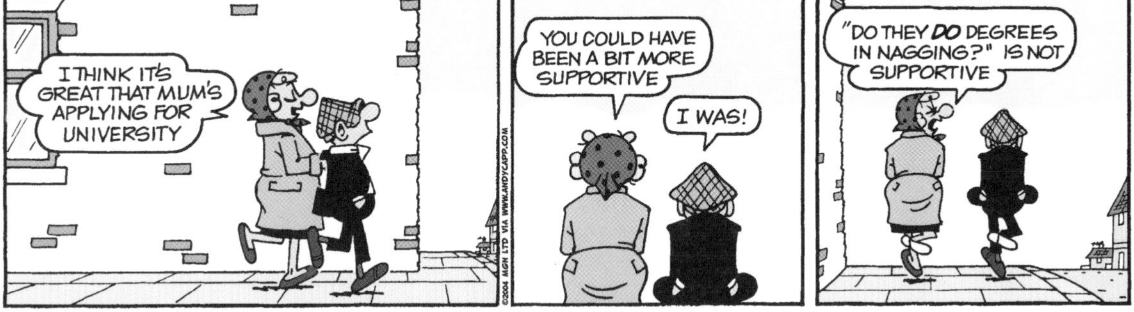

I THINK IT'S GREAT THAT MUM'S APPLYING FOR UNIVERSITY
©2004 MGN LTD VIA WWW.ANDYCAPP.COM
YOU COULD HAVE BEEN A BIT MORE SUPPORTIVE
I WAS!
"DO THEY DO DEGREES IN NAGGING?" IS NOT SUPPORTIVE

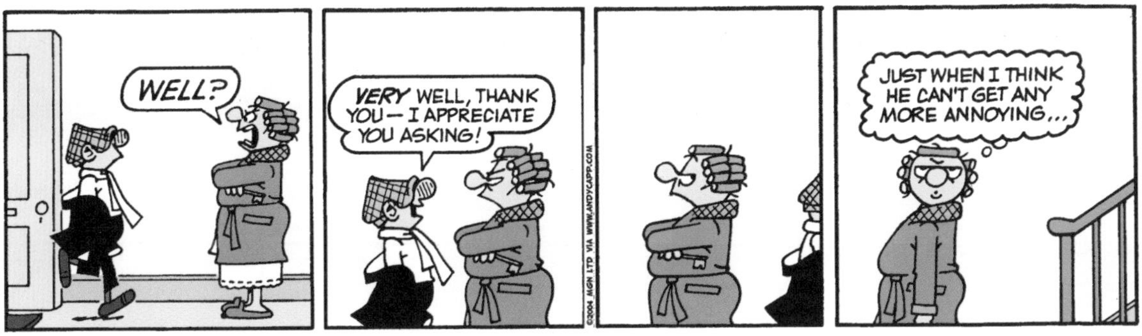
WELL?
VERY WELL, THANK YOU— I APPRECIATE YOU ASKING!
JUST WHEN I THINK HE CAN'T GET ANY MORE ANNOYING...

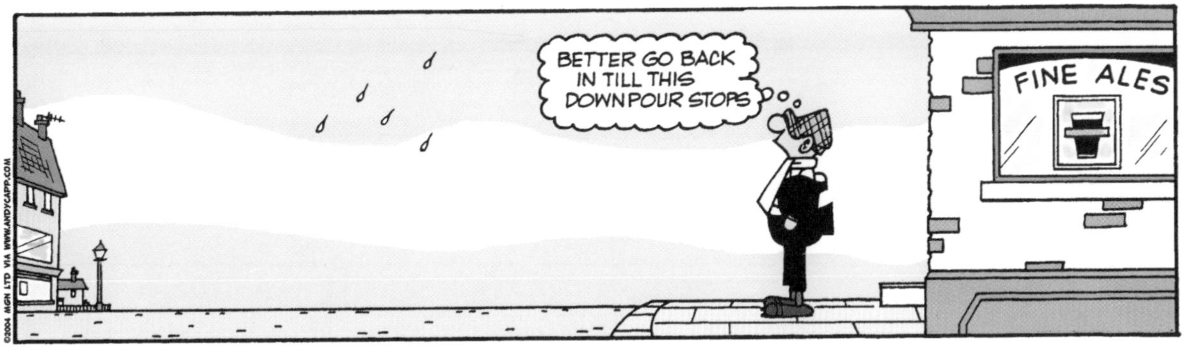
BETTER GO BACK IN TILL THIS DOWNPOUR STOPS
FINE ALES

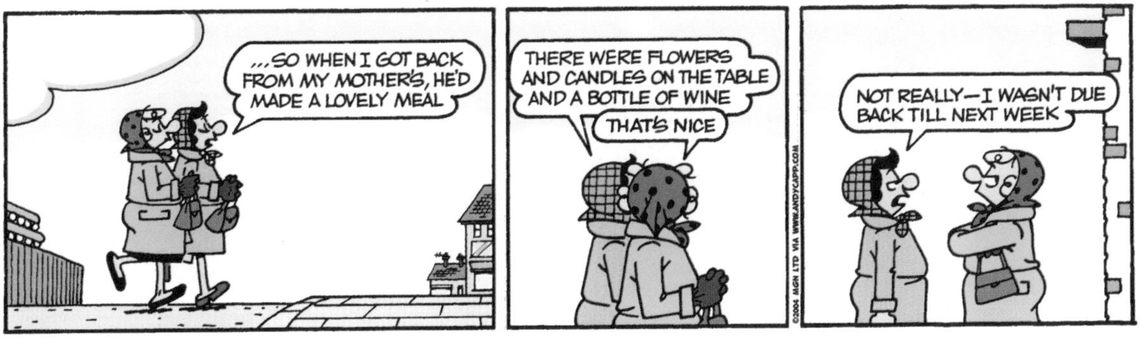
...SO WHEN I GOT BACK FROM MY MOTHER'S, HE'D MADE A LOVELY MEAL
THERE WERE FLOWERS AND CANDLES ON THE TABLE AND A BOTTLE OF WINE
THAT'S NICE
NOT REALLY—I WASN'T DUE BACK TILL NEXT WEEK

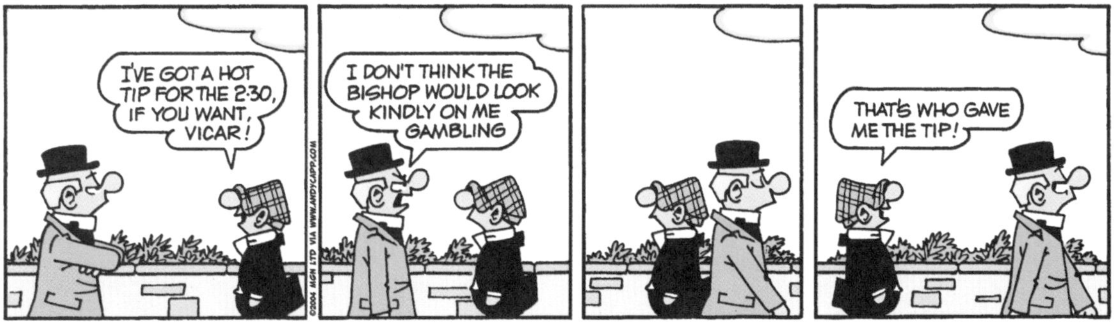
I'VE GOT A HOT TIP FOR THE 2:30, IF YOU WANT, VICAR!
I DON'T THINK THE BISHOP WOULD LOOK KINDLY ON ME GAMBLING
THAT'S WHO GAVE ME THE TIP!
©2004 MGN LTD VIA WWW.ANDYCAPP.COM

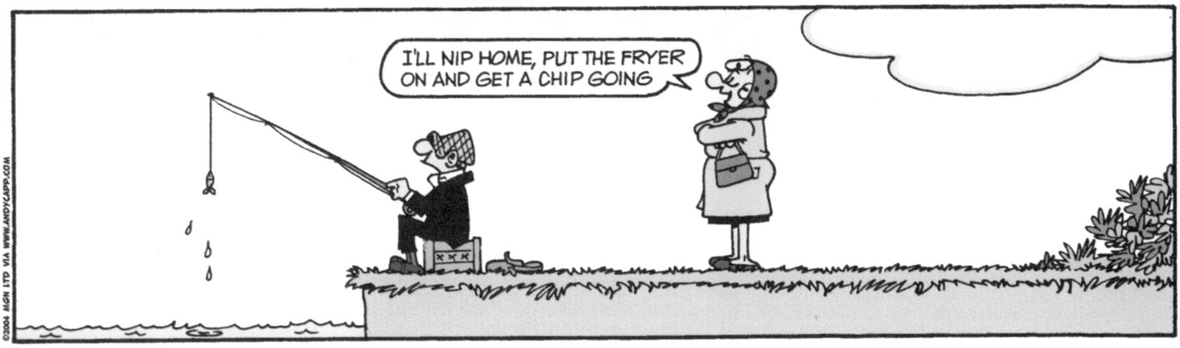
I'LL NIP HOME, PUT THE FRYER ON AND GET A CHIP GOING
©2004 MGN LTD VIA WWW.ANDYCAPP.COM

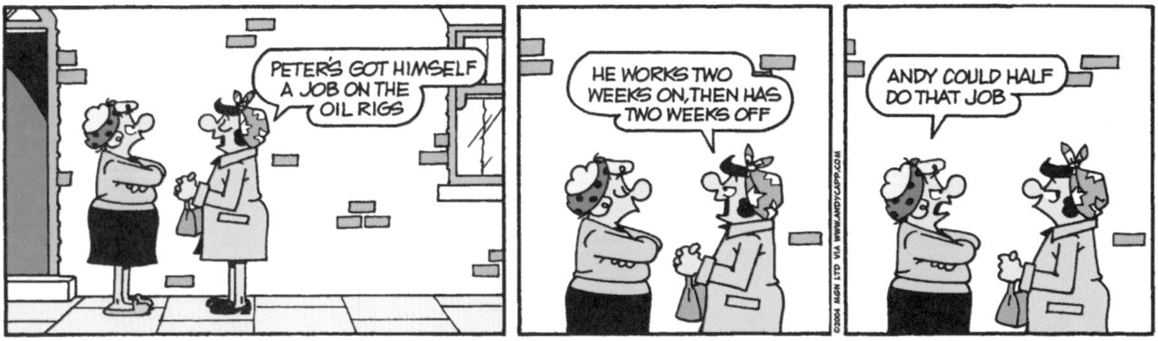
PETER'S GOT HIMSELF A JOB ON THE OIL RIGS
HE WORKS TWO WEEKS ON, THEN HAS TWO WEEKS OFF
ANDY COULD HALF DO THAT JOB
©2004 MGN LTD VIA WWW.ANDYCAPP.COM

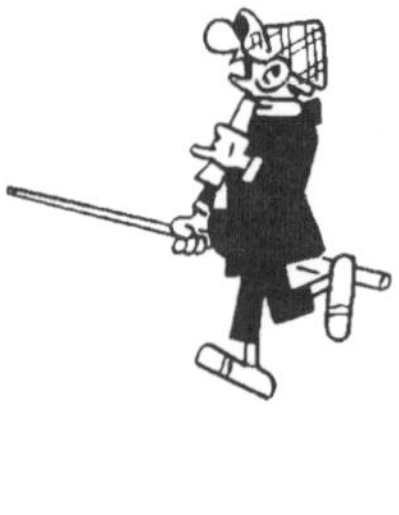

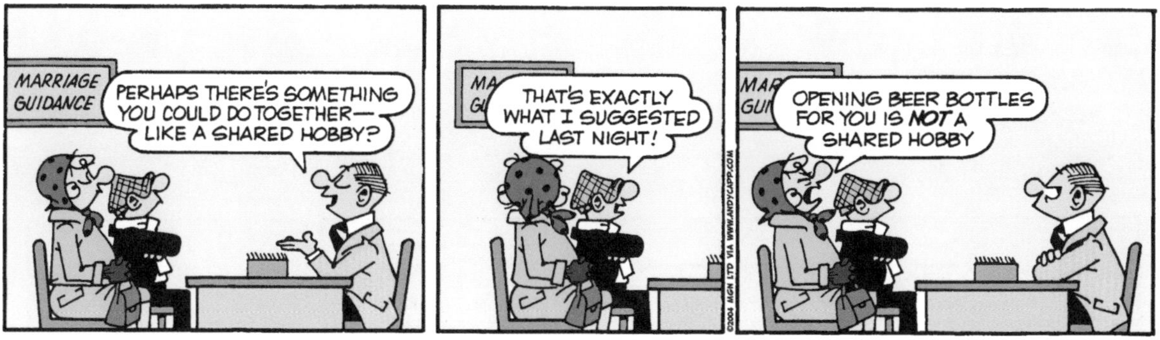
MARRIAGE GUIDANCE
PERHAPS THERE'S SOMETHING YOU COULD DO TOGETHER— LIKE A SHARED HOBBY?
THAT'S EXACTLY WHAT I SUGGESTED LAST NIGHT!
OPENING BEER BOTTLES FOR YOU IS NOT A SHARED HOBBY
©2004 MGN LTD VIA WWW.ANDYCAPP.COM

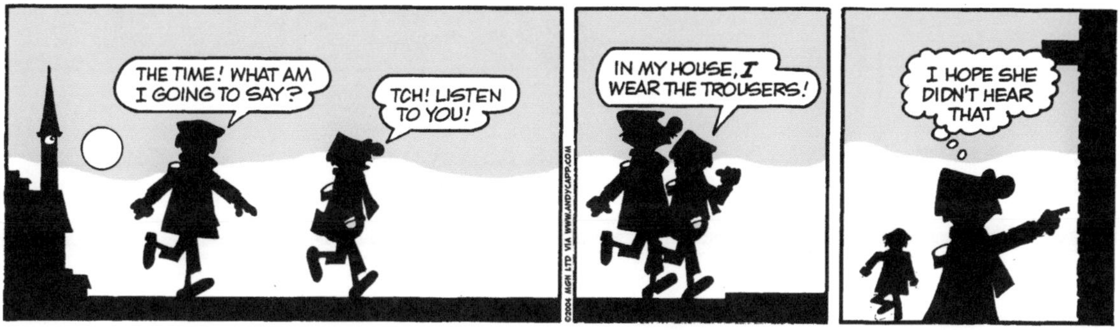
THE TIME! WHAT AM I GOING TO SAY?
TCH! LISTEN TO YOU!
IN MY HOUSE, I WEAR THE TROUSERS!
I HOPE SHE DIDN'T HEAR THAT
©2004 MGN LTD VIA WWW.ANDYCAPP.COM

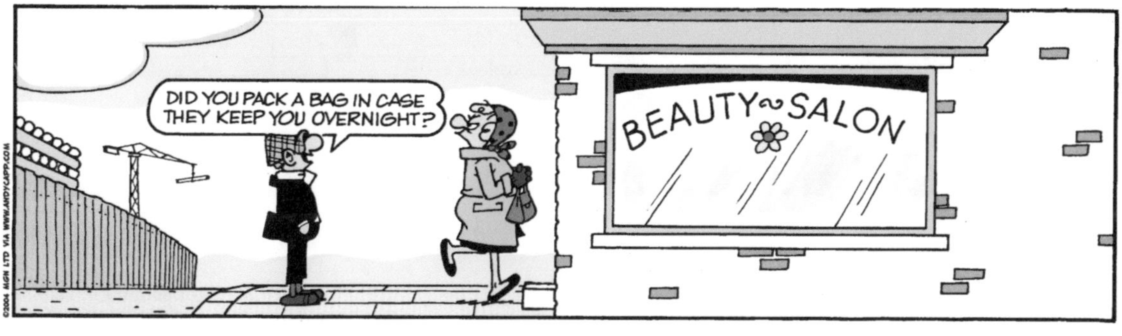
DID YOU PACK A BAG IN CASE THEY KEEP YOU OVERNIGHT?
BEAUTY SALON
©2004 MGN LTD VIA WWW.ANDYCAPP.COM

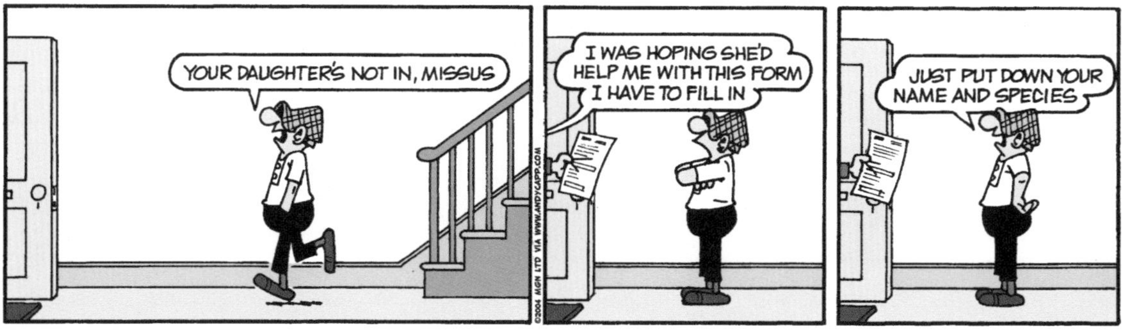
YOUR DAUGHTER'S NOT IN, MISSUS
©2004 MGN LTD VIA WWW.ANDYCAPP.COM
I WAS HOPING SHE'D HELP ME WITH THIS FORM I HAVE TO FILL IN
JUST PUT DOWN YOUR NAME AND SPECIES

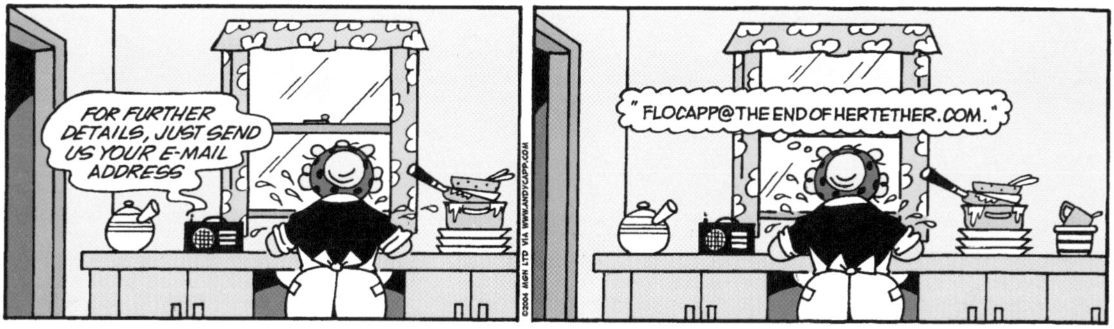
FOR FURTHER DETAILS, JUST SEND US YOUR E-MAIL ADDRESS
©2004 MGN LTD VIA WWW.ANDYCAPP.COM
"FLOCAPP@THE END OF HERTETHER.COM."

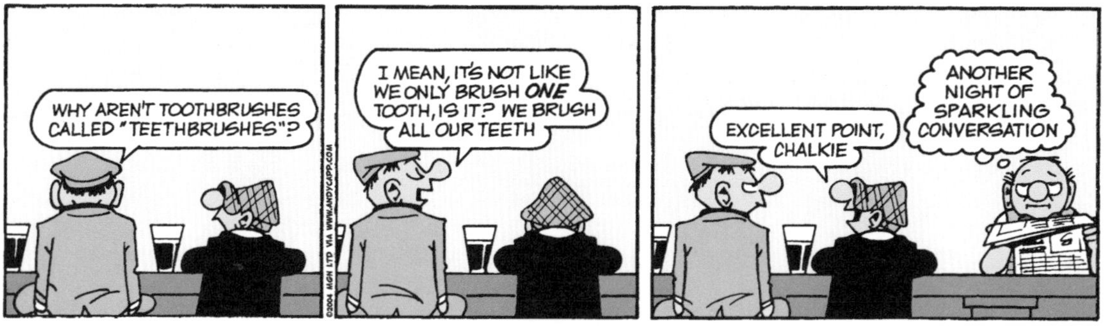
WHY AREN'T TOOTHBRUSHES CALLED "TEETHBRUSHES"?
©2004 MGN LTD VIA WWW.ANDYCAPP.COM
I MEAN, IT'S NOT LIKE WE ONLY BRUSH ONE TOOTH, IS IT? WE BRUSH ALL OUR TEETH
EXCELLENT POINT, CHALKIE
ANOTHER NIGHT OF SPARKLING CONVERSATION

MY NEPHEW'S DOING ENGLISH EXAMS AT THE MOMENT
©2004 MGN LTD VIA WWW.ANDYCAPP.COM
DON'T SEE THE POINT IN IT MYSELF
I MEAN, YOU'RE EITHER GOOD AT ENGLISH OR YOU ISN'T

I'M SORRY I'M LATE, PET, BUT I HAD TO BE FAIR TO THE OTHER LADS
©2004 MGN LTD VIA WWW.ANDYCAPP.COM
THEY DON'T HAVE A BEAUTIFUL WIFE TO COME HOME TO LIKE I DO!
YOU REALLY THOUGHT I'D SWALLOW THAT?
I WAS HOPEFUL BUT NOT CONFIDENT

I NOTICED YOU ROLLING OUT OF THE PUB AT MIDNIGHT, SINGING YOUR HEAD OFF
©2004 MGN LTD VIA WWW.ANDYCAPP.COM
I THINK THE LESS SAID ABOUT THAT, THE BETTER
SAY NO MORE, VICAR— NO ONE WILL HEAR FROM ME YOU WERE HANGING AROUND OUTSIDE THE PUB AT MIDNIGHT!

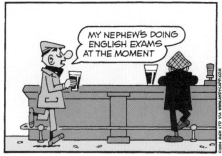

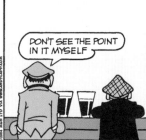

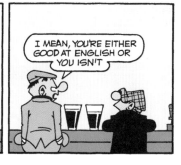

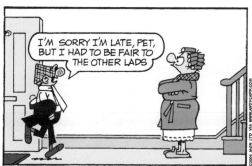

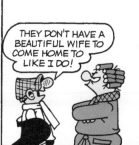

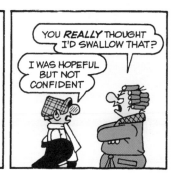

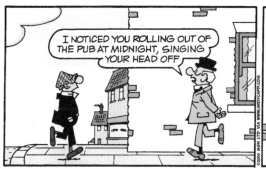

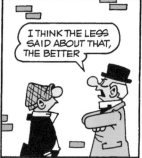

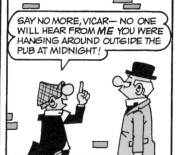

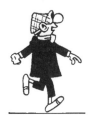

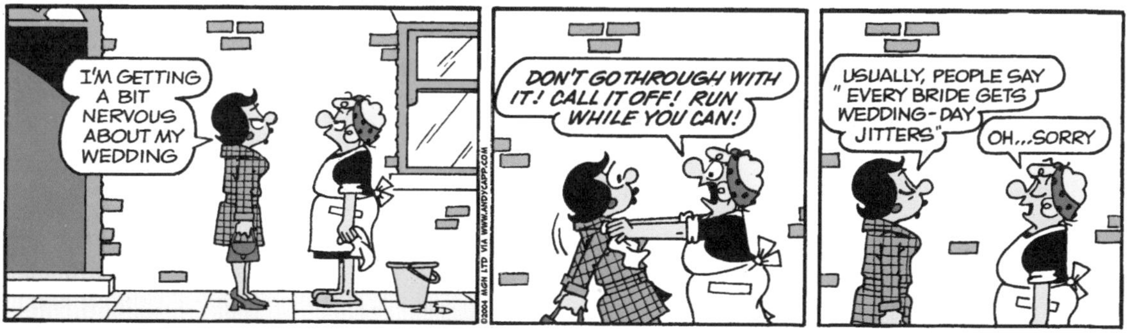
I'M GETTING A BIT NERVOUS ABOUT MY WEDDING
DON'T GO THROUGH WITH IT! CALL IT OFF! RUN WHILE YOU CAN!
USUALLY, PEOPLE SAY "EVERY BRIDE GETS WEDDING-DAY JITTERS"
OH... SORRY
©2004 MGN LTD VIA WWW.ANDYCAPP.COM

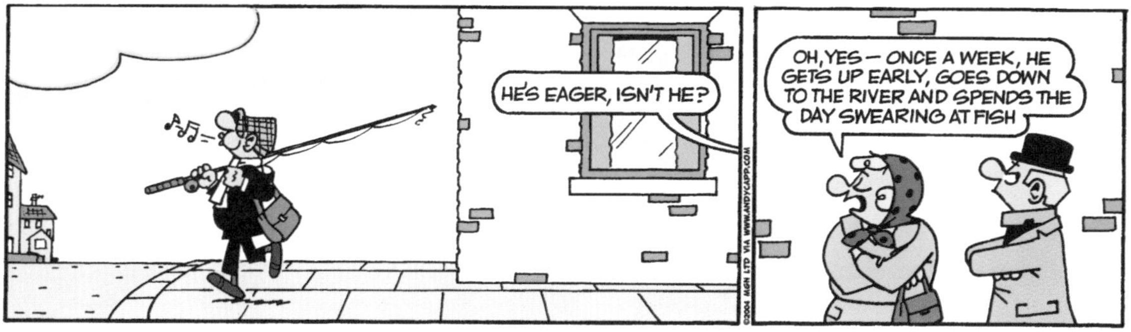
HE'S EAGER, ISN'T HE?
OH, YES — ONCE A WEEK, HE GETS UP EARLY, GOES DOWN TO THE RIVER AND SPENDS THE DAY SWEARING AT FISH
©2004 MGN LTD VIA WWW.ANDYCAPP.COM

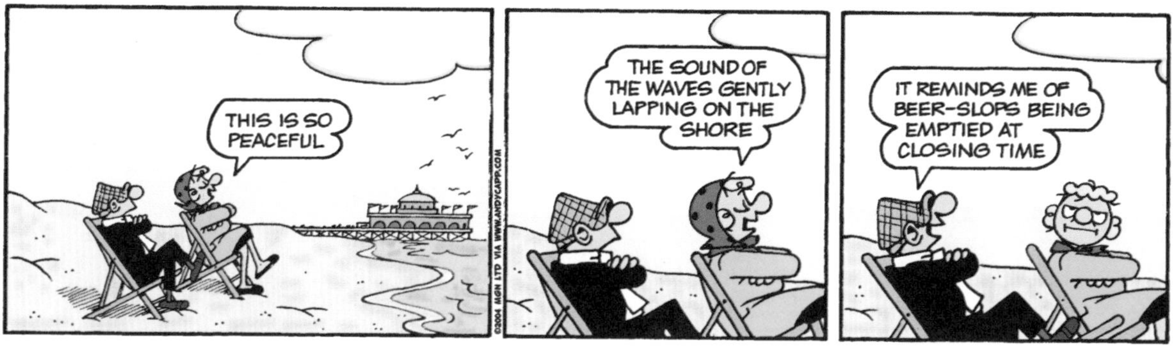
THIS IS SO PEACEFUL
THE SOUND OF THE WAVES GENTLY LAPPING ON THE SHORE
IT REMINDS ME OF BEER-SLOPS BEING EMPTIED AT CLOSING TIME
©2004 MGN LTD VIA WWW.ANDYCAPP.COM

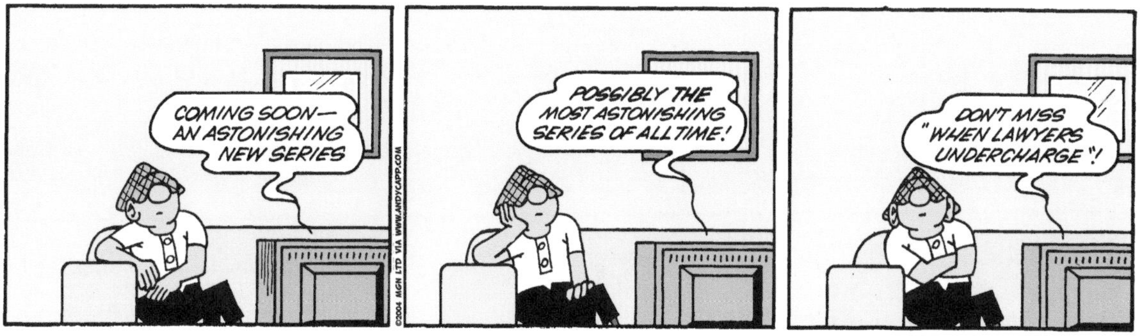
COMING SOON— AN ASTONISHING NEW SERIES
©2004 MGN LTD VIA WWW.ANDYCAPP.COM
POSSIBLY THE MOST ASTONISHING SERIES OF ALL TIME!
DON'T MISS "WHEN LAWYERS UNDERCHARGE"!

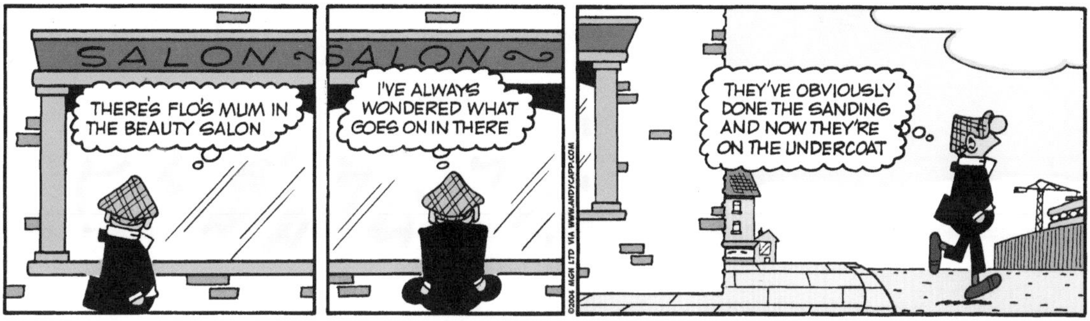
SALON
THERE'S FLO'S MUM IN THE BEAUTY SALON
SALON
I'VE ALWAYS WONDERED WHAT GOES ON IN THERE
©2004 MGN LTD VIA WWW.ANDYCAPP.COM
THEY'VE OBVIOUSLY DONE THE SANDING AND NOW THEY'RE ON THE UNDERCOAT

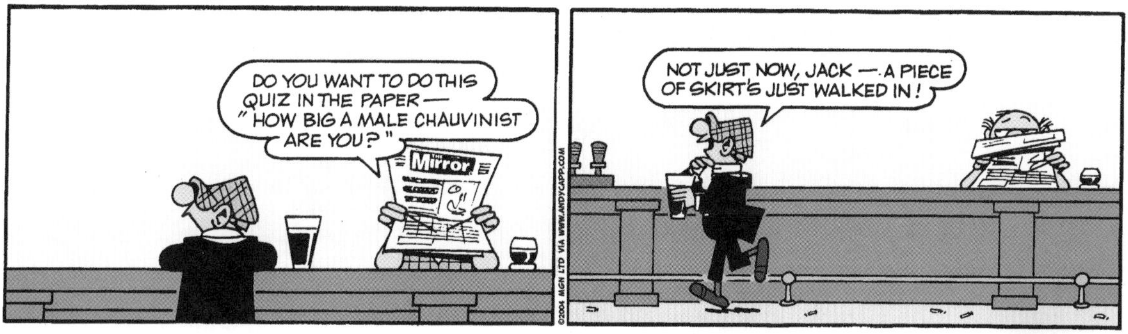
DO YOU WANT TO DO THIS QUIZ IN THE PAPER— "HOW BIG A MALE CHAUVINIST ARE YOU?"
Mirror
©2004 MGN LTD VIA WWW.ANDYCAPP.COM
NOT JUST NOW, JACK — A PIECE OF SKIRT'S JUST WALKED IN!

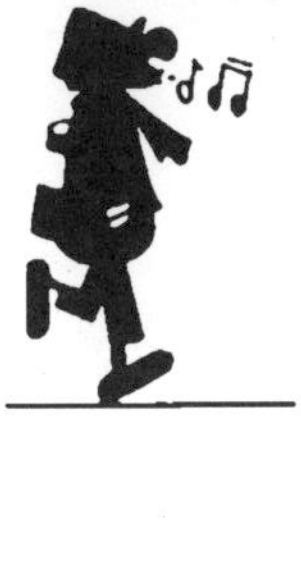

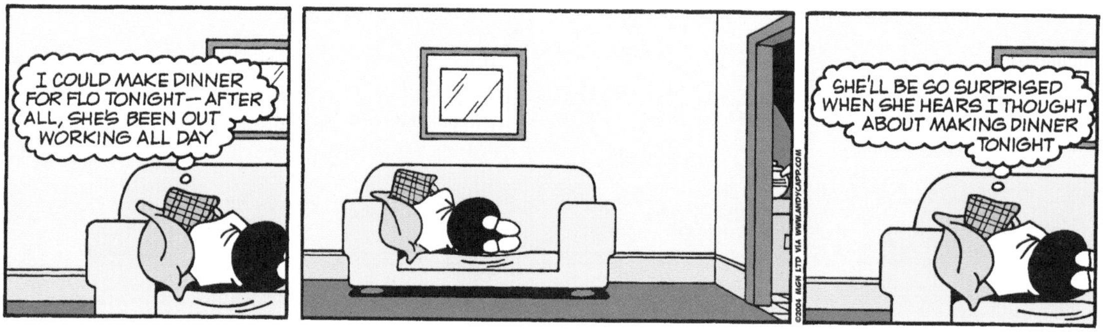
I COULD MAKE DINNER FOR FLO TONIGHT— AFTER ALL, SHE'S BEEN OUT WORKING ALL DAY
SHE'LL BE SO SURPRISED WHEN SHE HEARS I THOUGHT ABOUT MAKING DINNER TONIGHT

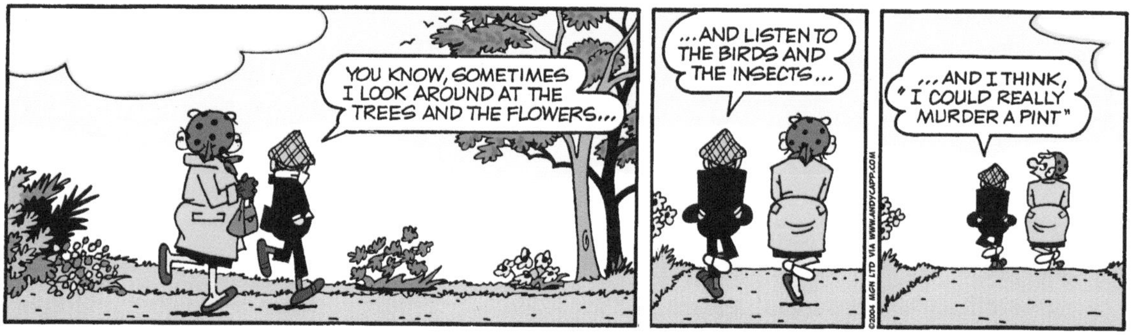
YOU KNOW, SOMETIMES I LOOK AROUND AT THE TREES AND THE FLOWERS...
...AND LISTEN TO THE BIRDS AND THE INSECTS...
...AND I THINK, "I COULD REALLY MURDER A PINT"

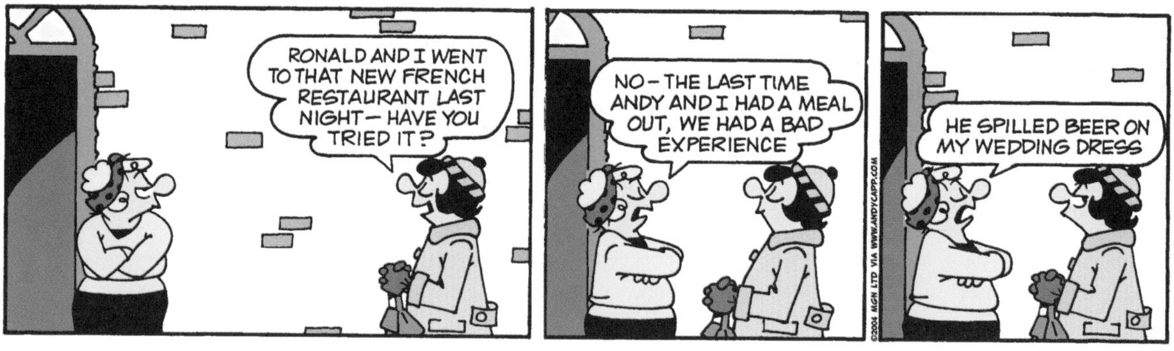
RONALD AND I WENT TO THAT NEW FRENCH RESTAURANT LAST NIGHT— HAVE YOU TRIED IT?
NO— THE LAST TIME ANDY AND I HAD A MEAL OUT, WE HAD A BAD EXPERIENCE
HE SPILLED BEER ON MY WEDDING DRESS

IF YOU PUT A POUND ON A HORSE AT 17–2 AND IT WINS, WHAT DO YOU GET?
©2004 MGN LTD VIA WWW.ANDYCAPP.COM
IN MY CASE, A SHOCK

IT'S A POSTCARD FROM THAT COUSIN OF YOURS WHO WENT TO AUSTRALIA
WELL, WELL, WELL! FROM THE COUSIN YOU SAID WAS TOO STUPID TO **FIND** AUSTRALIA — I'LL ACCEPT YOUR APOLOGY
©2004 MGN LTD VIA WWW.ANDYCAPP.COM
THE POSTCARD'S FROM GREENLAND

MY STARS SAY THERE'S LOVE ON THE HORIZON
OO, THAT'S EXCITING — WHAT DO MINE SAY?
©2004 MGN LTD VIA WWW.ANDYCAPP.COM
"IGNORE THIRSTY STRANGER AT YOUR PERIL!"

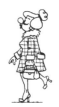

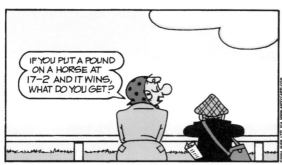

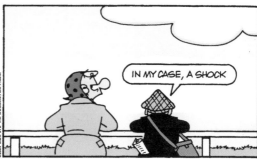

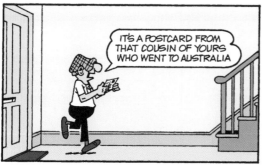

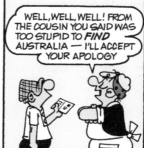

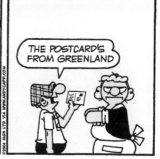

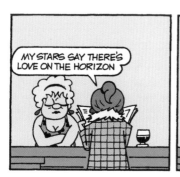

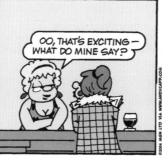

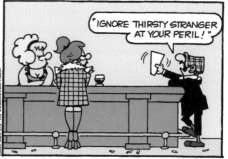

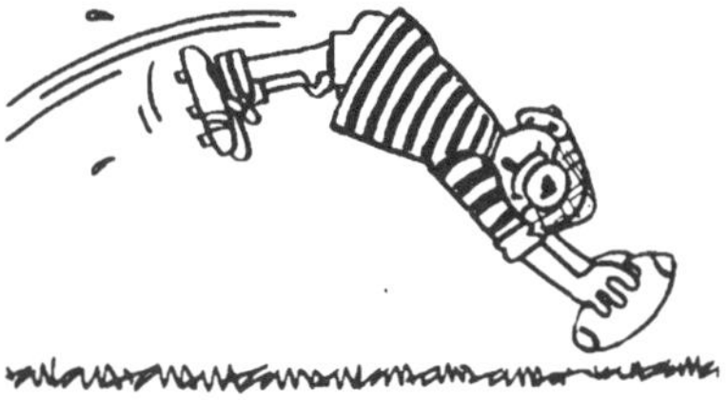

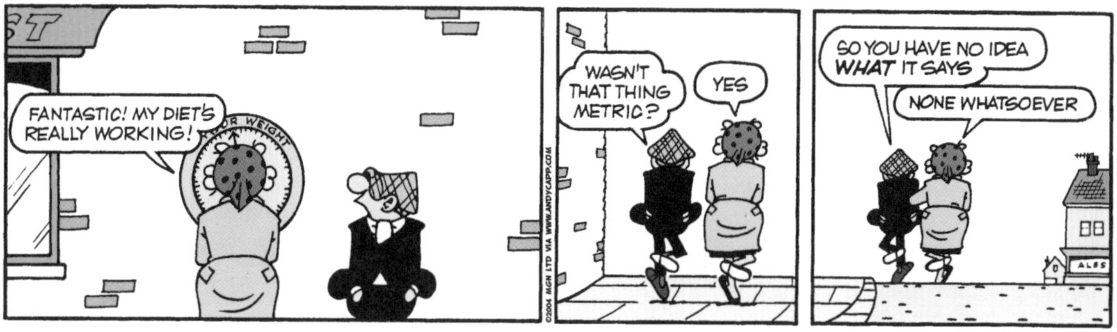
FANTASTIC! MY DIET'S REALLY WORKING!
©2004 MGN LTD VIA WWW.ANDYCAPP.COM
WASN'T THAT THING METRIC?
YES
SO YOU HAVE NO IDEA **WHAT** IT SAYS
NONE WHATSOEVER
ALES

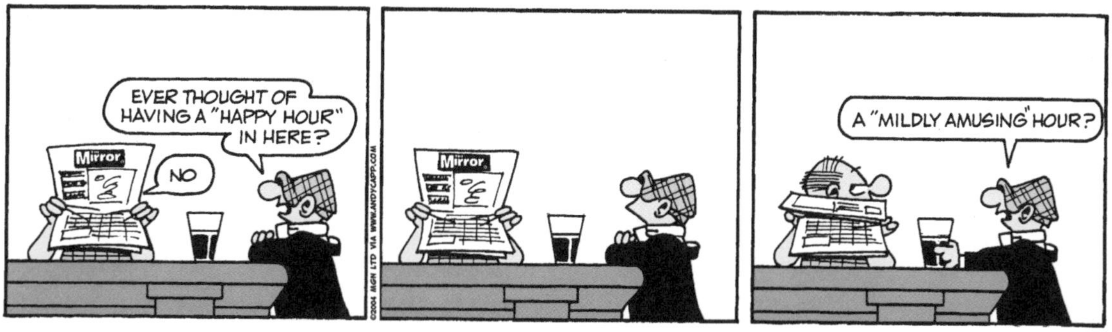
Mirror
EVER THOUGHT OF HAVING A "HAPPY HOUR" IN HERE?
NO
©2004 MGN LTD VIA WWW.ANDYCAPP.COM
Mirror
A "MILDLY AMUSING" HOUR?

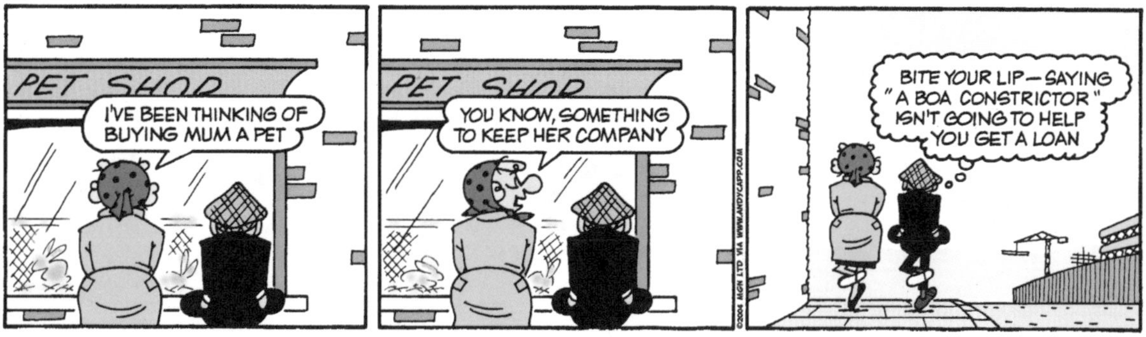
PET SHOP
I'VE BEEN THINKING OF BUYING MUM A PET
PET SHOP
YOU KNOW, SOMETHING TO KEEP HER COMPANY
©2004 MGN LTD VIA WWW.ANDYCAPP.COM
BITE YOUR LIP—SAYING "A BOA CONSTRICTOR" ISN'T GOING TO HELP YOU GET A LOAN

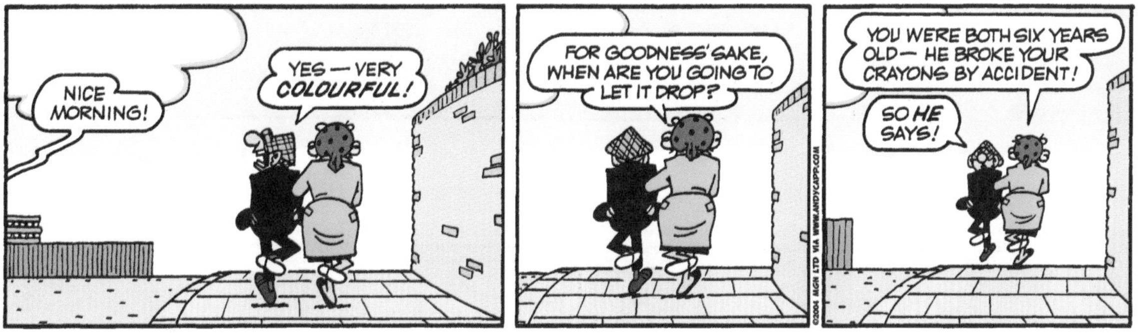
NICE MORNING!
YES — VERY COLOURFUL!
FOR GOODNESS' SAKE, WHEN ARE YOU GOING TO LET IT DROP?
YOU WERE BOTH SIX YEARS OLD— HE BROKE YOUR CRAYONS BY ACCIDENT!
SO HE SAYS!
©2004 MGN LTD VIA WWW.ANDYCAPP.COM

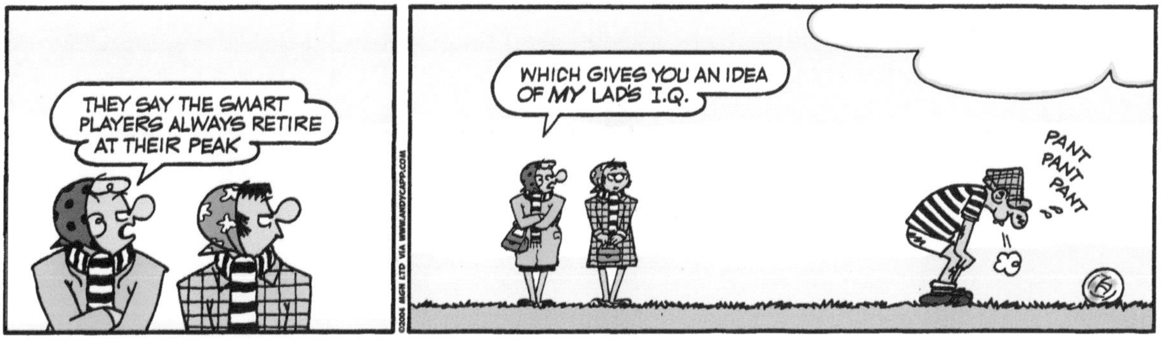
THEY SAY THE SMART PLAYERS ALWAYS RETIRE AT THEIR PEAK
©2004 MGN LTD VIA WWW.ANDYCAPP.COM
WHICH GIVES YOU AN IDEA OF MY LAD'S I.Q.
PANT
PANT
PANT

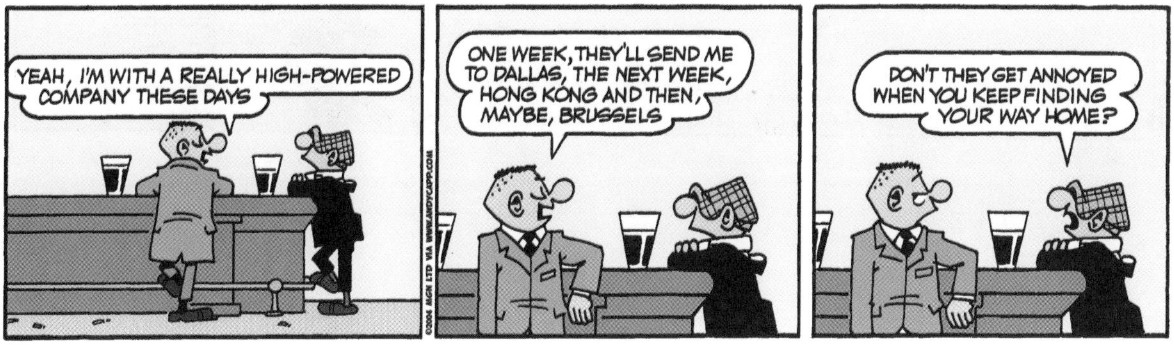
YEAH, I'M WITH A REALLY HIGH-POWERED COMPANY THESE DAYS
©2004 MGN LTD VIA WWW.ANDYCAPP.COM
ONE WEEK, THEY'LL SEND ME TO DALLAS, THE NEXT WEEK, HONG KONG AND THEN, MAYBE, BRUSSELS
DON'T THEY GET ANNOYED WHEN YOU KEEP FINDING YOUR WAY HOME?

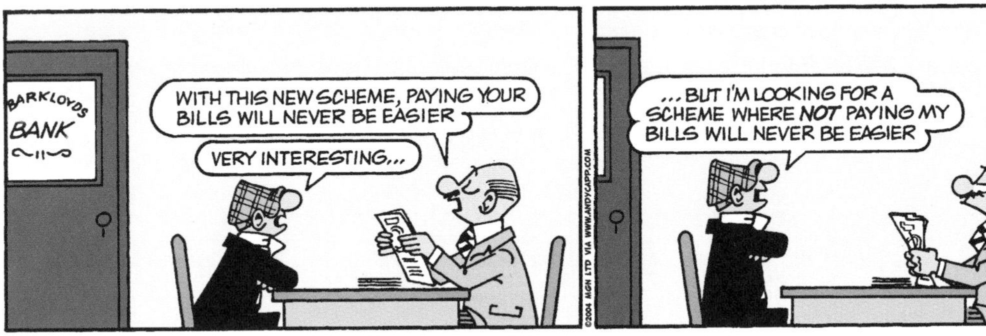
BARKLOYDS BANK
WITH THIS NEW SCHEME, PAYING YOUR BILLS WILL NEVER BE EASIER
VERY INTERESTING...
©2004 MGN LTD VIA WWW.ANDYCAPP.COM
... BUT I'M LOOKING FOR A SCHEME WHERE NOT PAYING MY BILLS WILL NEVER BE EASIER

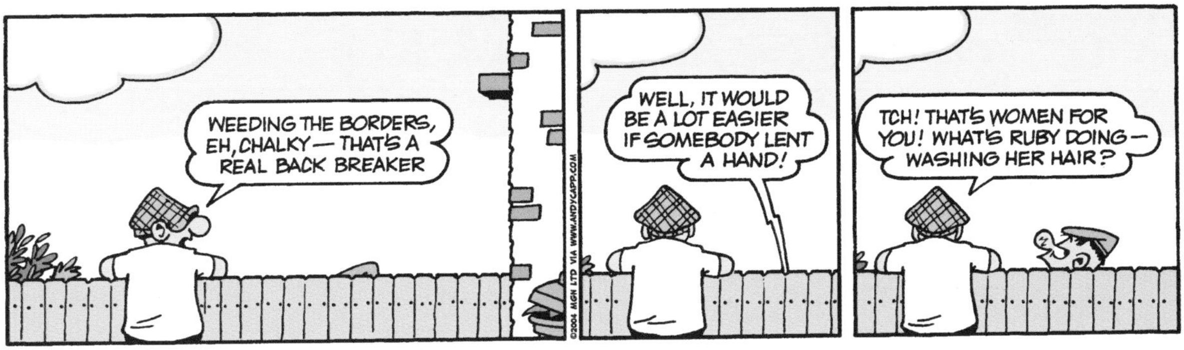
WEEDING THE BORDERS, EH, CHALKY — THAT'S A REAL BACK BREAKER
©2004 MGN LTD VIA WWW.ANDYCAPP.COM
WELL, IT WOULD BE A LOT EASIER IF SOMEBODY LENT A HAND!
TCH! THAT'S WOMEN FOR YOU! WHAT'S RUBY DOING — WASHING HER HAIR?

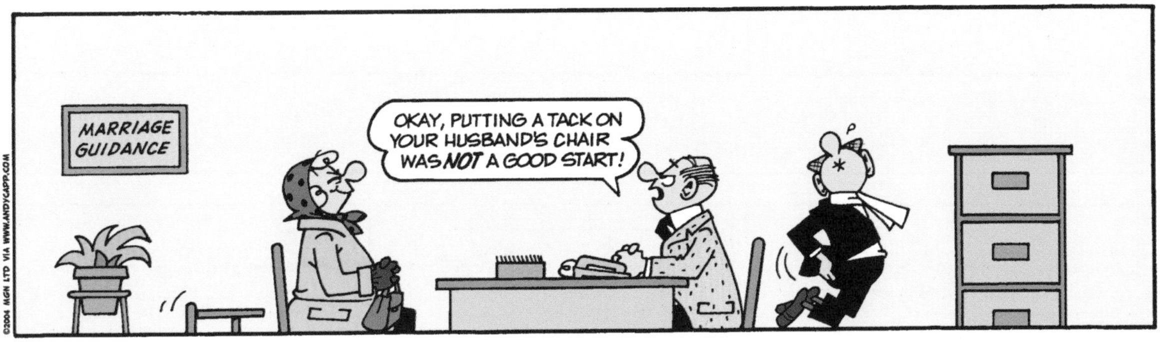
©2004 MGN LTD VIA WWW.ANDYCAPP.COM
MARRIAGE GUIDANCE
OKAY, PUTTING A TACK ON YOUR HUSBAND'S CHAIR WAS NOT A GOOD START!

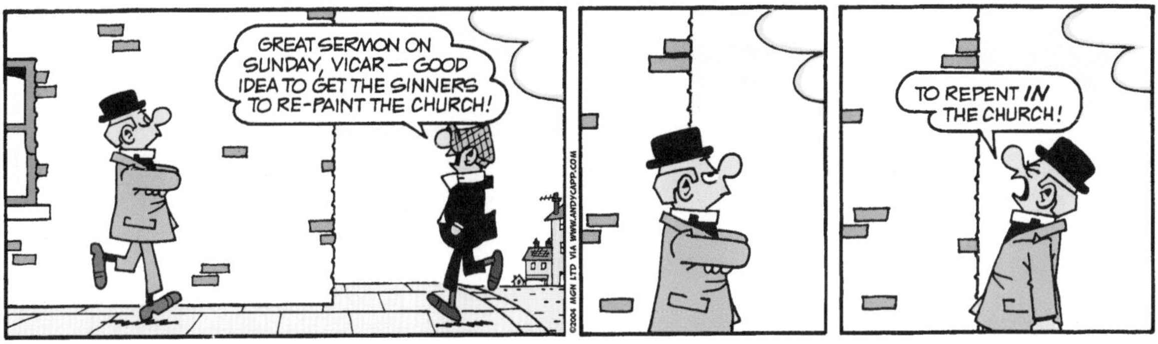
GREAT SERMON ON SUNDAY, VICAR — GOOD IDEA TO GET THE SINNERS TO RE-PAINT THE CHURCH!
©2004 MGN LTD VIA WWW.ANDYCAPP.COM
TO REPENT *IN* THE CHURCH!

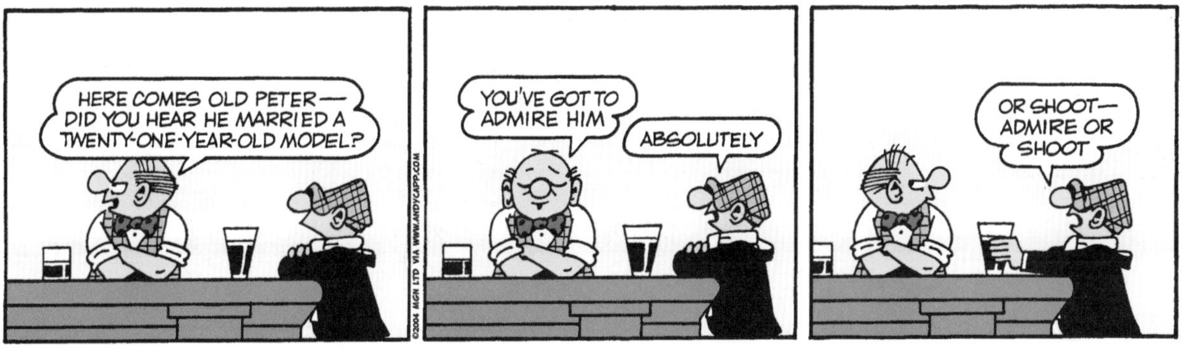
HERE COMES OLD PETER — DID YOU HEAR HE MARRIED A TWENTY-ONE-YEAR-OLD MODEL?
©2004 MGN LTD VIA WWW.ANDYCAPP.COM
YOU'VE GOT TO ADMIRE HIM
ABSOLUTELY
OR SHOOT — ADMIRE OR SHOOT

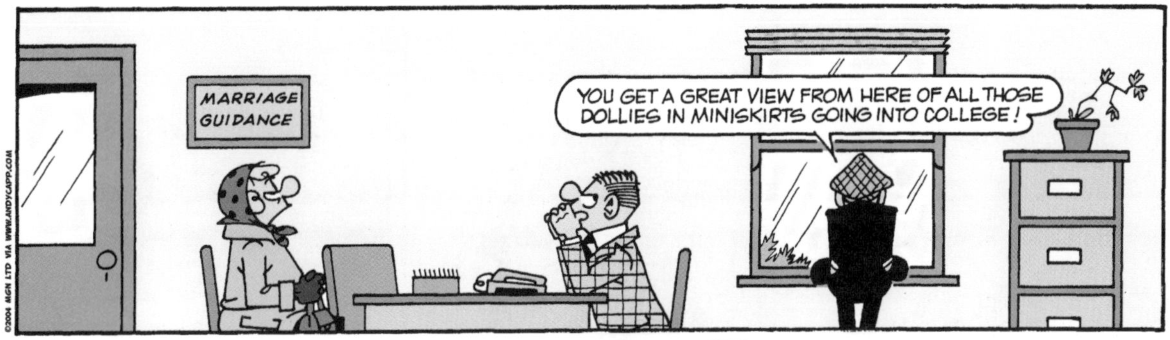
©2004 MGN LTD VIA WWW.ANDYCAPP.COM
MARRIAGE GUIDANCE
YOU GET A GREAT VIEW FROM HERE OF ALL THOSE DOLLIES IN MINISKIRTS GOING INTO COLLEGE!

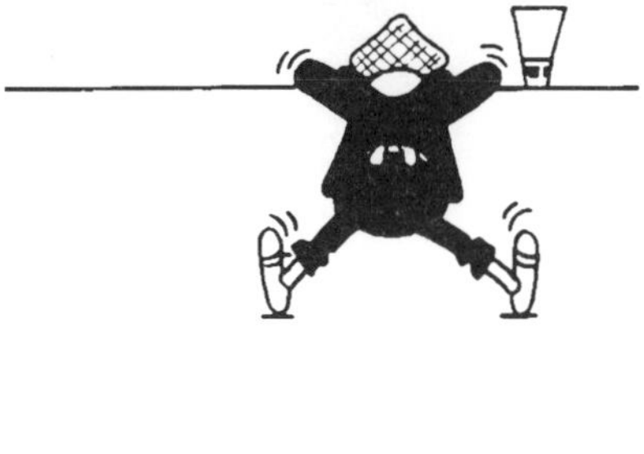

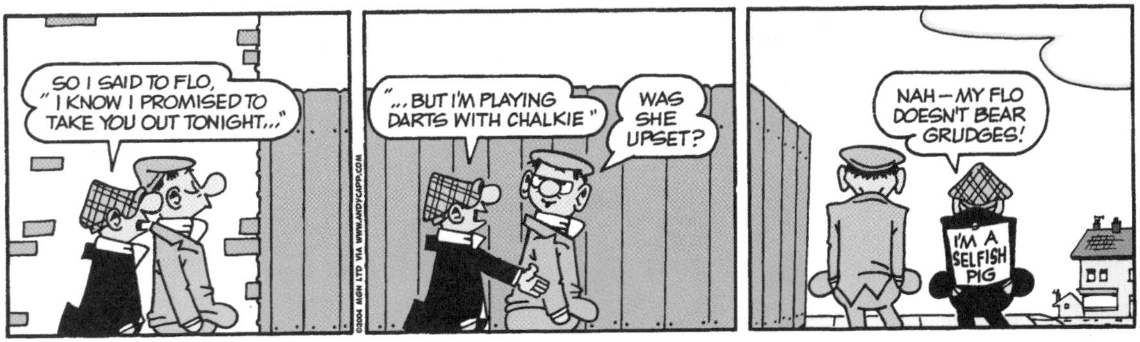
SO I SAID TO FLO, " I KNOW I PROMISED TO TAKE YOU OUT TONIGHT..."
"... BUT I'M PLAYING DARTS WITH CHALKIE"
WAS SHE UPSET?
NAH — MY FLO DOESN'T BEAR GRUDGES!
I'M A SELFISH PIG
©2004 MGN LTD VIA WWW.ANDYCAPP.COM

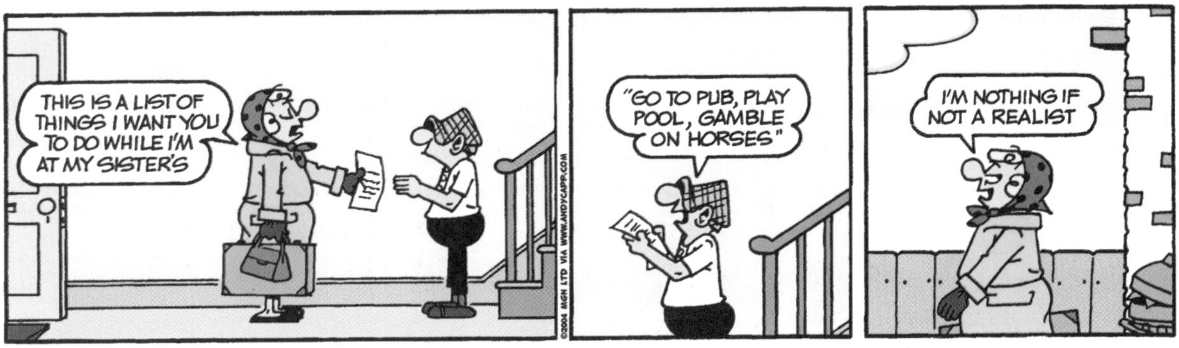
THIS IS A LIST OF THINGS I WANT YOU TO DO WHILE I'M AT MY SISTER'S
"GO TO PUB, PLAY POOL, GAMBLE ON HORSES"
I'M NOTHING IF NOT A REALIST
©2004 MGN LTD VIA WWW.ANDYCAPP.COM

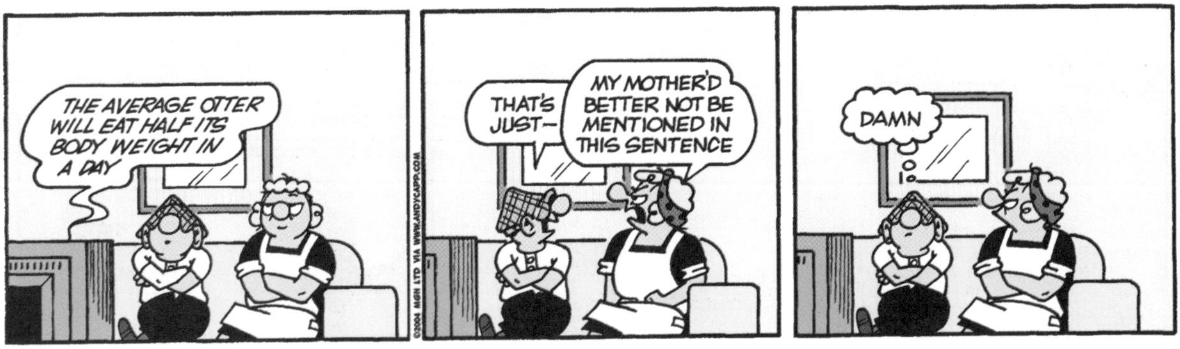
THE AVERAGE OTTER WILL EAT HALF ITS BODY WEIGHT IN A DAY
THAT'S JUST—
MY MOTHER'D BETTER NOT BE MENTIONED IN THIS SENTENCE
DAMN
©2004 MGN LTD VIA WWW.ANDYCAPP.COM

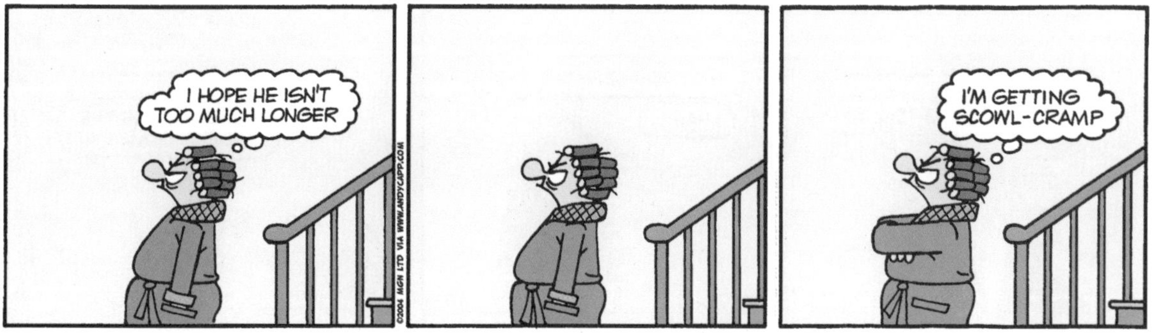
I HOPE HE ISN'T TOO MUCH LONGER
©2004 MGN LTD VIA WWW.ANDYCAPP.COM
I'M GETTING SCOWL-CRAMP

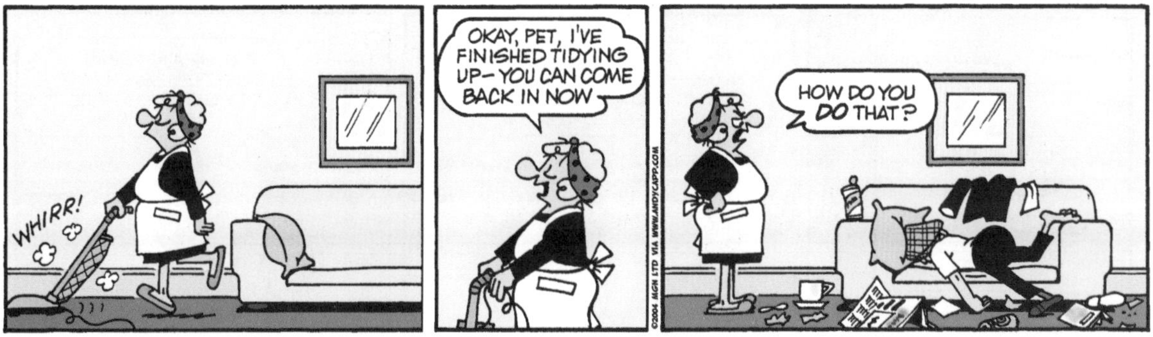
WHIRR!
OKAY, PET, I'VE FINISHED TIDYING UP– YOU CAN COME BACK IN NOW
©2004 MGN LTD VIA WWW.ANDYCAPP.COM
HOW DO YOU **DO** THAT?

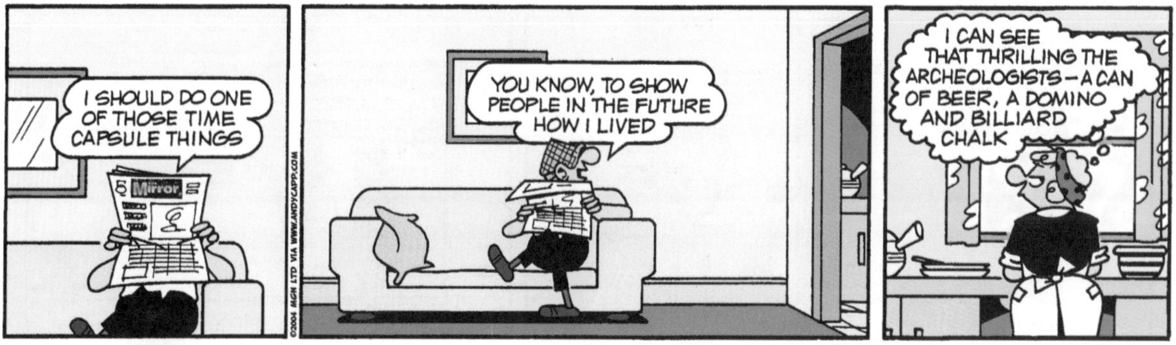
I SHOULD DO ONE OF THOSE TIME CAPSULE THINGS
Mirror
©2004 MGN LTD VIA WWW.ANDYCAPP.COM
YOU KNOW, TO SHOW PEOPLE IN THE FUTURE HOW I LIVED
I CAN SEE THAT THRILLING THE ARCHEOLOGISTS–A CAN OF BEER, A DOMINO AND BILLIARD CHALK

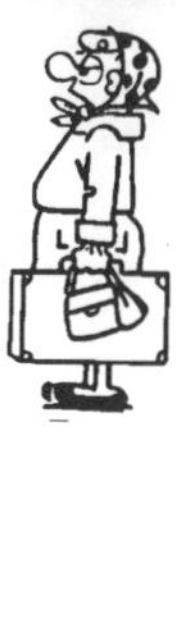

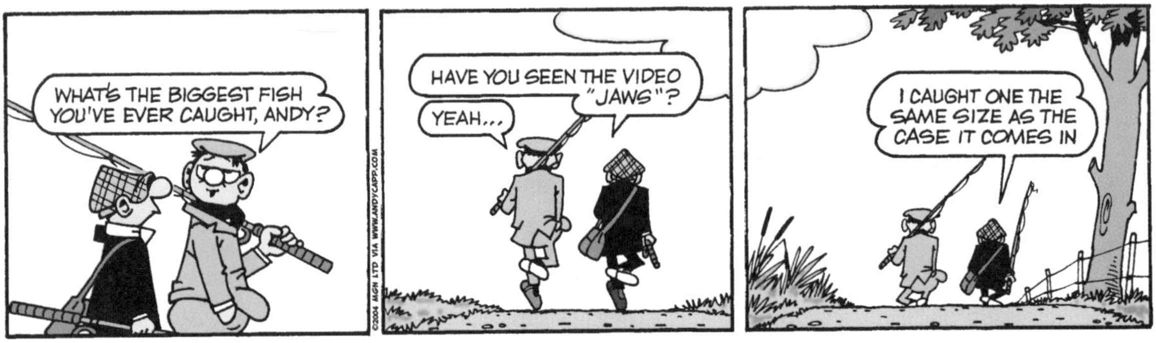
WHAT'S THE BIGGEST FISH YOU'VE EVER CAUGHT, ANDY?
©2004 MGN LTD VIA WWW.ANDYCAPP.COM
HAVE YOU SEEN THE VIDEO "JAWS"?
YEAH...
I CAUGHT ONE THE SAME SIZE AS THE CASE IT COMES IN

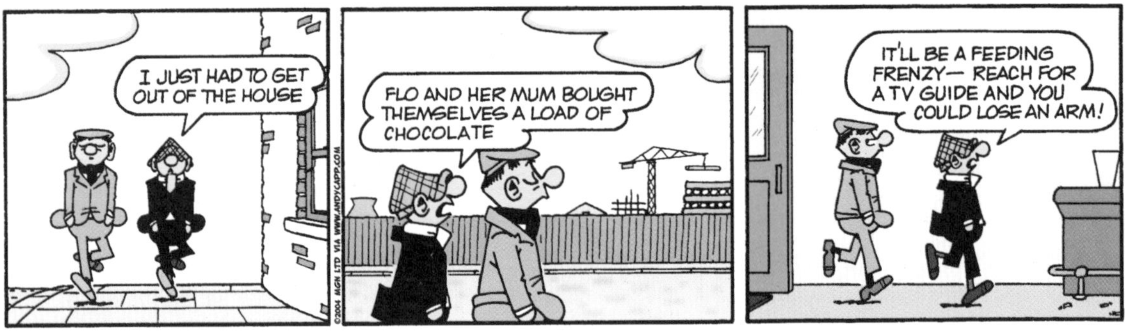
I JUST HAD TO GET OUT OF THE HOUSE
©2004 MGN LTD VIA WWW.ANDYCAPP.COM
FLO AND HER MUM BOUGHT THEMSELVES A LOAD OF CHOCOLATE
IT'LL BE A FEEDING FRENZY— REACH FOR A TV GUIDE AND YOU COULD LOSE AN ARM!

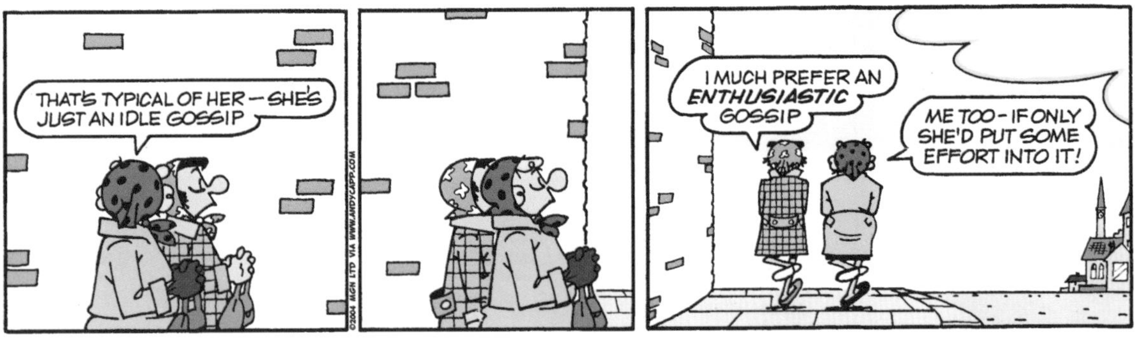
THAT'S TYPICAL OF HER — SHE'S JUST AN IDLE GOSSIP
©2004 MGN LTD VIA WWW.ANDYCAPP.COM
I MUCH PREFER AN ENTHUSIASTIC GOSSIP
ME TOO - IF ONLY SHE'D PUT SOME EFFORT INTO IT!

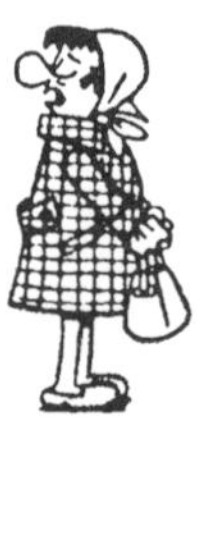

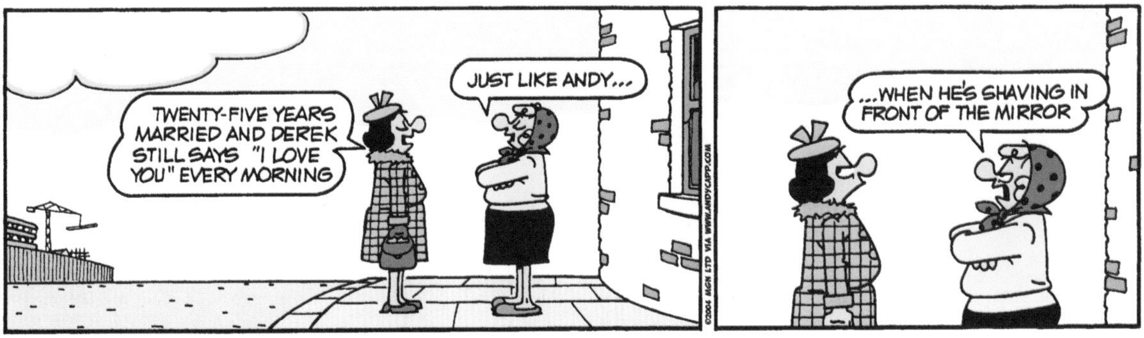
TWENTY-FIVE YEARS MARRIED AND DEREK STILL SAYS "I LOVE YOU" EVERY MORNING
JUST LIKE ANDY...
...WHEN HE'S SHAVING IN FRONT OF THE MIRROR
©2004 MGN LTD VIA WWW.ANDYCAPP.COM

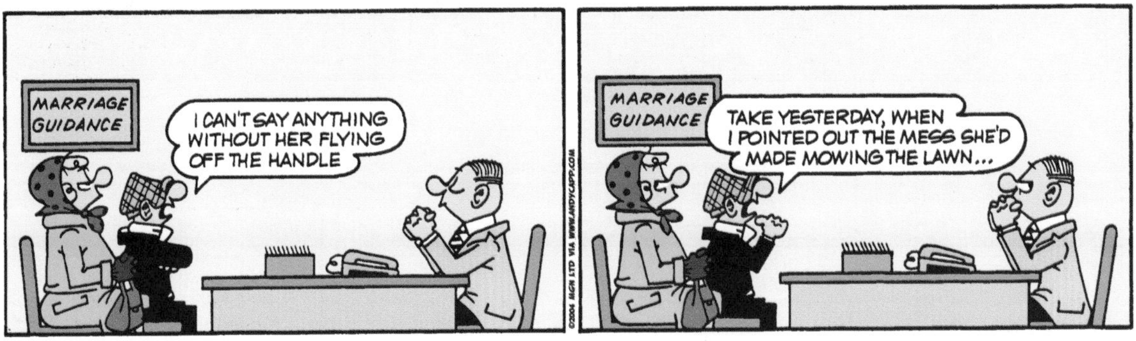
MARRIAGE GUIDANCE
I CAN'T SAY ANYTHING WITHOUT HER FLYING OFF THE HANDLE
MARRIAGE GUIDANCE
TAKE YESTERDAY, WHEN I POINTED OUT THE MESS SHE'D MADE MOWING THE LAWN...
©2004 MGN LTD VIA WWW.ANDYCAPP.COM

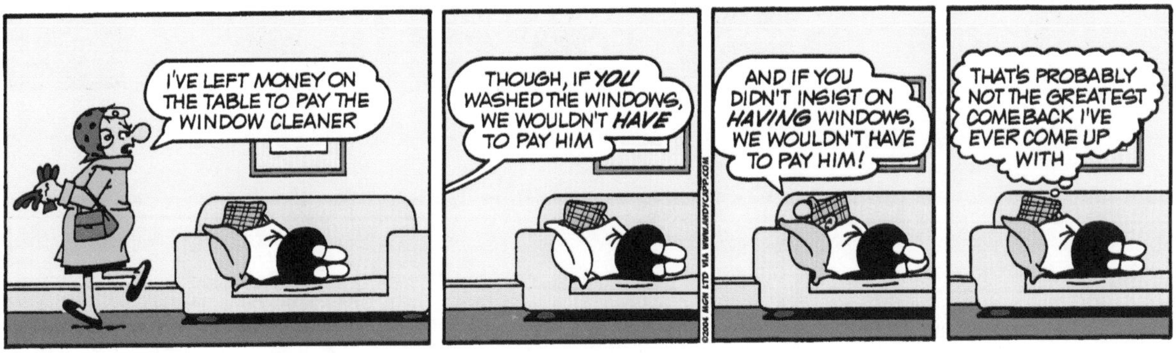
I'VE LEFT MONEY ON THE TABLE TO PAY THE WINDOW CLEANER
THOUGH, IF YOU WASHED THE WINDOWS, WE WOULDN'T HAVE TO PAY HIM
AND IF YOU DIDN'T INSIST ON HAVING WINDOWS, WE WOULDN'T HAVE TO PAY HIM!
THAT'S PROBABLY NOT THE GREATEST COMEBACK I'VE EVER COME UP WITH
©2004 MGN LTD VIA WWW.ANDYCAPP.COM

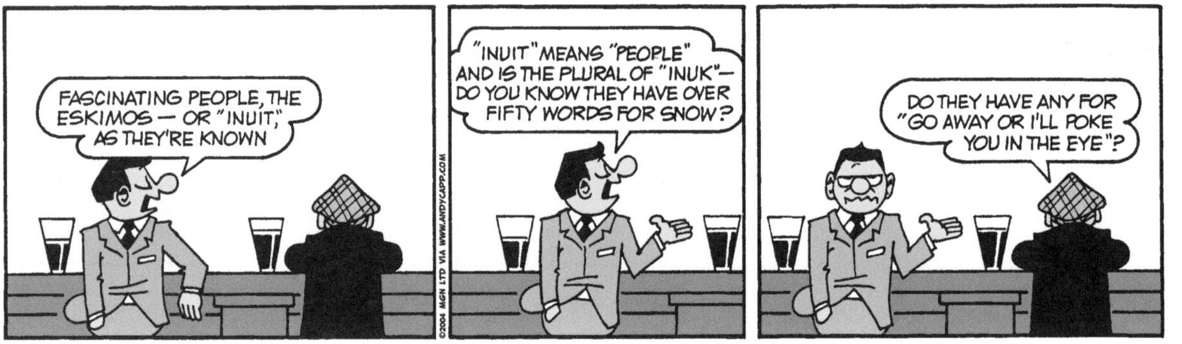
FASCINATING PEOPLE, THE ESKIMOS — OR "INUIT," AS THEY'RE KNOWN
©2004 MGN LTD VIA WWW.ANDYCAPP.COM
"INUIT" MEANS "PEOPLE" AND IS THE PLURAL OF "INUK"— DO YOU KNOW THEY HAVE OVER FIFTY WORDS FOR SNOW?
DO THEY HAVE ANY FOR "GO AWAY OR I'LL POKE YOU IN THE EYE"?

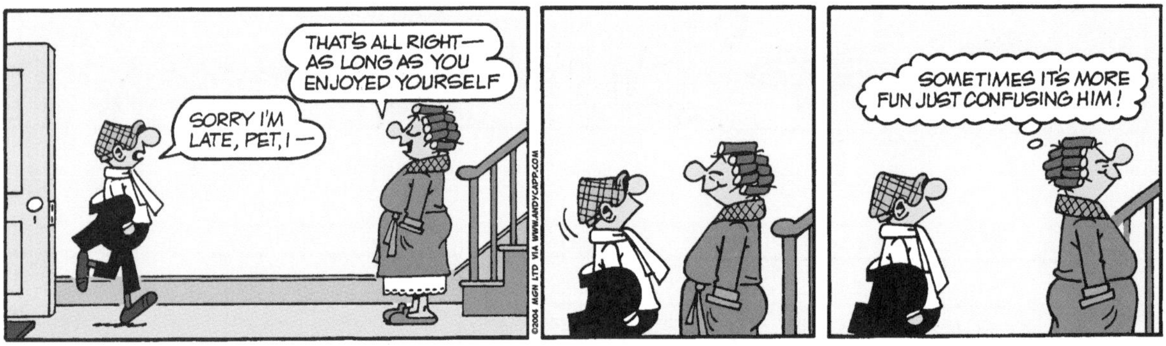
SORRY I'M LATE, PET, I —
THAT'S ALL RIGHT— AS LONG AS YOU ENJOYED YOURSELF
©2004 MGN LTD VIA WWW.ANDYCAPP.COM
SOMETIMES IT'S MORE FUN JUST CONFUSING HIM!

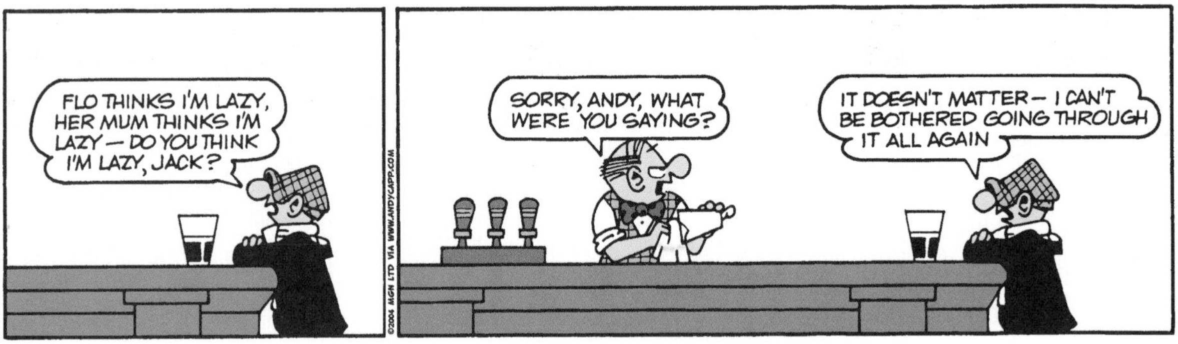
FLO THINKS I'M LAZY, HER MUM THINKS I'M LAZY — DO YOU THINK I'M LAZY, JACK?
©2004 MGN LTD VIA WWW.ANDYCAPP.COM
SORRY, ANDY, WHAT WERE YOU SAYING?
IT DOESN'T MATTER — I CAN'T BE BOTHERED GOING THROUGH IT ALL AGAIN

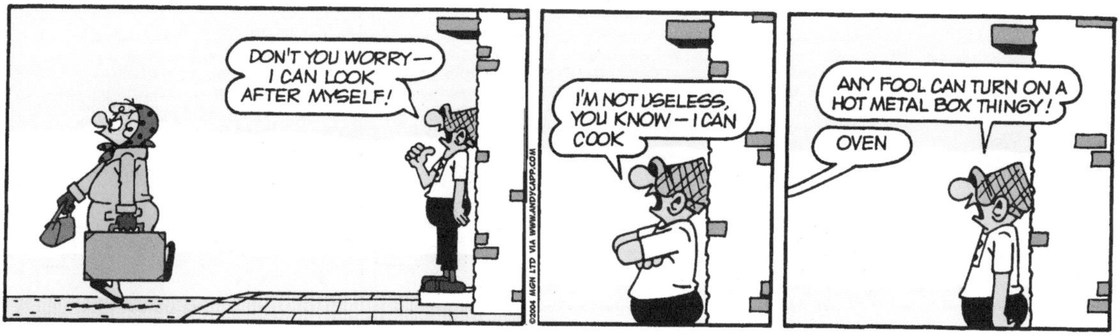
DON'T YOU WORRY— I CAN LOOK AFTER MYSELF!
©2004 MGN LTD VIA WWW.ANDYCAPP.COM
I'M NOT USELESS, YOU KNOW — I CAN COOK
ANY FOOL CAN TURN ON A HOT METAL BOX THINGY!
OVEN

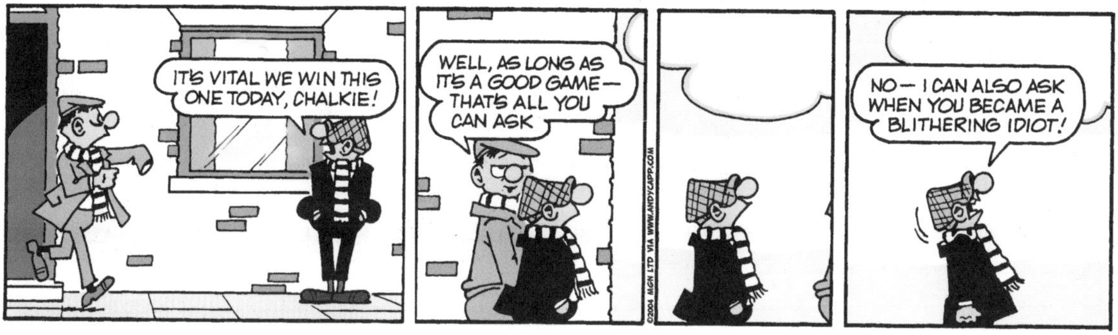
IT'S VITAL WE WIN THIS ONE TODAY, CHALKIE!
WELL, AS LONG AS IT'S A GOOD GAME— THAT'S ALL YOU CAN ASK
©2004 MGN LTD VIA WWW.ANDYCAPP.COM
NO— I CAN ALSO ASK WHEN YOU BECAME A BLITHERING IDIOT!

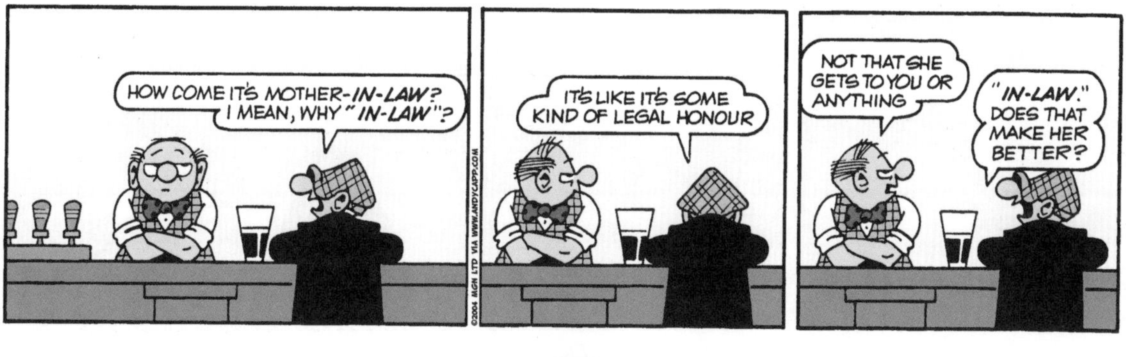
HOW COME IT'S MOTHER-IN-LAW? I MEAN, WHY "IN-LAW"?
©2004 MGN LTD VIA WWW.ANDYCAPP.COM
IT'S LIKE IT'S SOME KIND OF LEGAL HONOUR
NOT THAT SHE GETS TO YOU OR ANYTHING
"IN-LAW." DOES THAT MAKE HER BETTER?

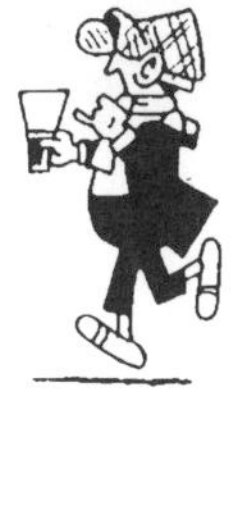

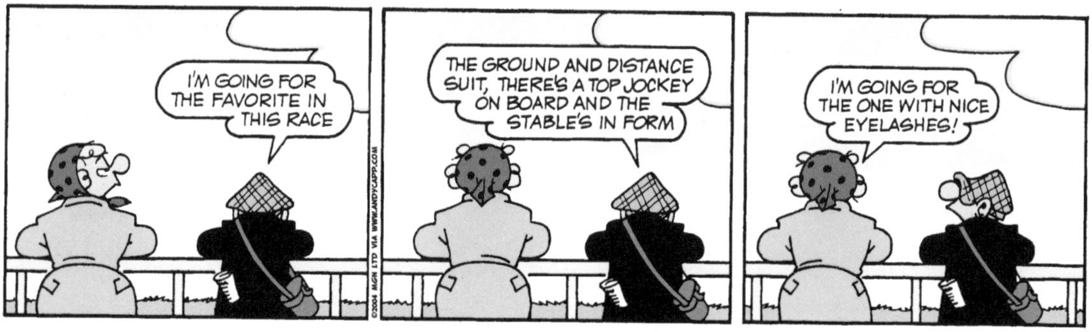
I'M GOING FOR THE FAVORITE IN THIS RACE
THE GROUND AND DISTANCE SUIT, THERE'S A TOP JOCKEY ON BOARD AND THE STABLE'S IN FORM
I'M GOING FOR THE ONE WITH NICE EYELASHES!

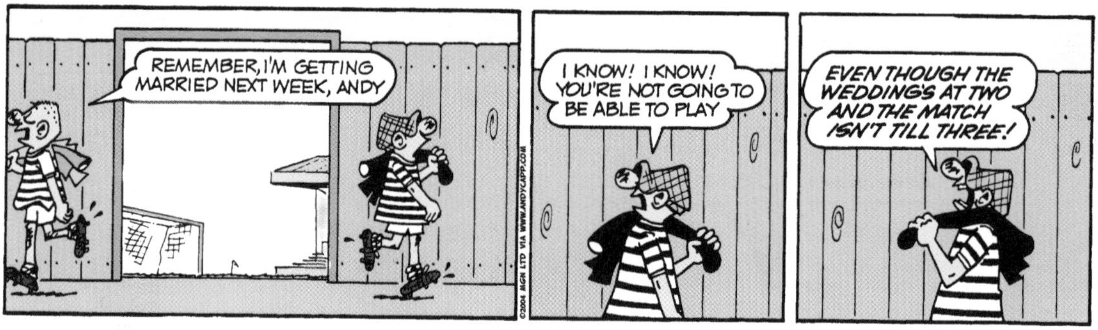
REMEMBER, I'M GETTING MARRIED NEXT WEEK, ANDY
I KNOW! I KNOW! YOU'RE NOT GOING TO BE ABLE TO PLAY
EVEN THOUGH THE WEDDING'S AT TWO AND THE MATCH ISN'T TILL THREE!

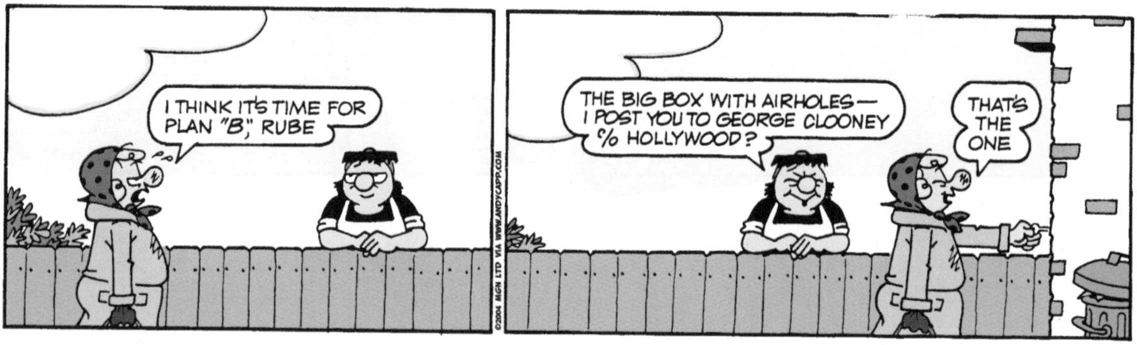
I THINK IT'S TIME FOR PLAN "B," RUBE
THE BIG BOX WITH AIRHOLES— I POST YOU TO GEORGE CLOONEY % HOLLYWOOD?
THAT'S THE ONE

MARRIAGE GUIDANCE
OKAY, I ACCEPT THAT SOMETIMES MY ATTITUDE TOWARD WOMEN IS A LITTLE OLD-FASHIONED,..
©2004 MGN LTD VIA WWW.ANDYCAPP.COM
...MEANWHILE, IF YOU'LL EXCUSE US, A CERTAIN LITTLE LADY HAS SOME DINNER TO COOK!

I'VE STARTED SOMETHING I CALL MY "HUBBY JAR"
©2004 MGN LTD VIA WWW.ANDYCAPP.COM
I PUT ASIDE A LITTLE EVERY WEEK SO I CAN TREAT MY GEORGE TO SOMETHING
I DO THE SAME WITH ANDY
EXCEPT I CALL IT "BAIL MONEY"

... SO I CAME OUT OF THE BACK DOOR OF THE GYM INTO THE ALLEY THAT RUNS BEHIND IT...
©2004 MGN LTD VIA WWW.ANDYCAPP.COM
...AND I COULDN'T BELIEVE IT— THERE MUST HAVE BEEN A HUNDRED RATS RUNNING AROUND!
YUK! I HATE GYMS!

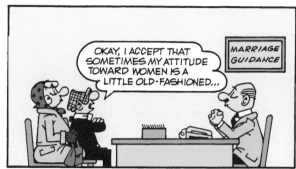

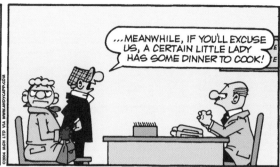

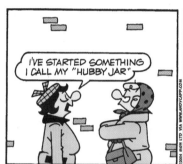

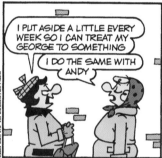

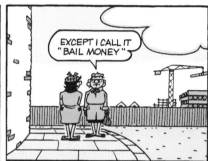

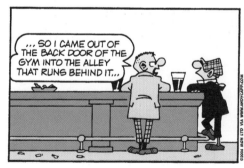

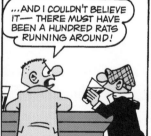

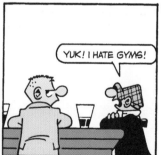

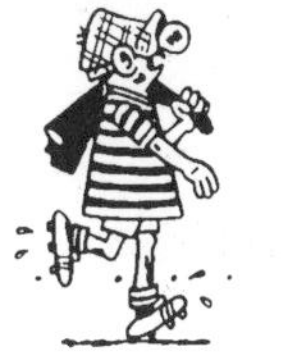

SO ANDY APPLIES FOR THE JOB AND HE GETS IT!
GO ON!
©2004 MGN LTD VIA WWW.ANDYCAPP.COM
AND WITHIN DAYS, HE'S MADE MANAGER WITH HIS OWN OFFICE!
NO!
THEN HE'S RIDING A GIANT HEN — I TOLD YOU IT WAS A WEIRD DREAM ...

SOMEONE'S SELLING A PIANO IN THE PAPER
Mirror
©2004 MGN LTD VIA WWW.ANDYCAPP.COM
THAT'S ONE OF THE GREAT REGRETS IN MY LIFE, PET
YOU KNOW, THAT I DON'T HAVE SOMETHING LIKE A PIANO TO SELL

YOUR MOTHER-IN-LAW STILL STAYING WITH YOU?
YEAH—AND SHE MAY BE GETTING ON A BIT, BUT SHE LIKES HER FOOD
©2004 MGN LTD VIA WWW.ANDYCAPP.COM
SHE'S GUMMING US OUT OF HOUSE AND HOME
ALES

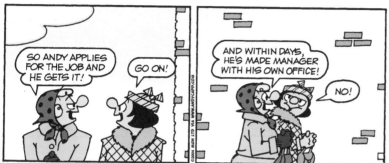

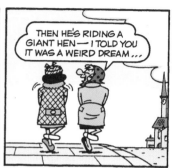

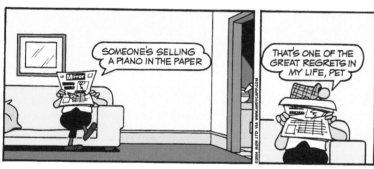

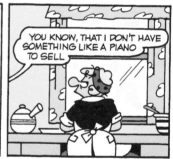

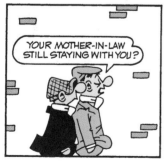

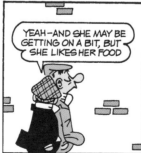

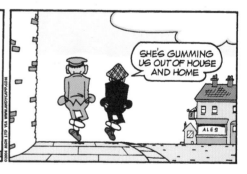

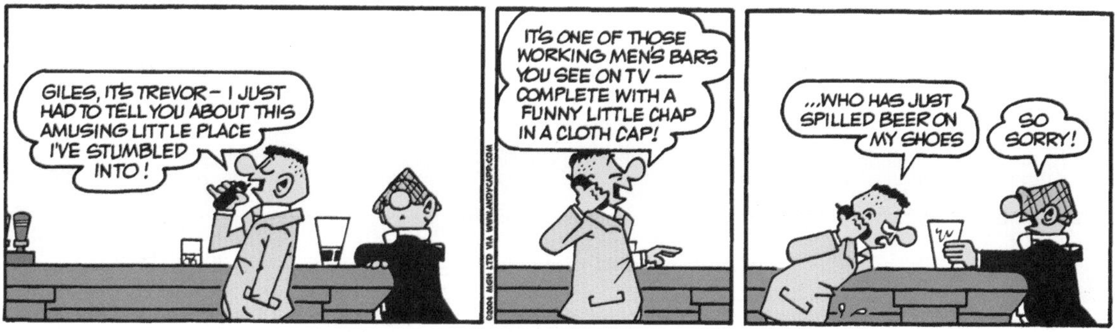
GILES, IT'S TREVOR – I JUST HAD TO TELL YOU ABOUT THIS AMUSING LITTLE PLACE I'VE STUMBLED INTO!
©2004 MGN LTD VIA WWW.ANDYCAPP.COM
IT'S ONE OF THOSE WORKING MEN'S BARS YOU SEE ON TV — COMPLETE WITH A FUNNY LITTLE CHAP IN A CLOTH CAP!
...WHO HAS JUST SPILLED BEER ON MY SHOES
SO SORRY!

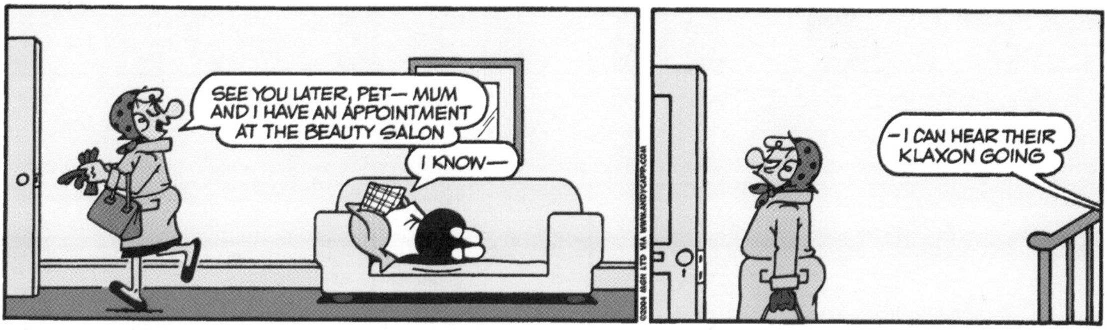
SEE YOU LATER, PET – MUM AND I HAVE AN APPOINTMENT AT THE BEAUTY SALON
I KNOW –
©2004 MGN LTD VIA WWW.ANDYCAPP.COM
– I CAN HEAR THEIR KLAXON GOING

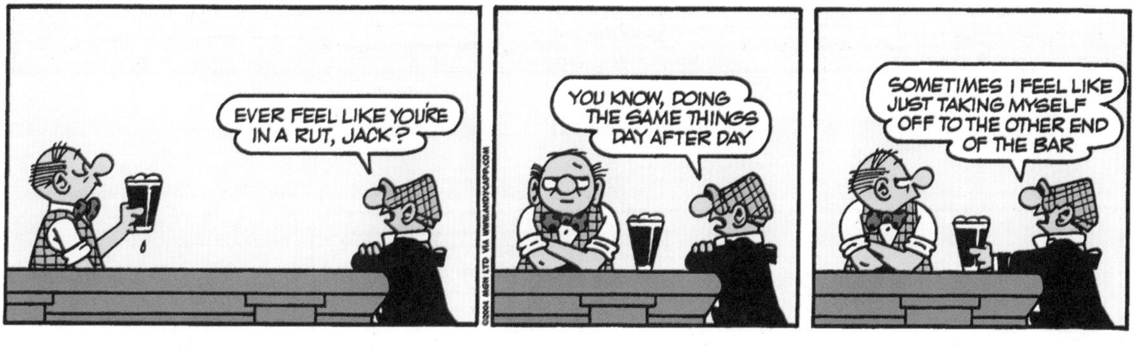
EVER FEEL LIKE YOU'RE IN A RUT, JACK?
©2004 MGN LTD VIA WWW.ANDYCAPP.COM
YOU KNOW, DOING THE SAME THINGS DAY AFTER DAY
SOMETIMES I FEEL LIKE JUST TAKING MYSELF OFF TO THE OTHER END OF THE BAR

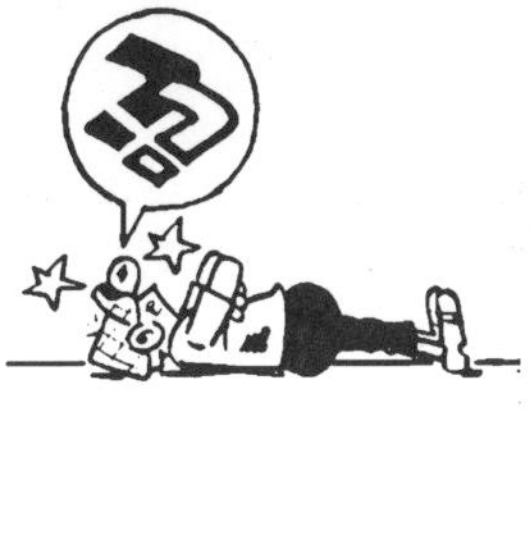

©2004 MGN LTD VIA WWW.ANDYCAPP.COM
I'D GO FOR THE SECOND ONE
I SPEAK YOUR WEIGHT
I LIE ABOUT IT

SPRING IS IN THE AIR— THE FLOWERS AND PLANTS ARE BLOOMING
©2004 MGN LTD VIA WWW.ANDYCAPP.COM
SHOULDN'T YOU BE LEANING ON THE FENCE, WATCHING OUR NEIGHBOR'S GARDENING ?

SHE'S NICE !
©2004 MGN LTD VIA WWW.ANDYCAPP.COM
WHAT MAKES YOU SAY THAT?
FORGET IT, CHALKIE — SHE'S WAY OUT OF YOUR LEAGUE
SHE CAN SEE YOU

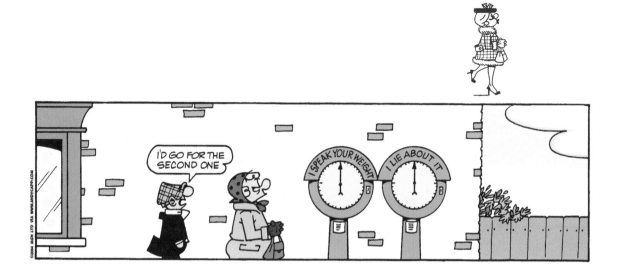

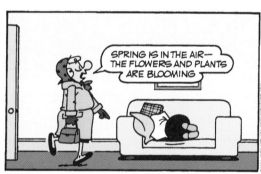

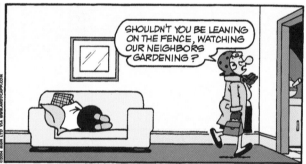

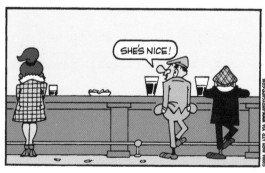

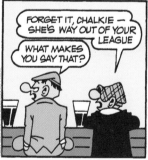

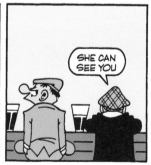

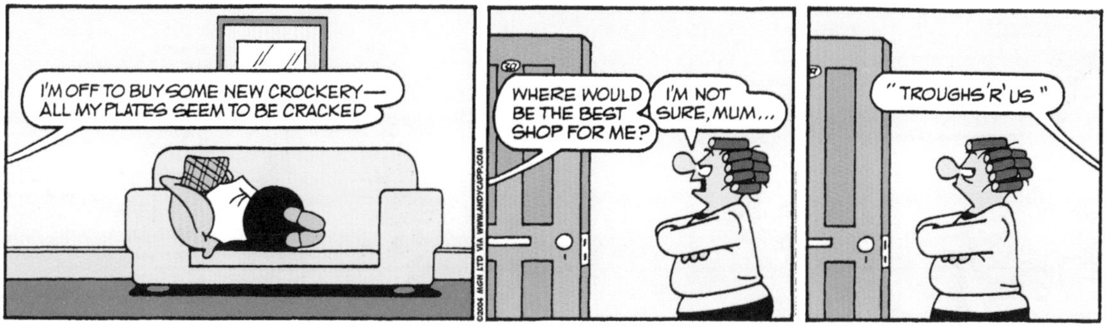
I'M OFF TO BUY SOME NEW CROCKERY— ALL MY PLATES SEEM TO BE CRACKED
©2004 MGN LTD VIA WWW.ANDYCAPP.COM
WHERE WOULD BE THE BEST SHOP FOR ME?
I'M NOT SURE, MUM...
"TROUGHS'R'US"

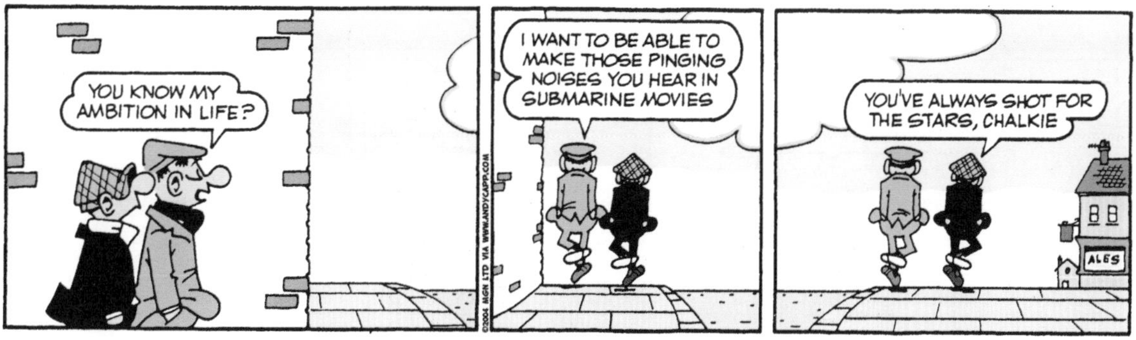
YOU KNOW MY AMBITION IN LIFE?
©2004 MGN LTD VIA WWW.ANDYCAPP.COM
I WANT TO BE ABLE TO MAKE THOSE PINGING NOISES YOU HEAR IN SUBMARINE MOVIES
YOU'VE ALWAYS SHOT FOR THE STARS, CHALKIE
ALES

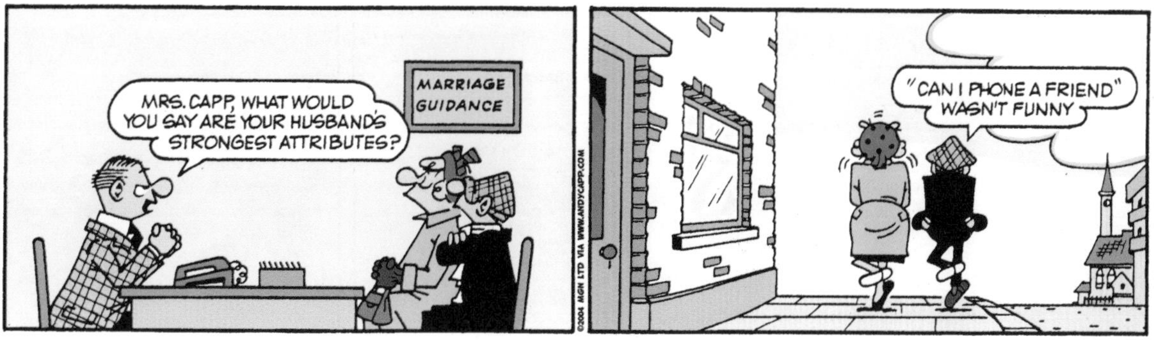
MARRIAGE GUIDANCE
MRS. CAPP, WHAT WOULD YOU SAY ARE YOUR HUSBAND'S STRONGEST ATTRIBUTES?
©2004 MGN LTD VIA WWW.ANDYCAPP.COM
"CAN I PHONE A FRIEND" WASN'T FUNNY

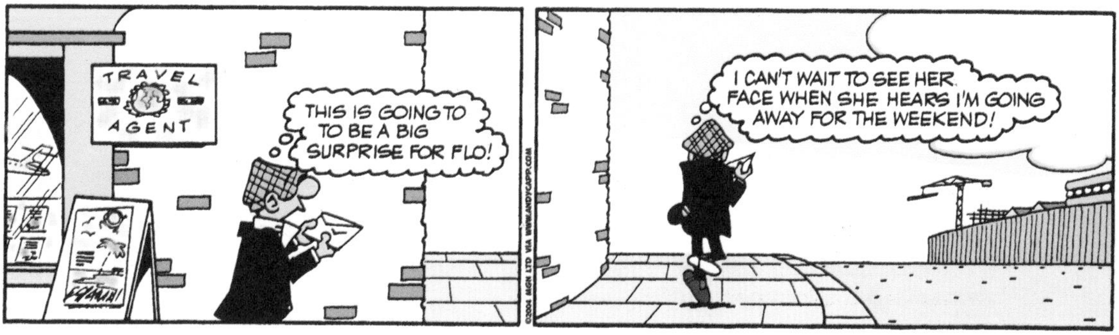
TRAVEL AGENT
THIS IS GOING TO TO BE A BIG SURPRISE FOR FLO!
©2004 MGN LTD VIA WWW.ANDYCAPP.COM
I CAN'T WAIT TO SEE HER FACE WHEN SHE HEARS I'M GOING AWAY FOR THE WEEKEND!

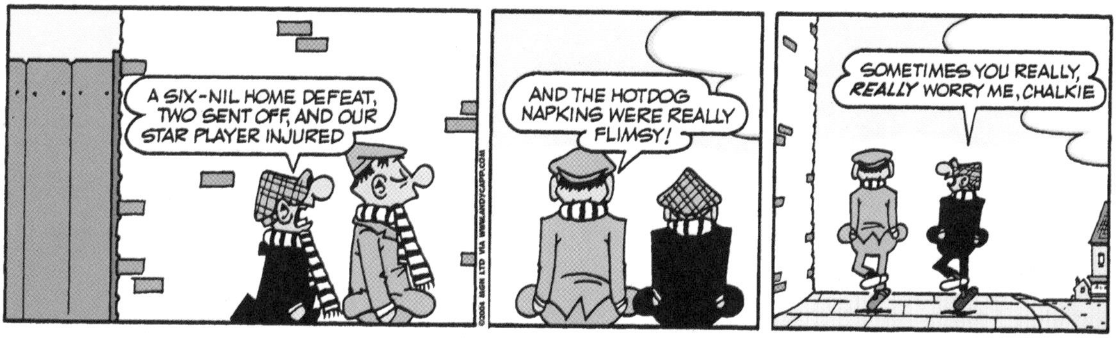
A SIX-NIL HOME DEFEAT, TWO SENT OFF, AND OUR STAR PLAYER INJURED
©2004 MGN LTD VIA WWW.ANDYCAPP.COM
AND THE HOTDOG NAPKINS WERE REALLY FLIMSY!
SOMETIMES YOU REALLY, *REALLY* WORRY ME, CHALKIE

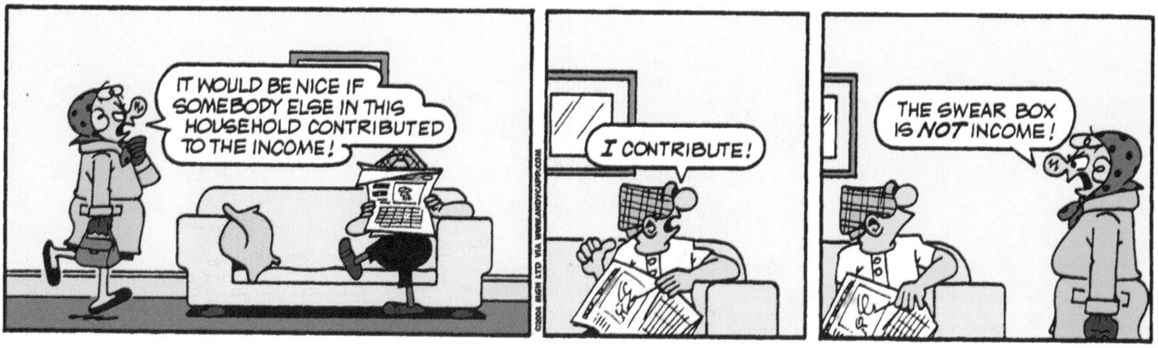
IT WOULD BE NICE IF SOMEBODY ELSE IN THIS HOUSEHOLD CONTRIBUTED TO THE INCOME!
©2004 MGN LTD VIA WWW.ANDYCAPP.COM
I CONTRIBUTE!
THE SWEAR BOX IS *NOT* INCOME!

DO YOU SEE MUCH OF ELSIE SMITH THESE DAYS?
I DO
©2004 MGN LTD VIA WWW.ANDYCAPP.COM
AAARGH!
SORRY—SAYING THOSE TWO WORDS BRINGS BACK SOME BAD MEMORIES

OKAY, I'LL LEND YOU SOME MONEY FOR THE PUB,,,
©2004 MGN LTD VIA WWW.ANDYCAPP.COM
IF YOU CAN TELL ME THE DATE OF OUR ANNIVERSARY
THAT'S NOT A LOAN—THAT'S A 364-1 SHOT!

HI, PAUL—SORRY TO HEAR THE NEWS
©2004 MGN LTD VIA WWW.ANDYCAPP.COM
IF YOU EVER WANT TO TALK TO SOMEONE, YOU KNOW WHERE I AM
THANKS, ANDY,,,
,,, MOST PEOPLE JUST SAY "CONGRATULATIONS ON YOUR ENGAGEMENT"!

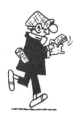

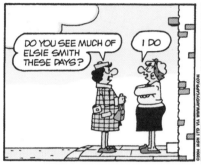

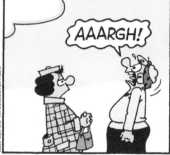

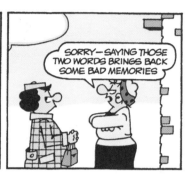

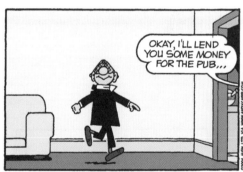

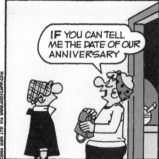

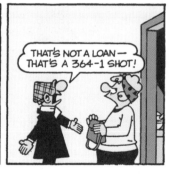

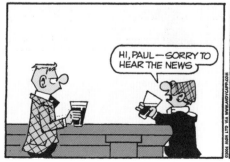

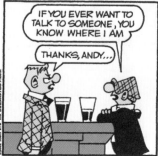

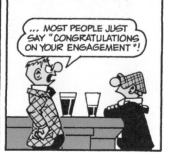

BANK
SO WHAT ARE THE CHANCES OF ME GETTING THE LOAN THEN?
I HAVE A FINANCIAL DIAGRAM HERE WHICH SHOULD ANSWER YOUR QUESTION
NOW, THIS IS A SNOWBALL AND THIS IS HELL...
©2004 MGN LTD VIA WWW.ANDYCAPP.COM

FASHIONS
I DON'T SEE WHY YOU NEED A NEW DRESS
©2004 MGN LTD VIA WWW.ANDYCAPP.COM
WHAT'S WRONG WITH THE LAST ONE YOU BOUGHT?
PEOPLE KEEP STANDING ON THE TRAIN

NEW AROUND HERE?
MOVED IN THIS WEEK
©2004 MGN LTD VIA WWW.ANDYCAPP.COM
WE HAVE AN OLD CUSTOM HERE WHERE NEWCOMERS HAVE TO BUY A LOCAL A DRINK — BEEN GOING ON FOR YEARS
I'M NEW TO THE AREA, MATE — NOT THE PLANET
GOOD TRY, ANDY!

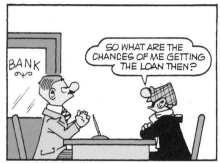

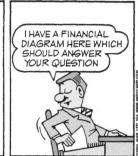

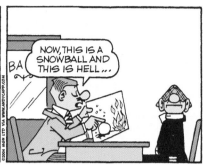

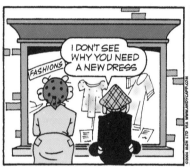

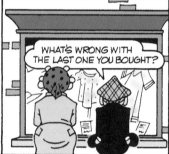

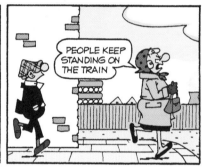

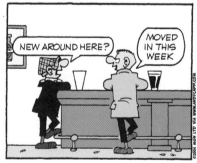

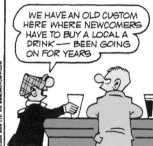

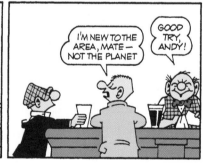

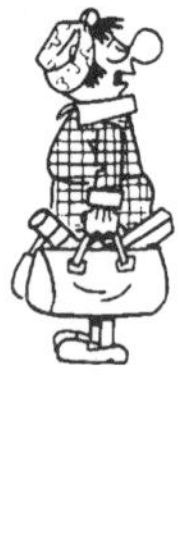

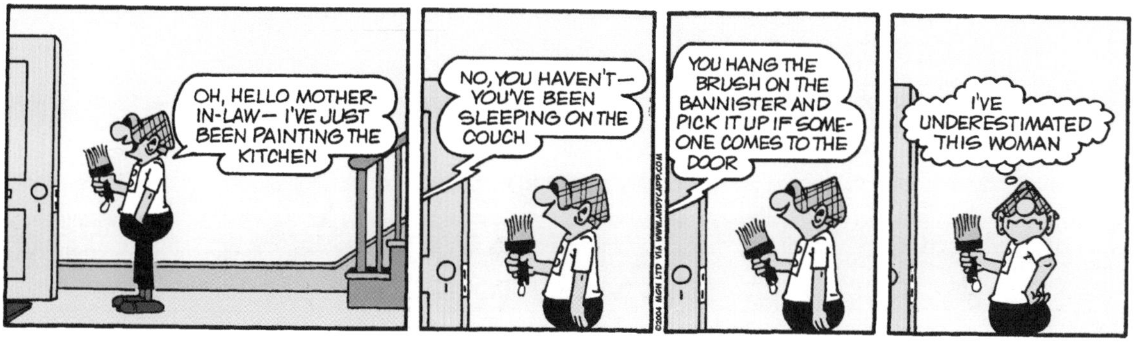
OH, HELLO MOTHER-IN-LAW— I'VE JUST BEEN PAINTING THE KITCHEN
NO, YOU HAVEN'T— YOU'VE BEEN SLEEPING ON THE COUCH
YOU HANG THE BRUSH ON THE BANNISTER AND PICK IT UP IF SOME-ONE COMES TO THE DOOR
©2004 MGN LTD VIA WWW.ANDYCAPP.COM
I'VE UNDERESTIMATED THIS WOMAN

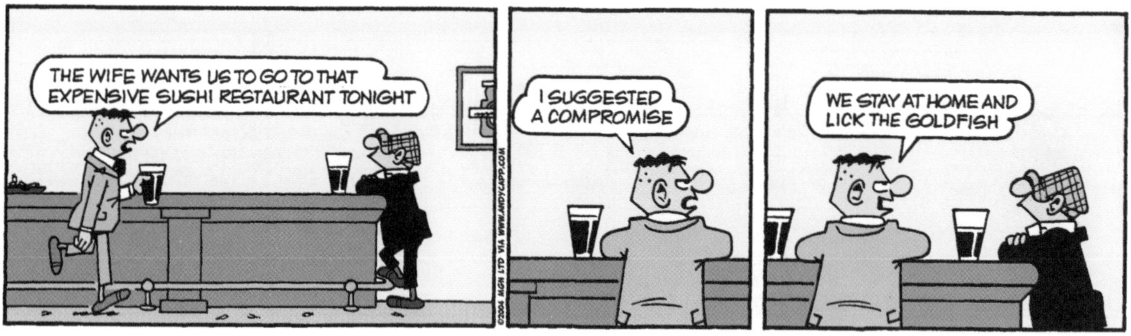
THE WIFE WANTS US TO GO TO THAT EXPENSIVE SUSHI RESTAURANT TONIGHT
©2004 MGN LTD VIA WWW.ANDYCAPP.COM
I SUGGESTED A COMPROMISE
WE STAY AT HOME AND LICK THE GOLDFISH

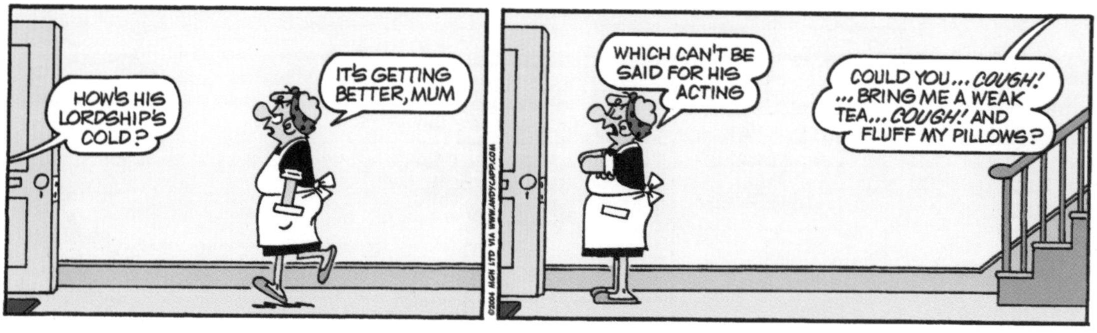
HOW'S HIS LORDSHIP'S COLD?
IT'S GETTING BETTER, MUM
©2004 MGN LTD VIA WWW.ANDYCAPP.COM
WHICH CAN'T BE SAID FOR HIS ACTING
COULD YOU... *COUGH!* ...BRING ME A WEAK TEA... *COUGH!* AND FLUFF MY PILLOWS?

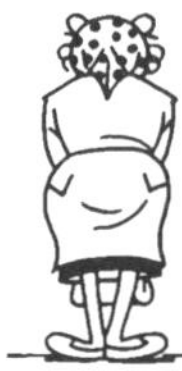

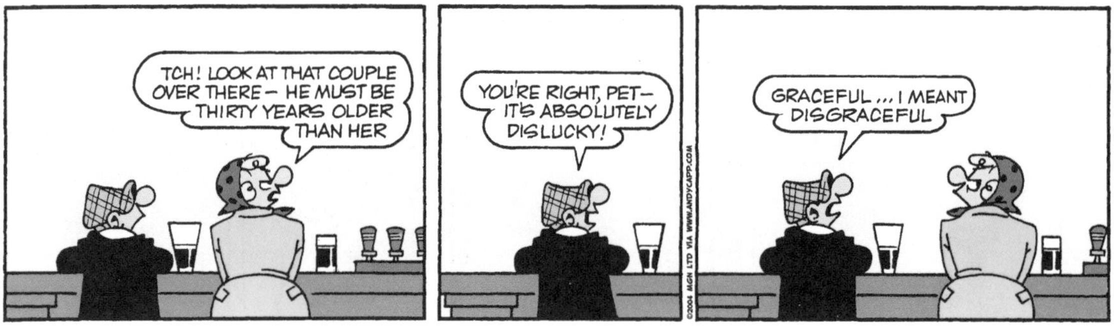
TCH! LOOK AT THAT COUPLE OVER THERE – HE MUST BE THIRTY YEARS OLDER THAN HER
YOU'RE RIGHT, PET– IT'S ABSOLUTELY DISLUCKY!
©2004 MGN LTD VIA WWW.ANDYCAPP.COM
GRACEFUL ... I MEANT DISGRACEFUL

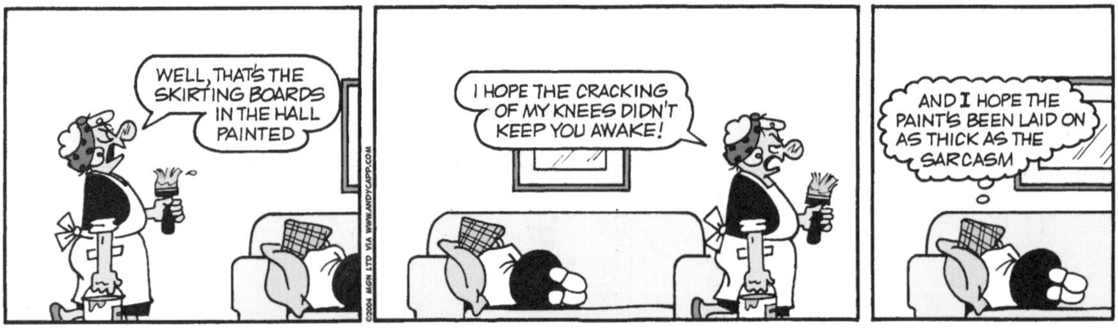
WELL, THAT'S THE SKIRTING BOARDS IN THE HALL PAINTED
©2004 MGN LTD VIA WWW.ANDYCAPP.COM
I HOPE THE CRACKING OF MY KNEES DIDN'T KEEP YOU AWAKE!
AND I HOPE THE PAINT'S BEEN LAID ON AS THICK AS THE SARCASM

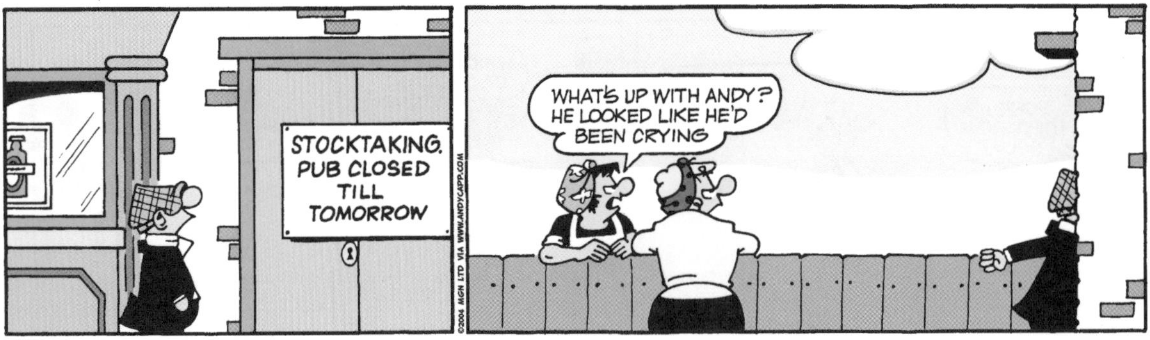
STOCKTAKING. PUB CLOSED TILL TOMORROW
©2004 MGN LTD VIA WWW.ANDYCAPP.COM
WHAT'S UP WITH ANDY? HE LOOKED LIKE HE'D BEEN CRYING

WE WERE TALKING AT WORK TODAY ABOUT HOW PEOPLE GROW TO LOOK LIKE THEIR PETS
©2004 MGN LTD VIA WWW.ANDYCAPP.COM
YOU MUST HAVE BEEN THE ONLY KID IN SCHOOL WITH A SLOTH

THAT MOTHER OF YOURS!
©2004 MGN LTD VIA WWW.ANDYCAPP.COM
I DON'T MIND HER ALWAYS HAVING THE LAST WORD...
...IT'S THE HUNDREDS SHE USES GETTING TO IT!

I'VE FOUND THE PERFECT JOB FOR YOU, PET — IT'S AT THE SLEEP RESEARCH CENTRE
©2004 MGN LTD VIA WWW.ANDYCAPP.COM
ALL YOU HAVE TO DO IS SLEEP, AND THEY GIVE YOU A BIG CHEQUE FOR IT!
A CHEQUE? DOES THAT MEAN I'D HAVE TO GO ALL THE WAY TO THE BANK TO CASH IT?

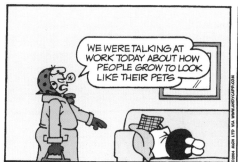

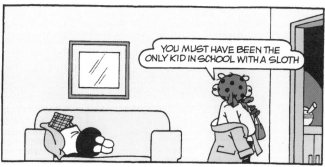

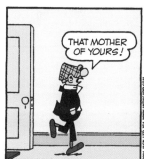

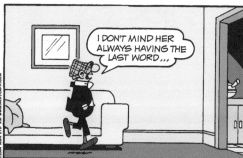

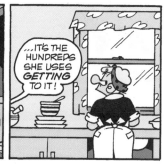

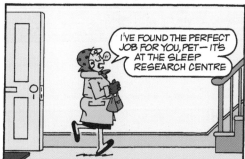

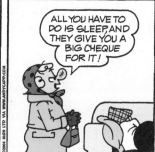

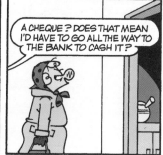

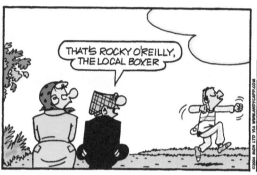

THAT'S ROCKY O'REILLY, THE LOCAL BOXER
©2004 MGN LTD VIA WWW.ANDYCAPP.COM
HE GOT DISQUALIFIED FOR TAKING A LUCKY SHAMROCK INTO THE RING
HOW COME?
IT WAS PAINTED ON THE HORSESHOE IN HIS GLOVE

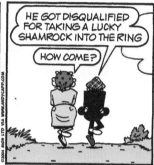

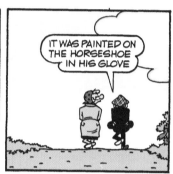

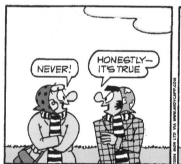

NEVER!
HONESTLY— IT'S TRUE
©2004 MGN LTD VIA WWW.ANDYCAPP.COM
I SHOULDN'T BE SURPRISED – SHE'S HAD A REPUTATION FOR YEARS
ABSOLUTELY
I HOPE MY GOAL CELEBRATIONS DIDN'T DROWN OUT YOUR CONVERSATION!

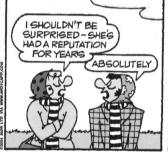

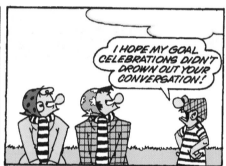

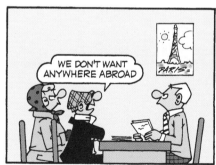

WE DON'T WANT ANYWHERE ABROAD
PARIS
WE WANT SOMEWHERE CHEAP, NEAR TO HOME AND EASY TO GET TO
I SEE
©2004 MGN LTD VIA WWW.ANDYCAPP.COM
HAVE YOU CONSIDERED YOUR GARDEN SHED?

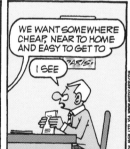

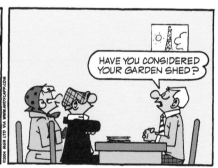

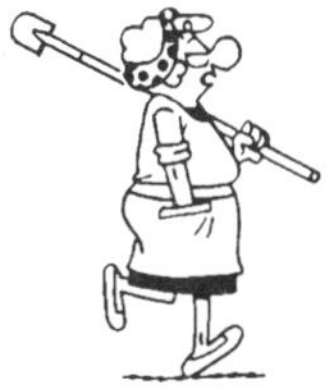

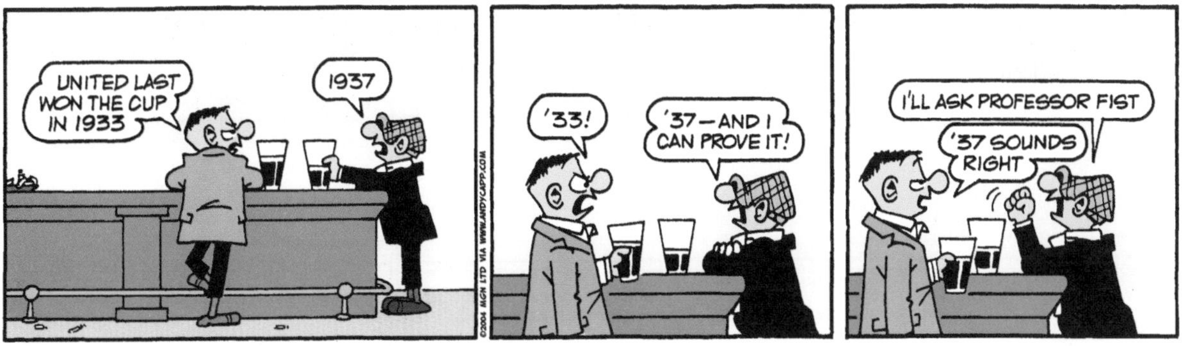

UNITED LAST WON THE CUP IN 1933
1937
©2004 MGN LTD VIA WWW.ANDYCAPP.COM
'33!
'37—AND I CAN PROVE IT!
I'LL ASK PROFESSOR FIST
'37 SOUNDS RIGHT

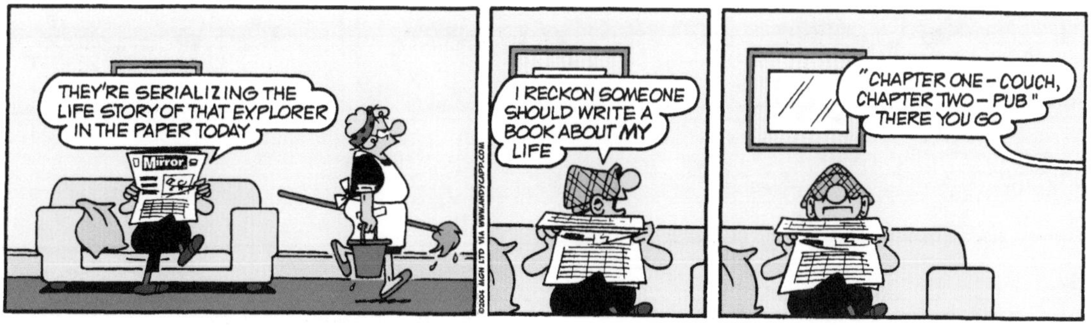

THEY'RE SERIALIZING THE LIFE STORY OF THAT EXPLORER IN THE PAPER TODAY
Mirror
©2004 MGN LTD VIA WWW.ANDYCAPP.COM
I RECKON SOMEONE SHOULD WRITE A BOOK ABOUT MY LIFE
"CHAPTER ONE - COUCH, CHAPTER TWO - PUB" THERE YOU GO

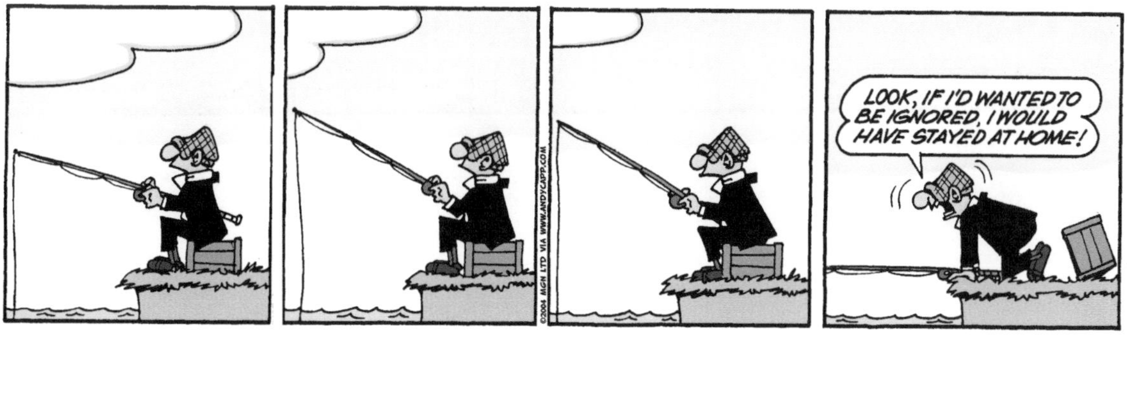

©2004 MGN LTD VIA WWW.ANDYCAPP.COM
LOOK, IF I'D WANTED TO BE IGNORED, I WOULD HAVE STAYED AT HOME!

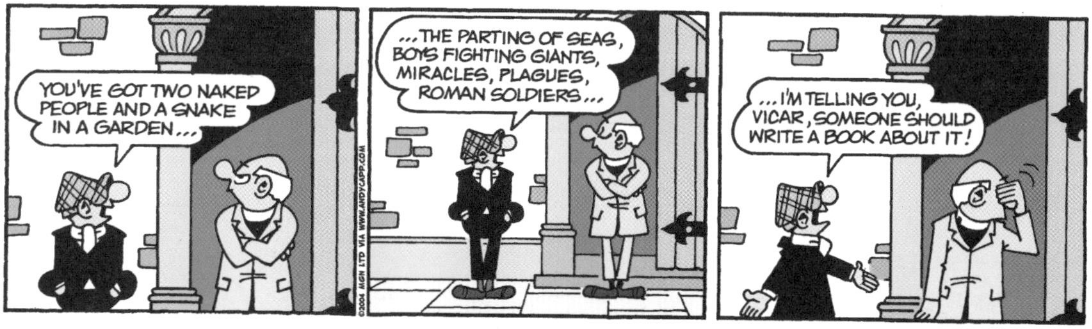
YOU'VE GOT TWO NAKED PEOPLE AND A SNAKE IN A GARDEN...
...THE PARTING OF SEAS, BOYS FIGHTING GIANTS, MIRACLES, PLAGUES, ROMAN SOLDIERS...
...I'M TELLING YOU, VICAR, SOMEONE SHOULD WRITE A BOOK ABOUT IT!
©2004 MGN LTD VIA WWW.ANDYCAPP.COM

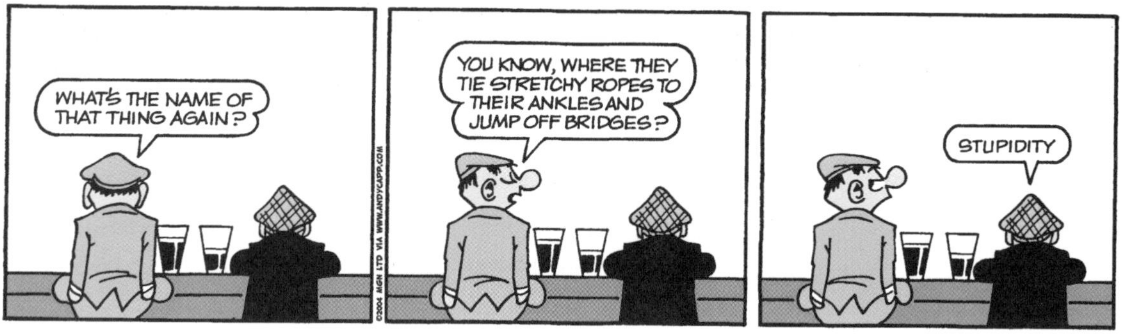
WHAT'S THE NAME OF THAT THING AGAIN?
YOU KNOW, WHERE THEY TIE STRETCHY ROPES TO THEIR ANKLES AND JUMP OFF BRIDGES?
STUPIDITY
©2004 MGN LTD VIA WWW.ANDYCAPP.COM

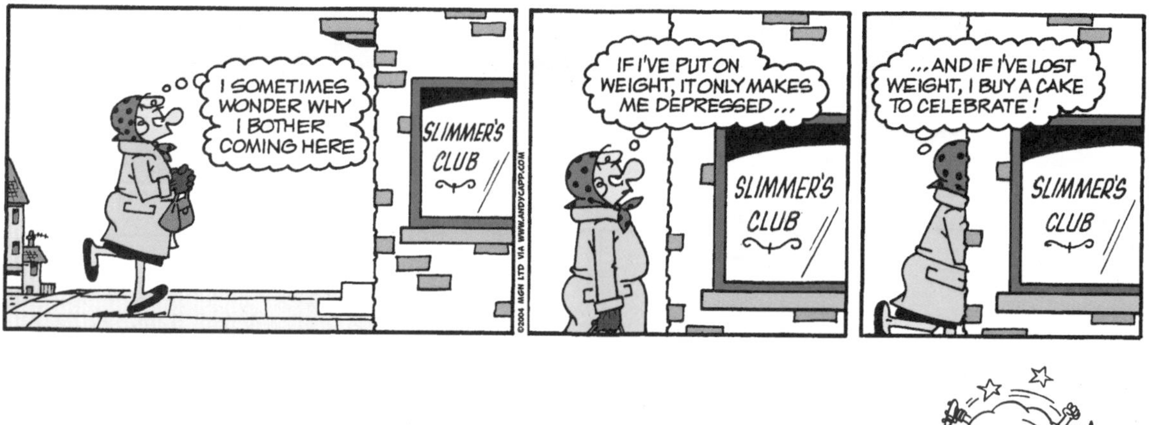
I SOMETIMES WONDER WHY I BOTHER COMING HERE
SLIMMER'S CLUB
IF I'VE PUT ON WEIGHT, IT ONLY MAKES ME DEPRESSED...
SLIMMER'S CLUB
...AND IF I'VE LOST WEIGHT, I BUY A CAKE TO CELEBRATE!
SLIMMER'S CLUB
©2004 MGN LTD VIA WWW.ANDYCAPP.COM

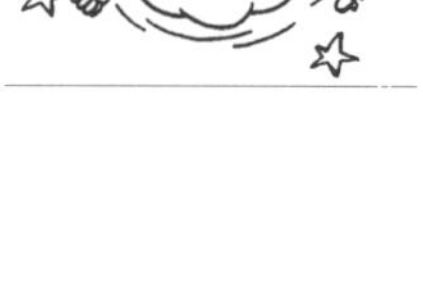

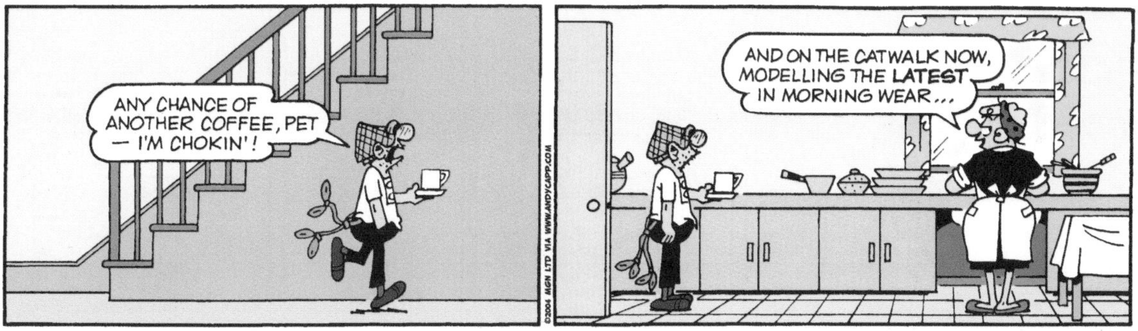
ANY CHANCE OF ANOTHER COFFEE, PET — I'M CHOKIN'!
AND ON THE CATWALK NOW, MODELLING THE **LATEST** IN MORNING WEAR...
©2004 MGN LTD VIA WWW.ANDYCAPP.COM

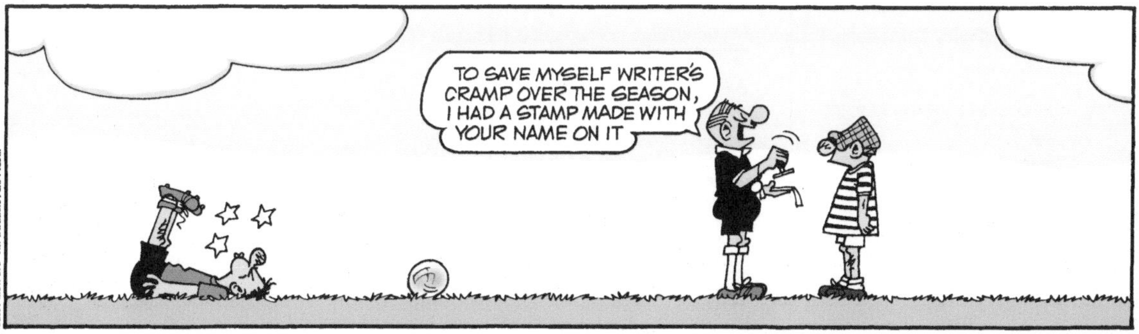
TO SAVE MYSELF WRITER'S CRAMP OVER THE SEASON, I HAD A STAMP MADE WITH YOUR NAME ON IT
©2004 MGN LTD VIA WWW.ANDYCAPP.COM

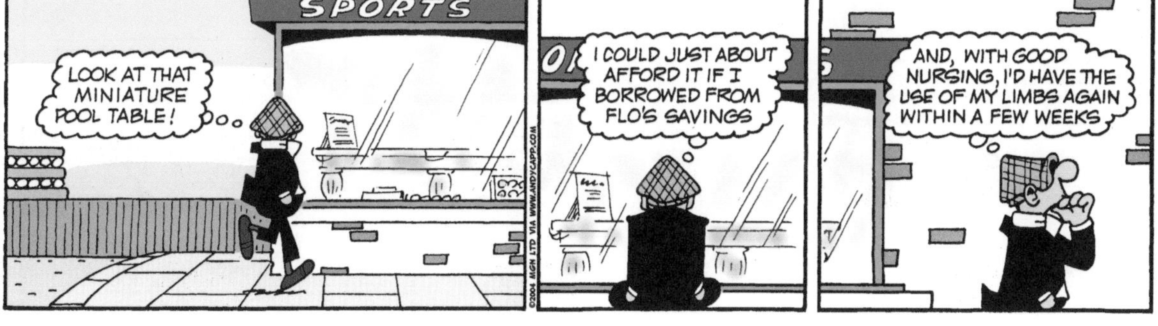
SPORTS
LOOK AT THAT MINIATURE POOL TABLE!
I COULD JUST ABOUT AFFORD IT IF I BORROWED FROM FLO'S SAVINGS
AND, WITH GOOD NURSING, I'D HAVE THE USE OF MY LIMBS AGAIN WITHIN A FEW WEEKS
©2004 MGN LTD VIA WWW.ANDYCAPP.COM

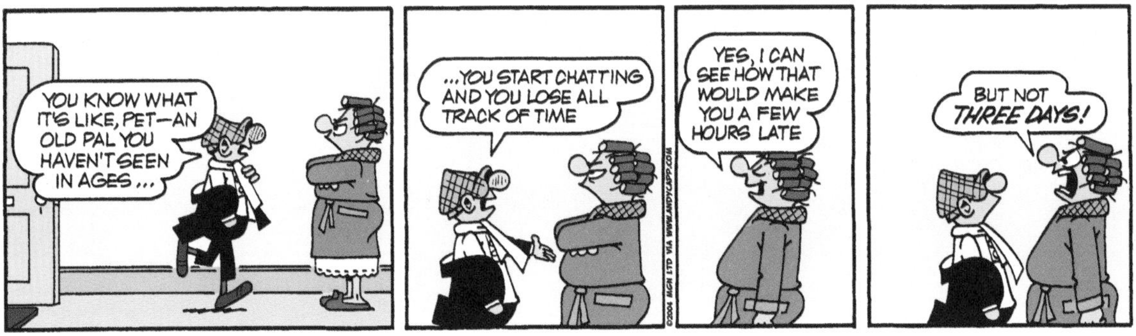
YOU KNOW WHAT IT'S LIKE, PET—AN OLD PAL YOU HAVEN'T SEEN IN AGES ...
...YOU START CHATTING AND YOU LOSE ALL TRACK OF TIME
YES, I CAN SEE HOW THAT WOULD MAKE YOU A FEW HOURS LATE
BUT NOT THREE DAYS!

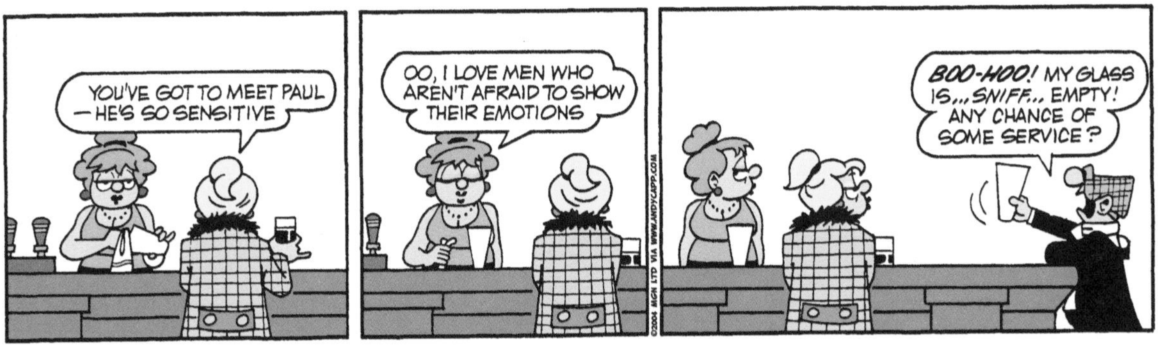
YOU'VE GOT TO MEET PAUL —HE'S SO SENSITIVE
OO, I LOVE MEN WHO AREN'T AFRAID TO SHOW THEIR EMOTIONS
BOO-HOO! MY GLASS IS... SNIFF... EMPTY! ANY CHANCE OF SOME SERVICE?

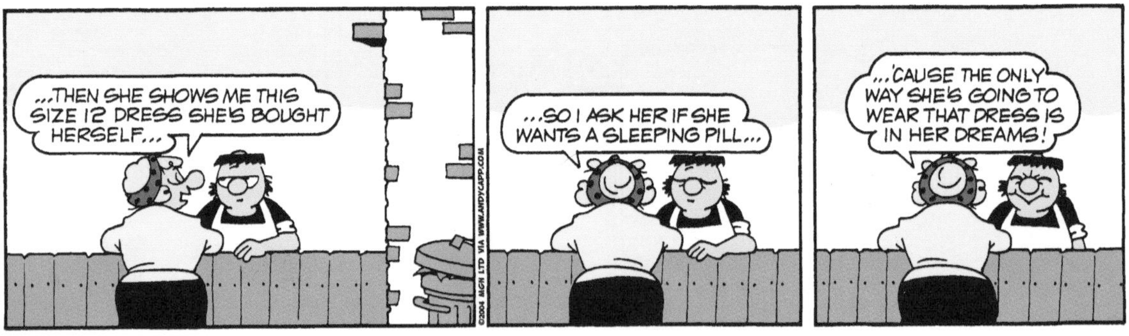
...THEN SHE SHOWS ME THIS SIZE 12 DRESS SHE'S BOUGHT HERSELF...
...SO I ASK HER IF SHE WANTS A SLEEPING PILL...
...'CAUSE THE ONLY WAY SHE'S GOING TO WEAR THAT DRESS IS IN HER DREAMS!

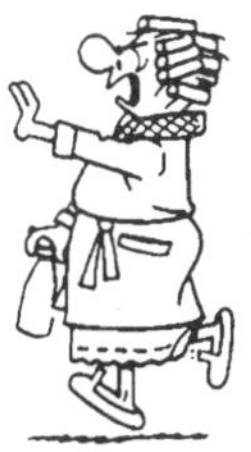

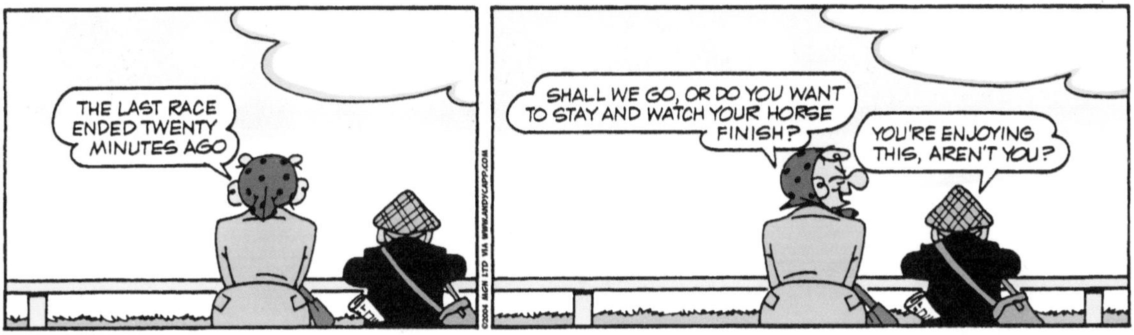

THE LAST RACE ENDED TWENTY MINUTES AGO
©2004 MGN LTD VIA WWW.ANDYCAPP.COM
SHALL WE GO, OR DO YOU WANT TO STAY AND WATCH YOUR HORSE FINISH?
YOU'RE ENJOYING THIS, AREN'T YOU?

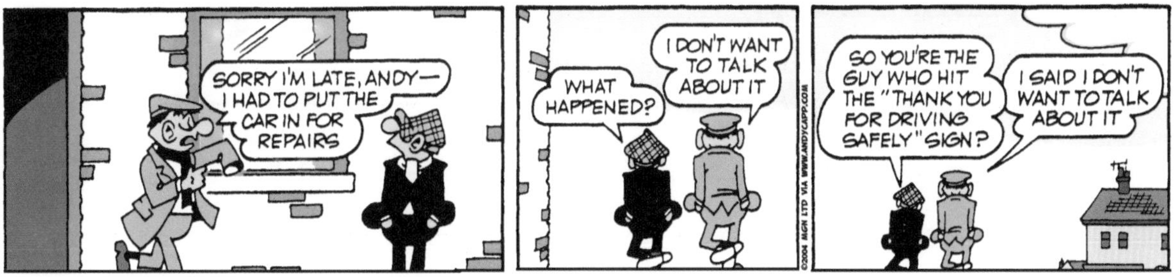

SORRY I'M LATE, ANDY— I HAD TO PUT THE CAR IN FOR REPAIRS
WHAT HAPPENED?
I DON'T WANT TO TALK ABOUT IT
©2004 MGN LTD VIA WWW.ANDYCAPP.COM
SO YOU'RE THE GUY WHO HIT THE "THANK YOU FOR DRIVING SAFELY" SIGN?
I SAID I DON'T WANT TO TALK ABOUT IT

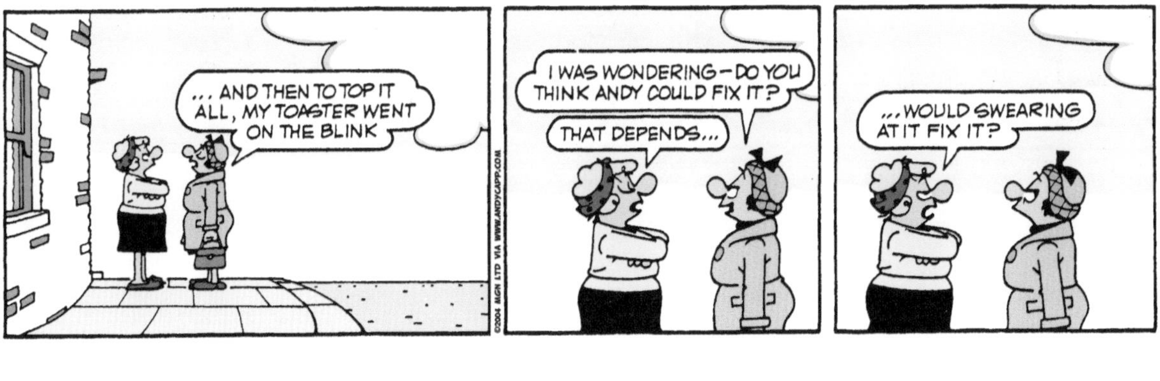

... AND THEN TO TOP IT ALL, MY TOASTER WENT ON THE BLINK
©2004 MGN LTD VIA WWW.ANDYCAPP.COM
I WAS WONDERING—DO YOU THINK ANDY COULD FIX IT?
THAT DEPENDS...
...WOULD SWEARING AT IT FIX IT?

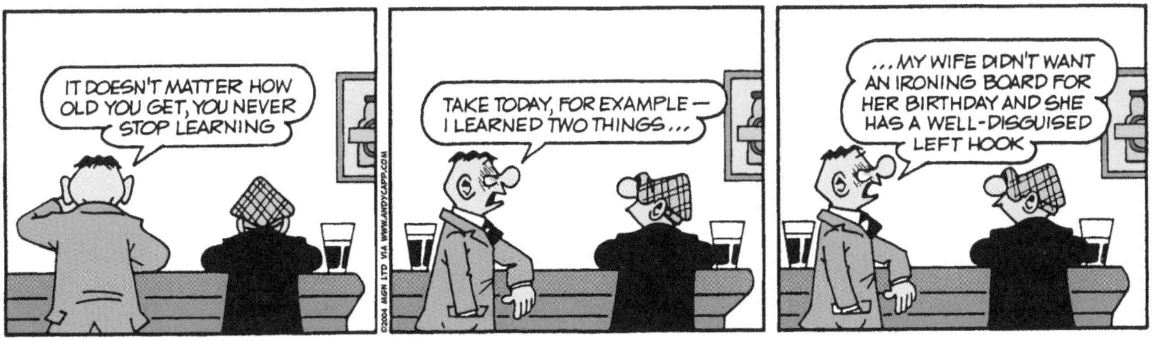
IT DOESN'T MATTER HOW OLD YOU GET, YOU NEVER STOP LEARNING
©2004 MGN LTD VIA WWW.ANDYCAPP.COM
TAKE TODAY, FOR EXAMPLE — I LEARNED TWO THINGS...
...MY WIFE DIDN'T WANT AN IRONING BOARD FOR HER BIRTHDAY AND SHE HAS A WELL-DISGUISED LEFT HOOK

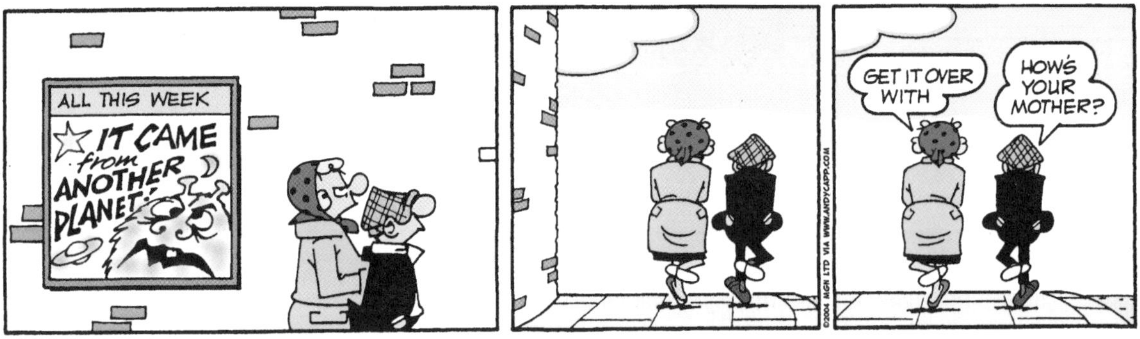
ALL THIS WEEK
IT CAME from ANOTHER PLANET!
©2004 MGN LTD VIA WWW.ANDYCAPP.COM
GET IT OVER WITH
HOW'S YOUR MOTHER?

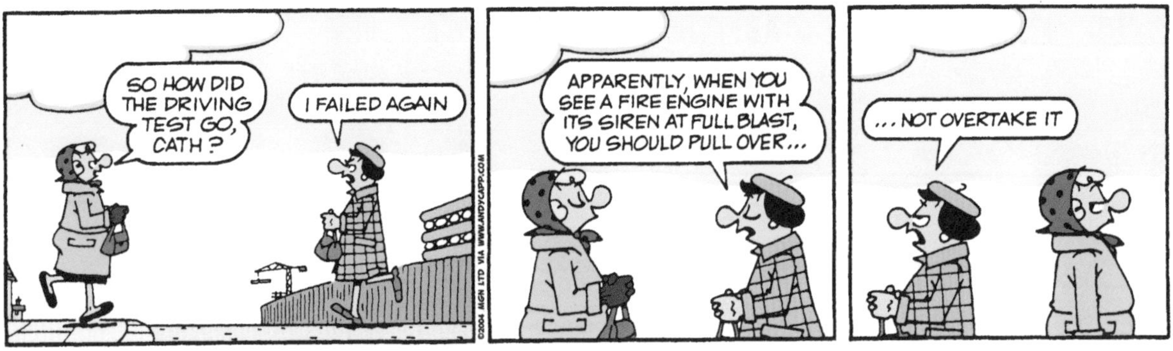
SO HOW DID THE DRIVING TEST GO, CATH?
I FAILED AGAIN
©2004 MGN LTD VIA WWW.ANDYCAPP.COM
APPARENTLY, WHEN YOU SEE A FIRE ENGINE WITH ITS SIREN AT FULL BLAST, YOU SHOULD PULL OVER...
...NOT OVERTAKE IT

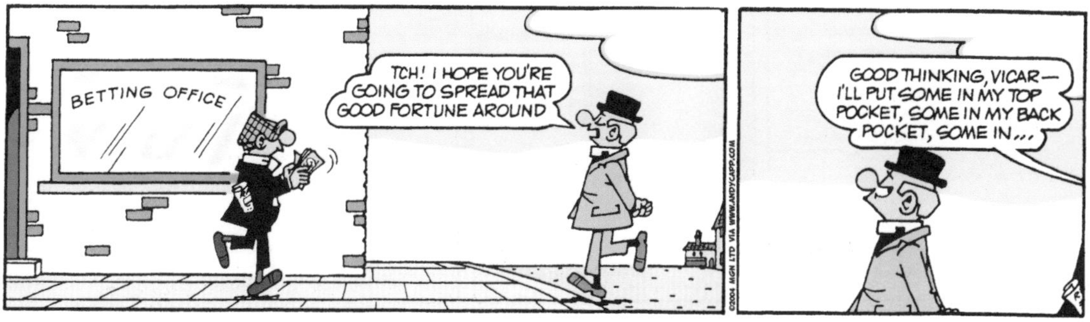
BETTING OFFICE
TCH! I HOPE YOU'RE GOING TO SPREAD THAT GOOD FORTUNE AROUND
©2004 MGN LTD VIA WWW.ANDYCAPP.COM
GOOD THINKING, VICAR— I'LL PUT SOME IN MY TOP POCKET, SOME IN MY BACK POCKET, SOME IN...

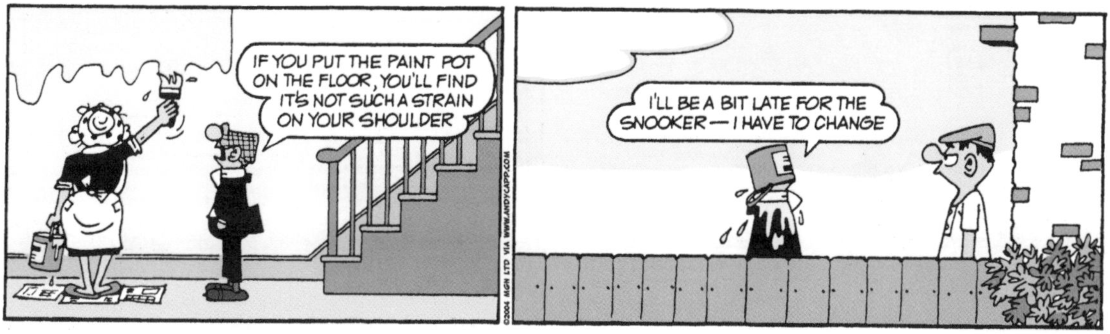
IF YOU PUT THE PAINT POT ON THE FLOOR, YOU'LL FIND IT'S NOT SUCH A STRAIN ON YOUR SHOULDER
©2004 MGN LTD VIA WWW.ANDYCAPP.COM
I'LL BE A BIT LATE FOR THE SNOOKER — I HAVE TO CHANGE

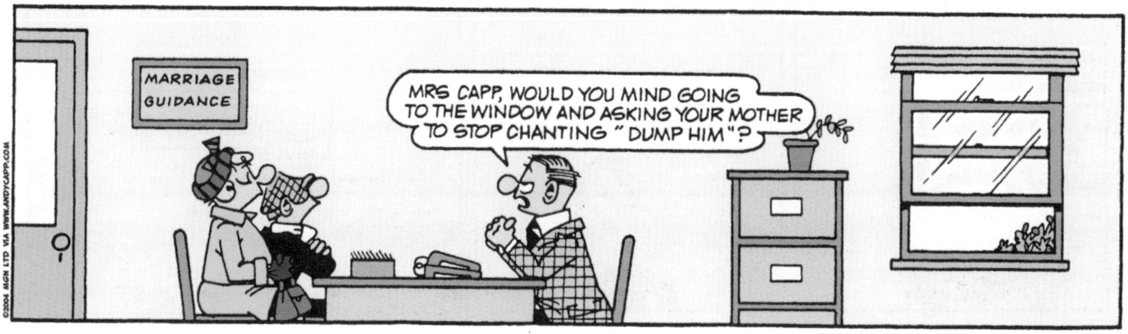
©2004 MGN LTD VIA WWW.ANDYCAPP.COM
MARRIAGE GUIDANCE
MRS CAPP, WOULD YOU MIND GOING TO THE WINDOW AND ASKING YOUR MOTHER TO STOP CHANTING "DUMP HIM"?

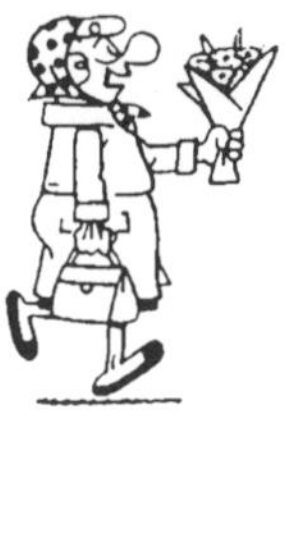

JUST LOOK AT YOU – IT'S TWO IN THE AFTERNOON, AND YOU'RE FLAT ON YOUR BACK ON A COUCH
YOU KNOW YOU ONLY GET TO SLEEP ON YOUR SIDE
©2004 MGN LTD VIA WWW.ANDYCAPP.COM

POLICE SUSPECT THAT THE MAN THEY ARE HUNTING IS OF LOW INTELLIGENCE
LIKE THAT NARROWS IT DOWN
©2004 MGN LTD VIA WWW.ANDYCAPP.COM

IS IT... A) ISTANBUL... ...B) ATHENS...
...C) CAIRO... ...D) PALERMO?
OR E) THE DOG AND DUCK FOR A BEER
©2004 MGN LTD VIA WWW.ANDYCAPP.COM

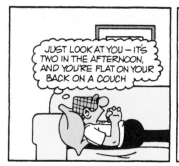

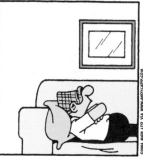

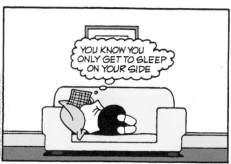

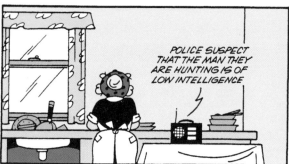

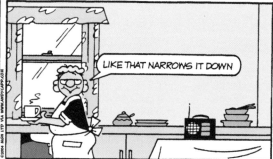

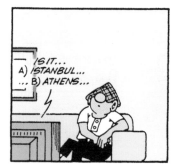

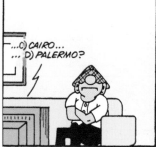

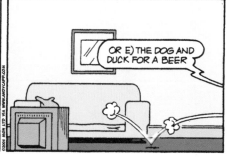

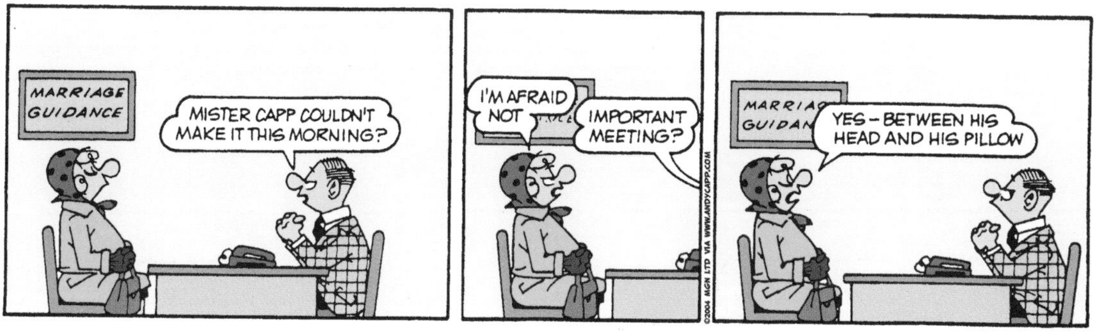
MARRIAGE GUIDANCE
MISTER CAPP COULDN'T MAKE IT THIS MORNING?
I'M AFRAID NOT
IMPORTANT MEETING?
YES – BETWEEN HIS HEAD AND HIS PILLOW
©2004 MGN LTD VIA WWW.ANDYCAPP.COM

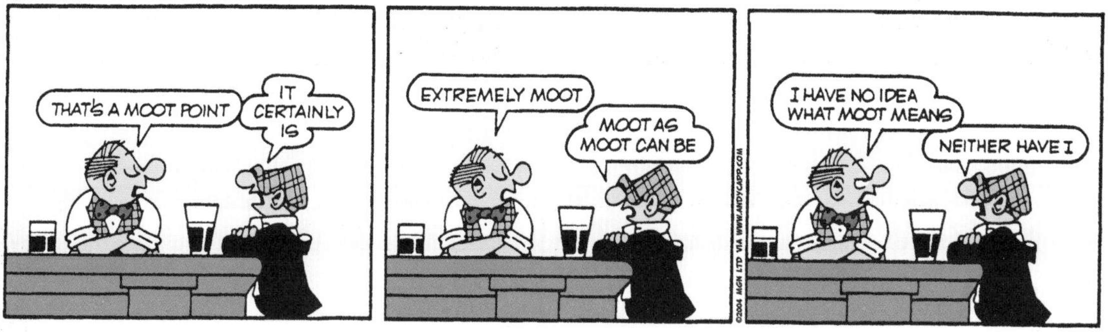
THAT'S A MOOT POINT
IT CERTAINLY IS
EXTREMELY MOOT
MOOT AS MOOT CAN BE
I HAVE NO IDEA WHAT MOOT MEANS
NEITHER HAVE I
©2004 MGN LTD VIA WWW.ANDYCAPP.COM

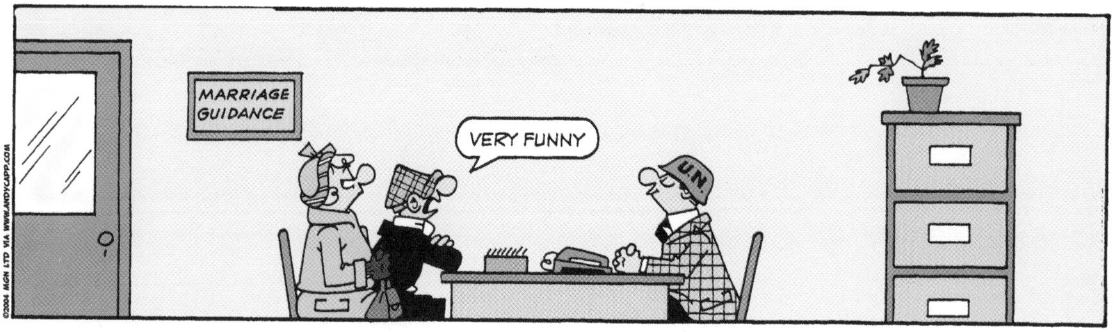
MARRIAGE GUIDANCE
VERY FUNNY
U.N.
©2004 MGN LTD VIA WWW.ANDYCAPP.COM

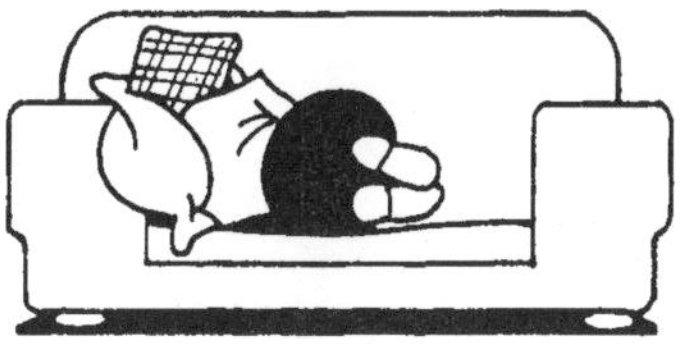

AND WHO HAVE WE HERE? IS HEAVEN MISSING AN ANGEL?
I NEEDN'T ASK WHO WON THE DOMINOES TOURNAMENT TONIGHT
©2004 MGN LTD VIA WWW.ANDYCAPP.COM

TCH! LATE AGAIN!
WHY AM I ALWAYS LATE? THERE MUST BE SOME REASON
I SHOULD GO BACK TO THE PUB AND THINK ABOUT THIS
©2004 MGN LTD VIA WWW.ANDYCAPP.COM

I AM!
DON'T BE STUPID— I AM!
THIS STARTED AS A DISCUSSION ABOUT WHO WAS THE MOST PLACID
©2004 MGN LTD VIA WWW.ANDYCAPP.COM

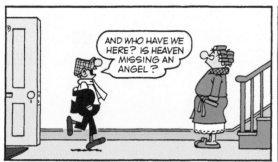

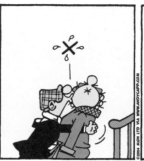

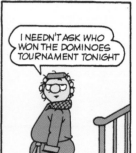

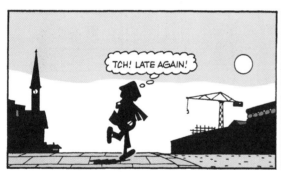

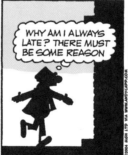

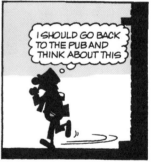

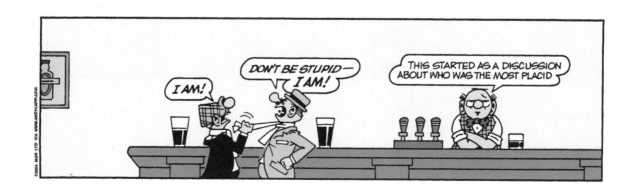

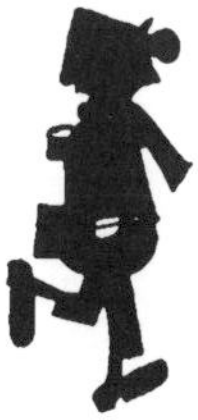

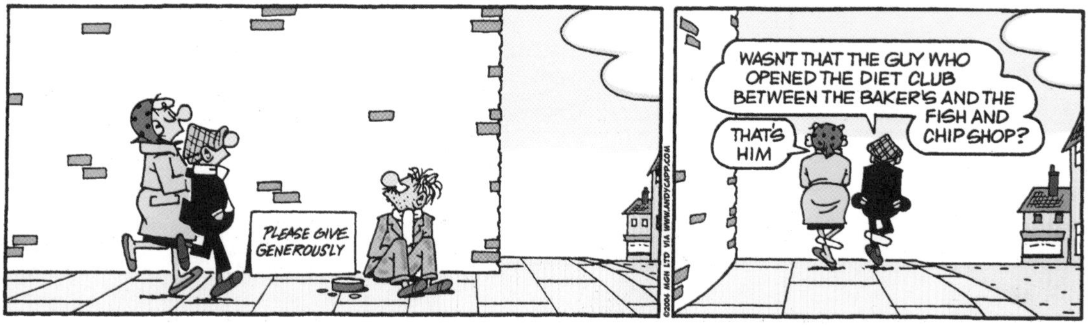
PLEASE GIVE GENEROUSLY
©2004 MGN LTD VIA WWW.ANDYCAPP.COM
WASN'T THAT THE GUY WHO OPENED THE DIET CLUB BETWEEN THE BAKER'S AND THE FISH AND CHIP SHOP?
THAT'S HIM

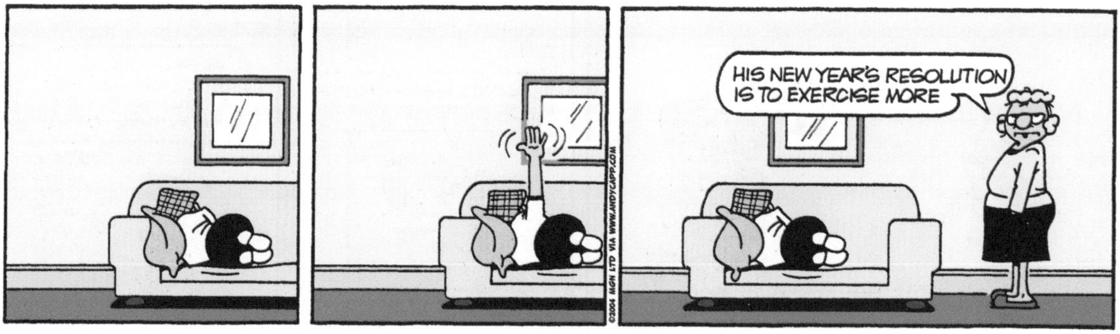
©2004 MGN LTD VIA WWW.ANDYCAPP.COM
HIS NEW YEAR'S RESOLUTION IS TO EXERCISE MORE

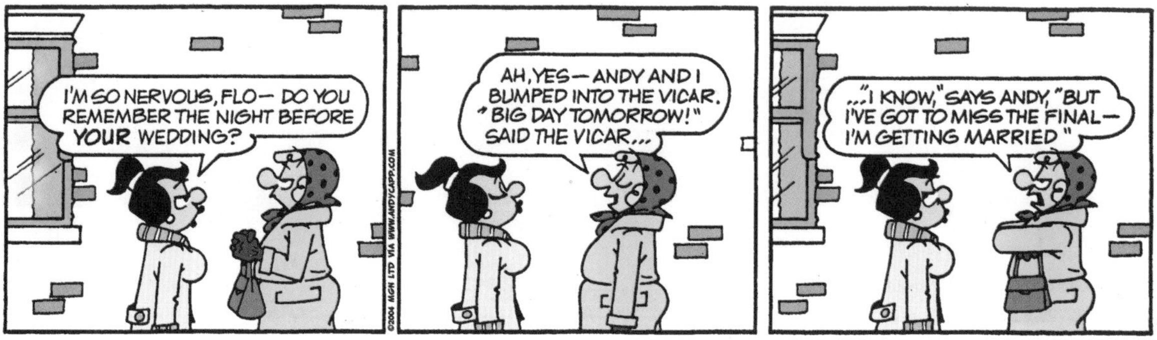
I'M SO NERVOUS, FLO— DO YOU REMEMBER THE NIGHT BEFORE YOUR WEDDING?
©2004 MGN LTD VIA WWW.ANDYCAPP.COM
AH, YES— ANDY AND I BUMPED INTO THE VICAR. "BIG DAY TOMORROW!" SAID THE VICAR...
..."I KNOW," SAYS ANDY, "BUT I'VE GOT TO MISS THE FINAL— I'M GETTING MARRIED"

RACING POST
I WAS SPEAKING TO MUM EARLIER
SHE'S GOT HERSELF A PART-TIME JOB IN THE LOCAL FLORIST'S
©2004 MGN LTD VIA WWW.ANDYCAPP.COM
THEY HAVE **BOUNCERS** IN FLORISTS NOW?

HI, ANDY
HI, MOTH
THAT'S A FUNNY NAME – HOW DID HE GET THAT?
©2004 MGN LTD VIA WWW.ANDYCAPP.COM
HE PANICKED IN A TATTOOIST'S AND RAN OFF HALFWAY THROUGH HIS "MOTHER" TATTOO

DON'T YOU WORRY ABOUT ME – I CAN LOOK AFTER ALL MY NEEDS!
©2004 MGN LTD VIA WWW.ANDYCAPP.COM
I DOUBT IT – I'VE TAKEN THE REMOTE AND THE BOTTLE OPENER!

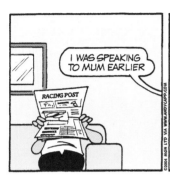

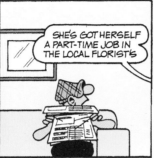

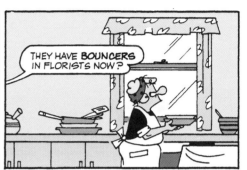

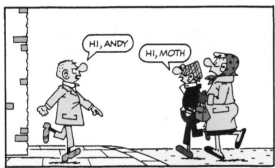

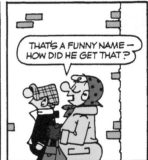

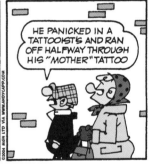

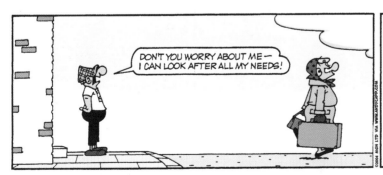

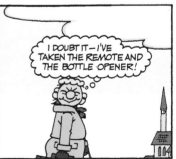

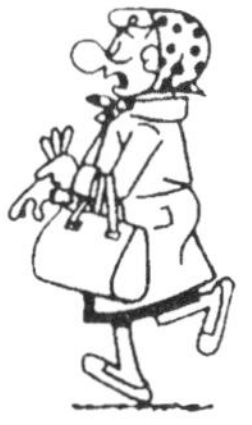

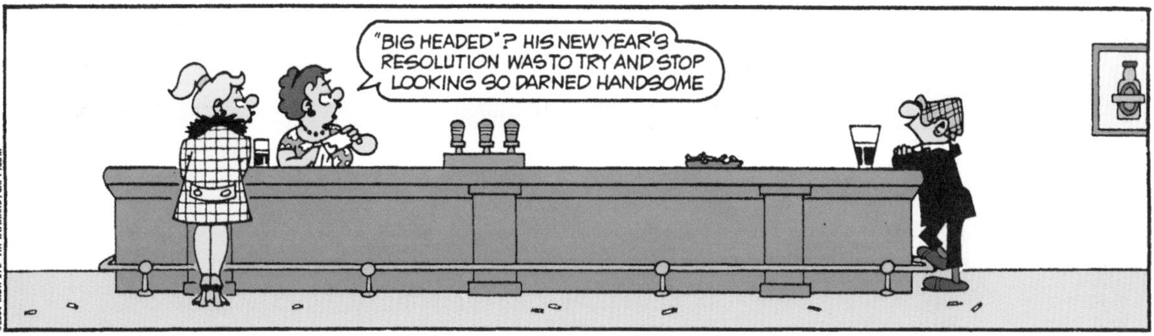
"BIG HEADED"? HIS NEW YEAR'S RESOLUTION WAS TO TRY AND STOP LOOKING SO DARNED HANDSOME
©2004 MGN LTD VIA WWW.ANDYCAPP.COM

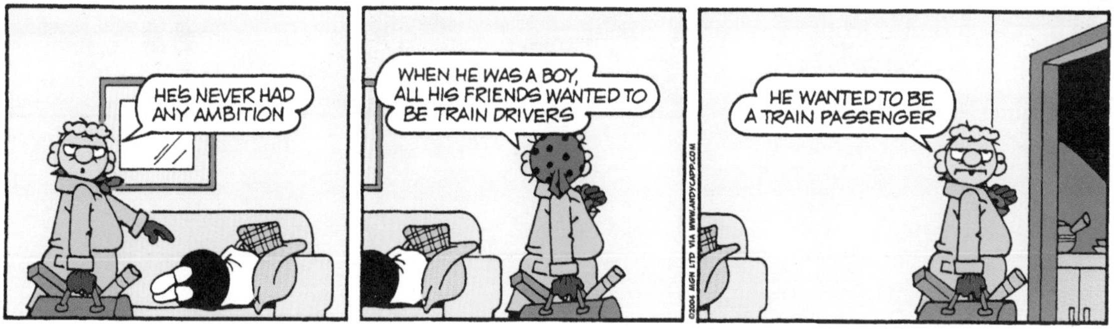
HE'S NEVER HAD ANY AMBITION
WHEN HE WAS A BOY, ALL HIS FRIENDS WANTED TO BE TRAIN DRIVERS
HE WANTED TO BE A TRAIN PASSENGER
©2004 MGN LTD VIA WWW.ANDYCAPP.COM

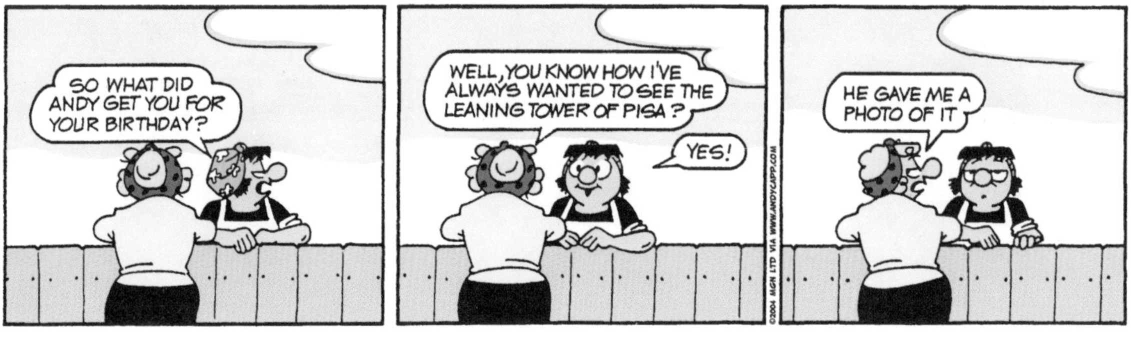
SO WHAT DID ANDY GET YOU FOR YOUR BIRTHDAY?
WELL, YOU KNOW HOW I'VE ALWAYS WANTED TO SEE THE LEANING TOWER OF PISA?
YES!
HE GAVE ME A PHOTO OF IT
©2004 MGN LTD VIA WWW.ANDYCAPP.COM

A CRAZY GAME, CRICKET
Mirror
A SIX-FOOT-SIX BOWLER CHUCKS A ROCK-HARD BALL AT NINETY MILES AN HOUR STRAIGHT AT A BATSMAN'S THROAT,..
©2004 MGN LTD VIA WWW.ANDYCAPP.COM
... THEN THEY STOP FOR TEA AND SANDWICHES!

CINEMA
NOW SHOWING
TCH! THERE WAS NOTHING BUT NAKED MEN IN THE ENTIRE FILM!
©2004 MGN LTD VIA WWW.ANDYCAPP.COM
SAME SEATS TOMORROW?
A BIT NEARER THE FRONT

MARRIAGE GUIDANCE
WELL, DID YOU TAKE THE ADVICE I GAVE YOU LAST WEEK?
©2004 MGN LTD VIA WWW.ANDYCAPP.COM
DID YOU GO FOR A NICE MEAL IN A QUIET RESTAURANT?
YES, I DID— AND SHE'S STILL FURIOUS

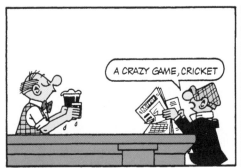

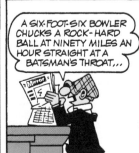

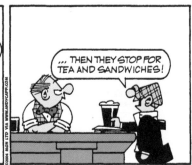

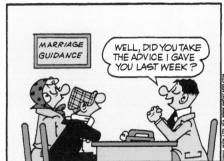

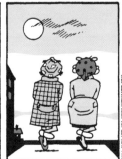

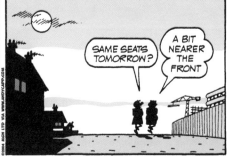

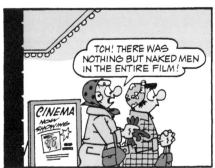

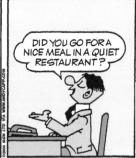

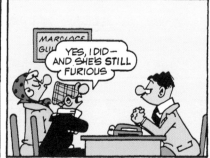

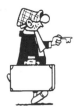

ARE YOU READY FOR THE SNOOKER, CHALKIE?
I CAN'T, ANDY— I PROMISED RUBY I'D TAKE HER TO THE CINEMA
WHAT WERE YOUR EXACT WORDS – DID YOU SAY YOU'D STAY FOR THE FILM?
©2004 MGN LTD VIA WWW.ANDYCAPP.COM

YOU LOOK TROUBLED, HARRY
YOU KNOW THE OLD SAYING — "BUY A FRIEND A BEER AND YOUR TROUBLES DISAPPEAR"
THAT'S NOT A SAYING!
IT MIGHT BE
©2004 MGN LTD VIA WWW.ANDYCAPP.COM

MISTER CAPP, HOW OFTEN WOULD YOU SAY YOU SURPRISE YOUR WIFE WITH A GIFT?
MARRIAGE GUIDANCE
IS LAUNDRY A GIFT?
©2004 MGN LTD VIA WWW.ANDYCAPP.COM

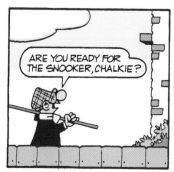

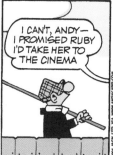

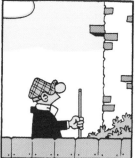

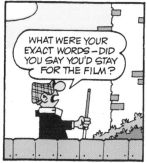

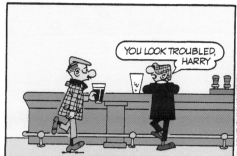

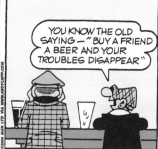

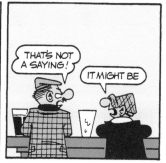

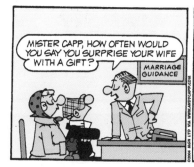

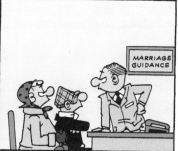

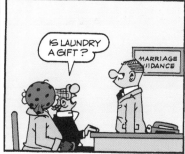

SIGH! I AM **REALLY** GETTING OLD
©2004 MGN LTD VIA WWW.ANDYCAPP.COM
FLO'S STAYING WITH HER SISTER FOR THE NIGHT— THAT USED TO BE A CUE FOR A PARTY
NOW MY MOTTO IS "WHEN THE CAT'S AWAY, THE MICE WILL NAP"

FLO, HOW DID ANDY'S JOB INTERVIEW GO?
HE SAYS IT WENT REALLY WELL
©2004 MGN LTD VIA WWW.ANDYCAPP.COM
HE DOESN'T WANT TO COUNT HIS CHICKENS, BUT HE'S PRETTY SURE HE DIDN'T GET IT

REFEREE, THAT DECISION WAS UNJUST AND SUGGESTED A DEGREE OF PARTISANSHIP!
©2004 MGN LTD VIA WWW.ANDYCAPP.COM
OH, DEAR— SOMETIMES I GET QUITE CARRIED AWAY!
YOU'RE AN ANIMAL, VICAR, AN ANIMAL

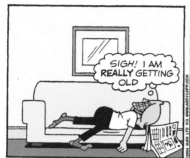

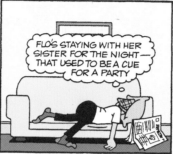

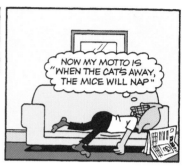

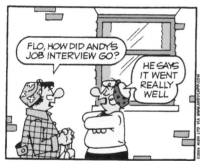

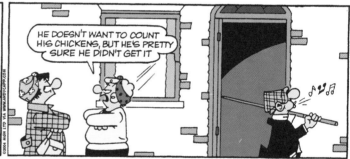

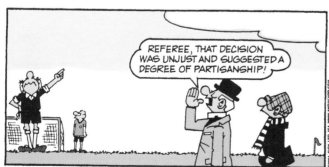

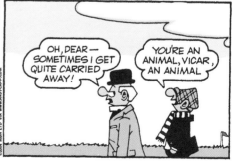

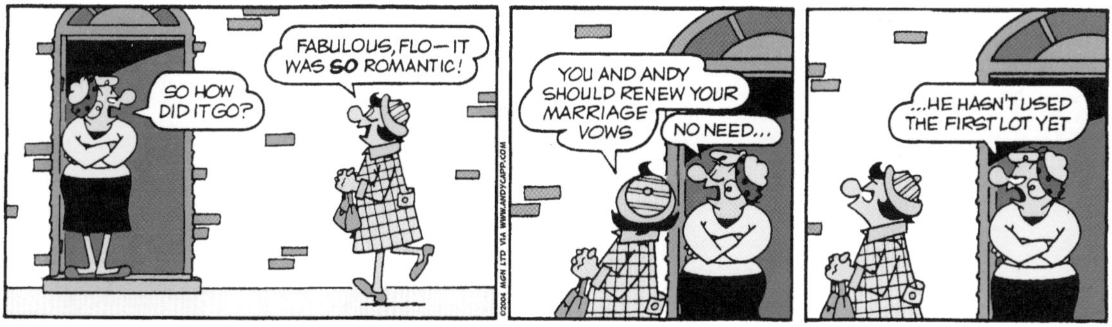
SO HOW DID IT GO?
FABULOUS, FLO— IT WAS SO ROMANTIC!
©2004 MGN LTD VIA WWW.ANDYCAPP.COM
YOU AND ANDY SHOULD RENEW YOUR MARRIAGE VOWS
NO NEED...
...HE HASN'T USED THE FIRST LOT YET

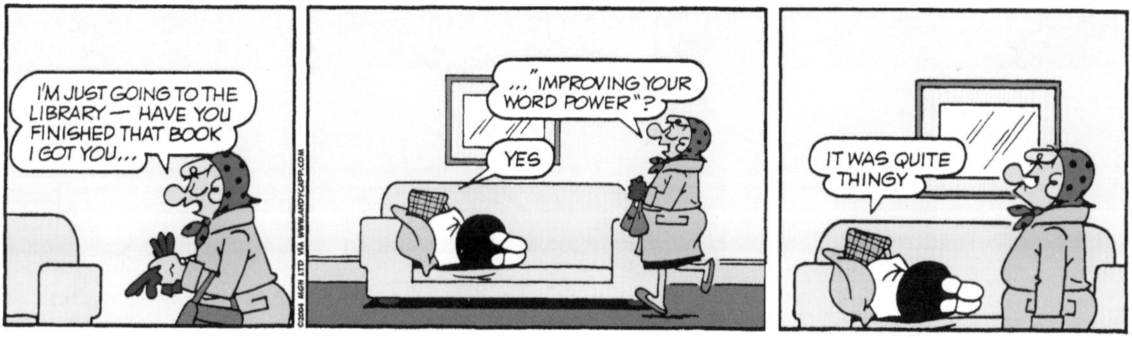
I'M JUST GOING TO THE LIBRARY — HAVE YOU FINISHED THAT BOOK I GOT YOU...
©2004 MGN LTD VIA WWW.ANDYCAPP.COM
..."IMPROVING YOUR WORD POWER"?
YES
IT WAS QUITE THINGY

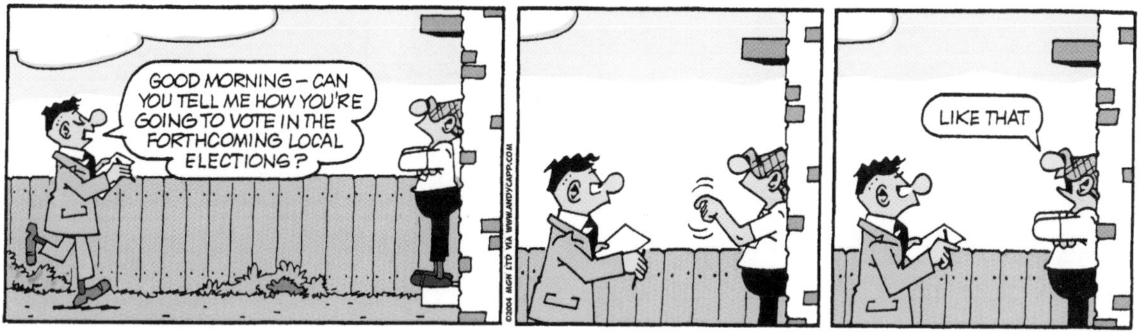
GOOD MORNING — CAN YOU TELL ME HOW YOU'RE GOING TO VOTE IN THE FORTHCOMING LOCAL ELECTIONS?
©2004 MGN LTD VIA WWW.ANDYCAPP.COM
LIKE THAT

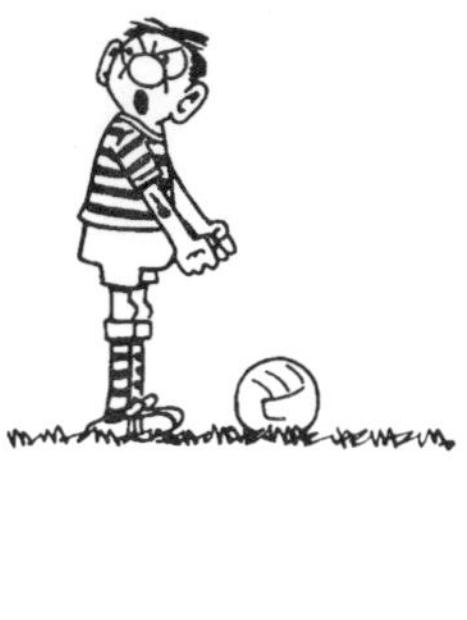

BACON SANDWICH FOR TEA — OKAY?
WELL...
BEFORE YOU ANSWER, I'VE HAD A ROTTEN DAY AT WORK, I'VE WALKED HOME IN THE RAIN...
©2004 MGN LTD VIA WWW.ANDYCAPP.COM
...I'M WET, TIRED AND HAVE A ROLLED-UP BUT DANGEROUS UMBRELLA IN MY HAND
YUM! YUM! BACON SANDWICH!

SO WHAT ARE YOU BUYING FLO FOR HER BIRTHDAY?
©2004 MGN LTD VIA WWW.ANDYCAPP.COM
NO IDEA – SHE IS SO DIFFICULT TO SHOP FOR
FOR A START, I HAVE TO RULE OUT ANYTHING THAT COULD DOUBLE AS A WEAPON

THE SIGNS ARE THERE FOR ALL TO SEE
©2004 MGN LTD VIA WWW.ANDYCAPP.COM
I'M DEFINITELY GETTING SLOWER
I USED TO GET SENT OFF IN THE FIRST HALF

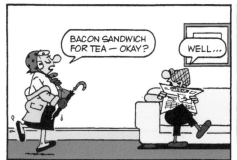

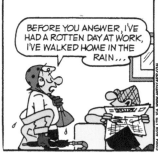

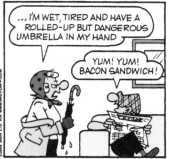

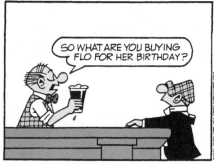

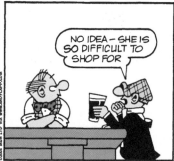

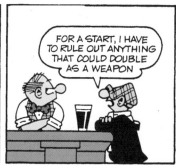

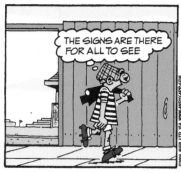

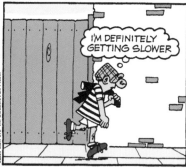

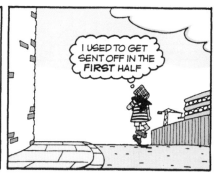

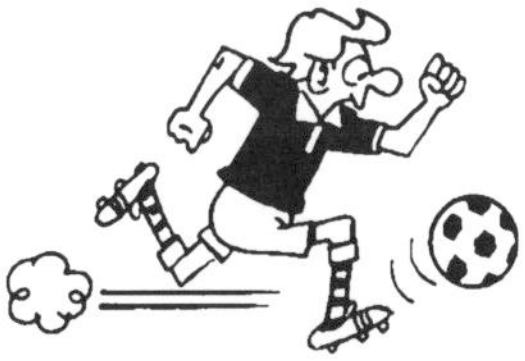

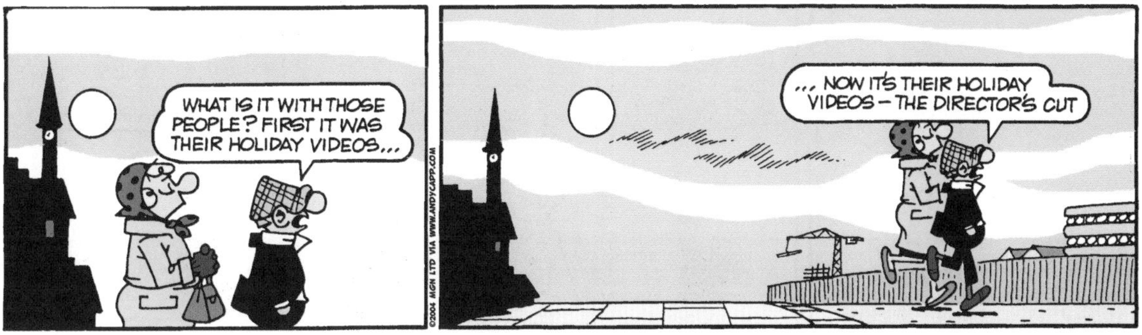

WHAT IS IT WITH THOSE PEOPLE? FIRST IT WAS THEIR HOLIDAY VIDEOS...
©2004 MGN LTD VIA WWW.ANDYCAPP.COM
... NOW IT'S THEIR HOLIDAY VIDEOS – THE DIRECTOR'S CUT

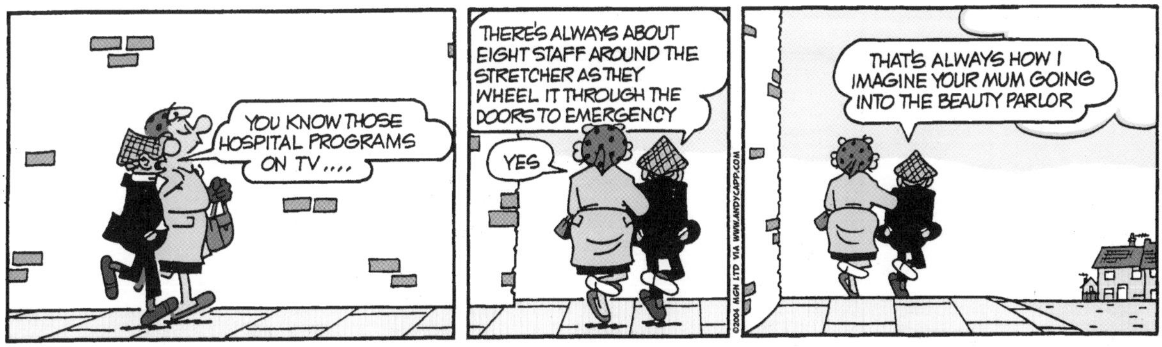

YOU KNOW THOSE HOSPITAL PROGRAMS ON TV....
THERE'S ALWAYS ABOUT EIGHT STAFF AROUND THE STRETCHER AS THEY WHEEL IT THROUGH THE DOORS TO EMERGENCY
YES
©2004 MGN LTD VIA WWW.ANDYCAPP.COM
THAT'S ALWAYS HOW I IMAGINE YOUR MUM GOING INTO THE BEAUTY PARLOR

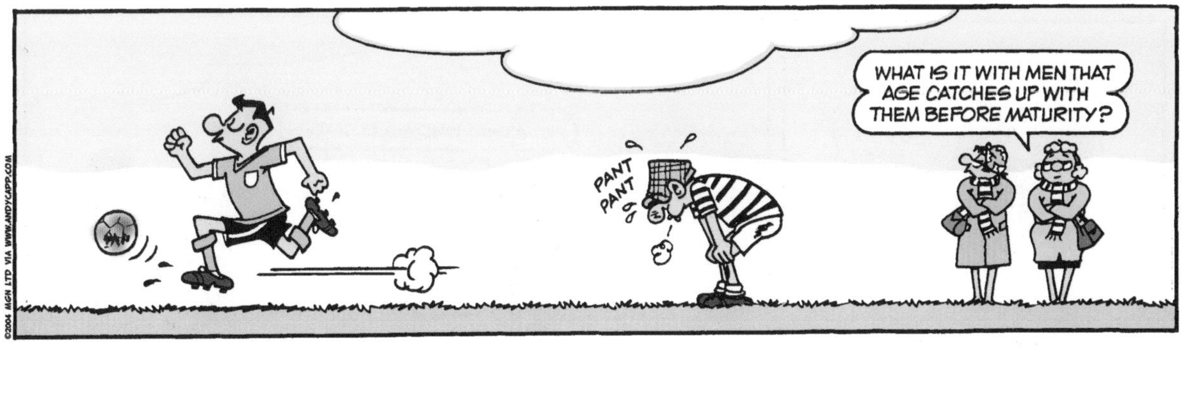

©2004 MGN LTD VIA WWW.ANDYCAPP.COM
PANT PANT
WHAT IS IT WITH MEN THAT AGE CATCHES UP WITH THEM BEFORE MATURITY?

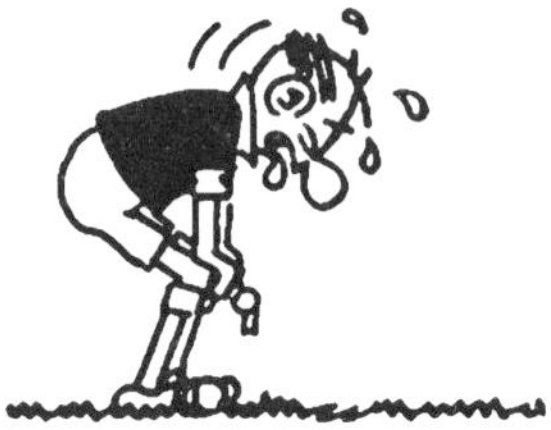

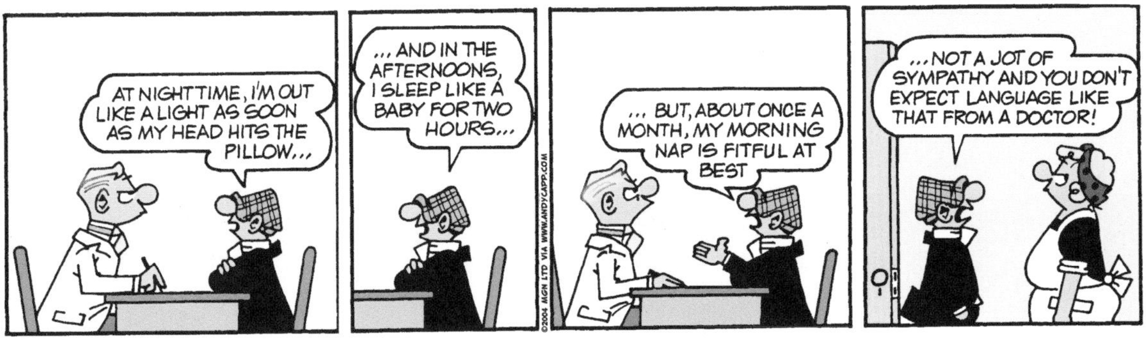

AT NIGHT TIME, I'M OUT LIKE A LIGHT AS SOON AS MY HEAD HITS THE PILLOW...
...AND IN THE AFTERNOONS, I SLEEP LIKE A BABY FOR TWO HOURS...
... BUT, ABOUT ONCE A MONTH, MY MORNING NAP IS FITFUL AT BEST
...NOT A JOT OF SYMPATHY AND YOU DON'T EXPECT LANGUAGE LIKE THAT FROM A DOCTOR!
©2004 MGN LTD VIA WWW.ANDYCAPP.COM

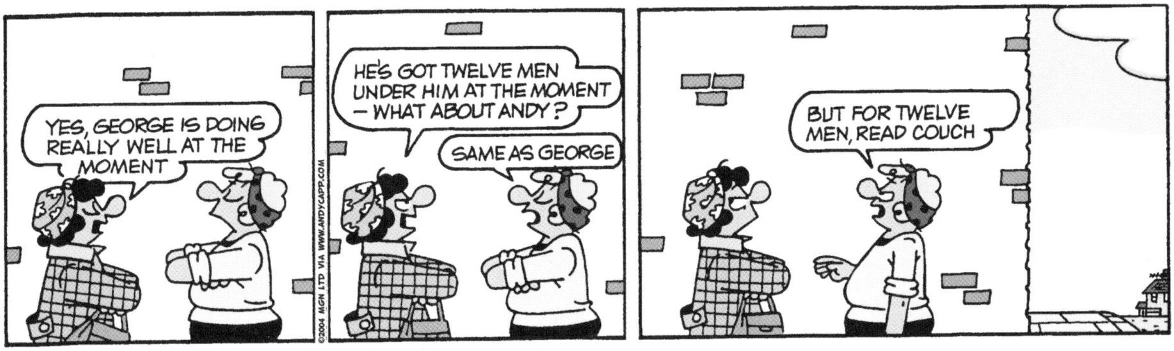

YES, GEORGE IS DOING REALLY WELL AT THE MOMENT
HE'S GOT TWELVE MEN UNDER HIM AT THE MOMENT – WHAT ABOUT ANDY?
SAME AS GEORGE
BUT FOR TWELVE MEN, READ COUCH
©2004 MGN LTD VIA WWW.ANDYCAPP.COM

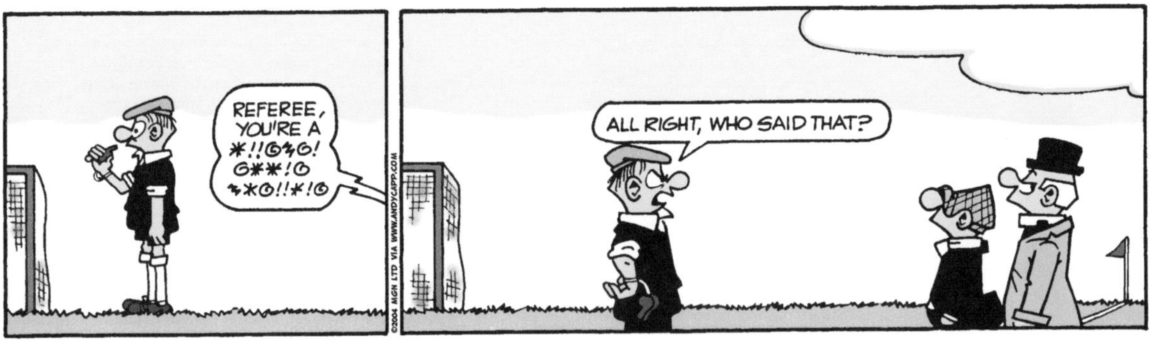

REFEREE, YOU'RE A
ALL RIGHT, WHO SAID THAT?
©2004 MGN LTD VIA WWW.ANDYCAPP.COM

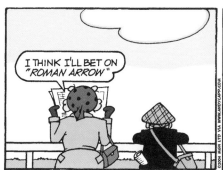

I THINK I'LL BET ON "ROMAN ARROW"
©2004 MGN LTD VIA WWW.ANDYCAPP.COM
AUNT JEAN WENT TO ROME ONCE, AND SHE LIKED JOHN WAYNE FILMS, WHICH OFTEN HAD ARROWS IN THEM
AND HERE'S ME THINKING THE UNBEATEN, ODDS-ON FAVORITE MIGHT HAVE A CHANCE

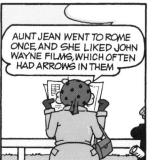

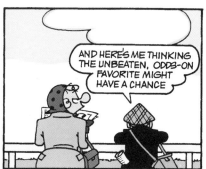

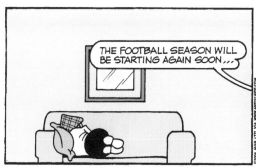

THE FOOTBALL SEASON WILL BE STARTING AGAIN SOON...
©2004 MGN LTD VIA WWW.ANDYCAPP.COM
SHOULDN'T YOU BE OUT PRACTICING SWEARING AT REFEREES?

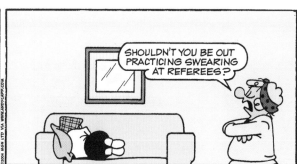

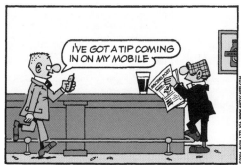

I'VE GOT A TIP COMING IN ON MY MOBILE
RACING POST
©2004 MGN LTD VIA WWW.ANDYCAPP.COM
IT'S STRAIGHT FROM THE HORSE'S MOUTH
WHAT DOES IT SAY?
RACING POST
"WHINNY"

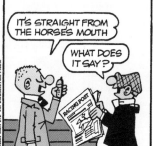

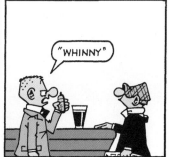

MARRIAGE GUIDANCE
I RECOMMEND YOU SET ASIDE SOME TIME FOR TALKING...
©2004 MGN LTD VIA WWW.ANDYCAPP.COM
...MAYBE TWENTY MINUTES IN THE EVENING —JUST TO DISCUSS YOUR DAY
FAIR ENOUGH,...
MARRIAG GUIDANC
...I SUPPOSE I COULD PHONE FROM THE PUB

MY SHOULDERS ARE REALLY ACHING
©2004 MGN LTD VIA WWW.ANDYCAPP.COM
THE GUTTER ON OUR ROOF HAS NEEDED REPAIRING FOR AGES
THREE HOURS I WAS HOLDING THAT LADDER FOR FLO!

THAT NEW DRESS SHOP IS FANTASTIC!
©2004 MGN LTD VIA WWW.ANDYCAPP.COM
I JUST HAVE TO MAKE SURE I DON'T SPEND ALL MY MONEY!
THE LAST TIME I BOUGHT A NEW DRESS, I JUST HAD TO MAKE SURE IT DIDN'T CLASH WITH MY BRIDESMAIDS'

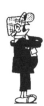

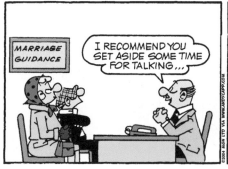

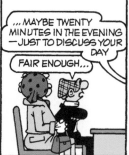

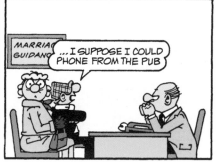

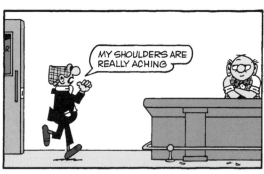

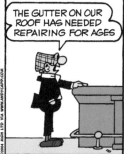

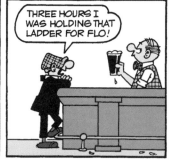

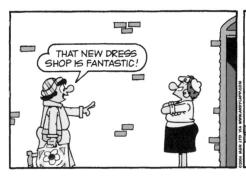

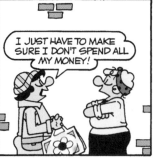

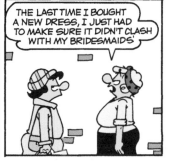

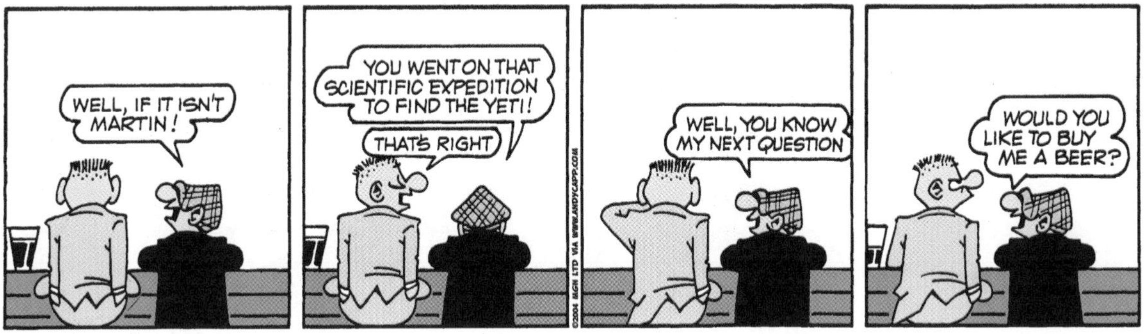
WELL, IF IT ISN'T MARTIN!
YOU WENT ON THAT SCIENTIFIC EXPEDITION TO FIND THE YETI!
THAT'S RIGHT
©2004 MGN LTD VIA WWW.ANDYCAPP.COM
WELL, YOU KNOW MY NEXT QUESTION
WOULD YOU LIKE TO BUY ME A BEER?

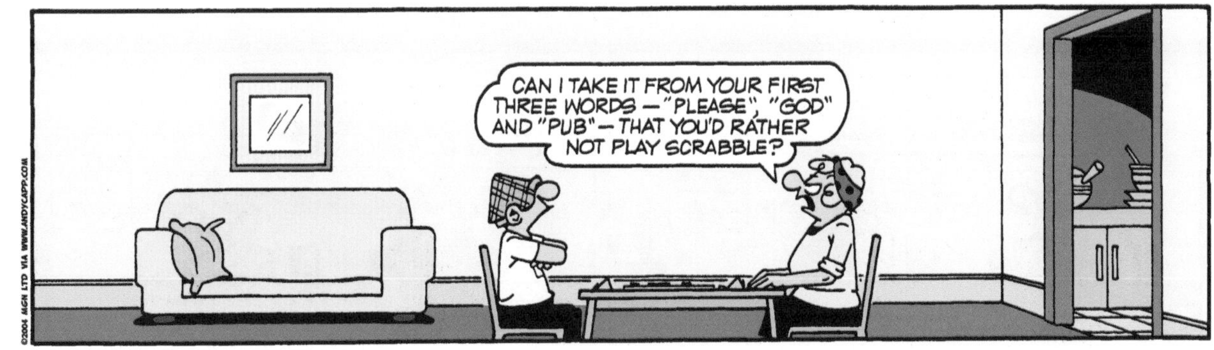
©2004 MGN LTD VIA WWW.ANDYCAPP.COM
CAN I TAKE IT FROM YOUR FIRST THREE WORDS — "PLEASE", "GOD" AND "PUB" — THAT YOU'D RATHER NOT PLAY SCRABBLE?

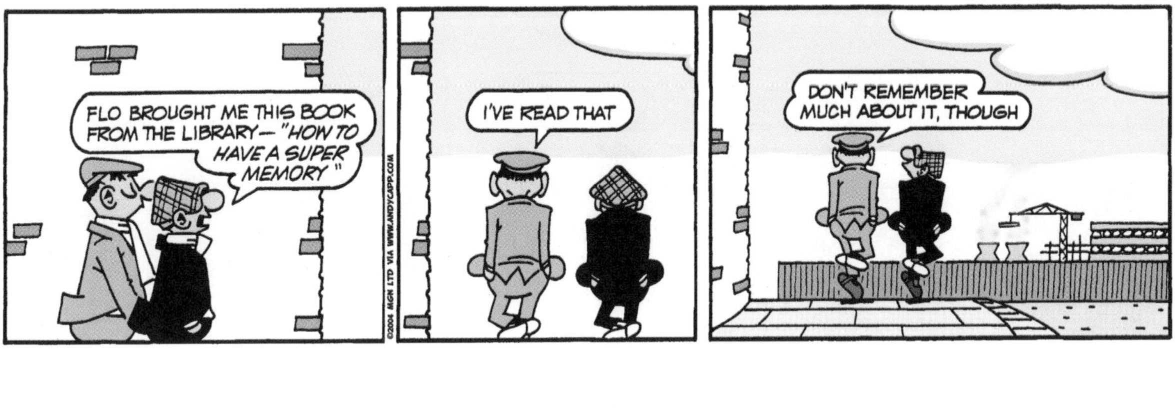
FLO BROUGHT ME THIS BOOK FROM THE LIBRARY— *"HOW TO HAVE A SUPER MEMORY"*
©2004 MGN LTD VIA WWW.ANDYCAPP.COM
I'VE READ THAT
DON'T REMEMBER MUCH ABOUT IT, THOUGH

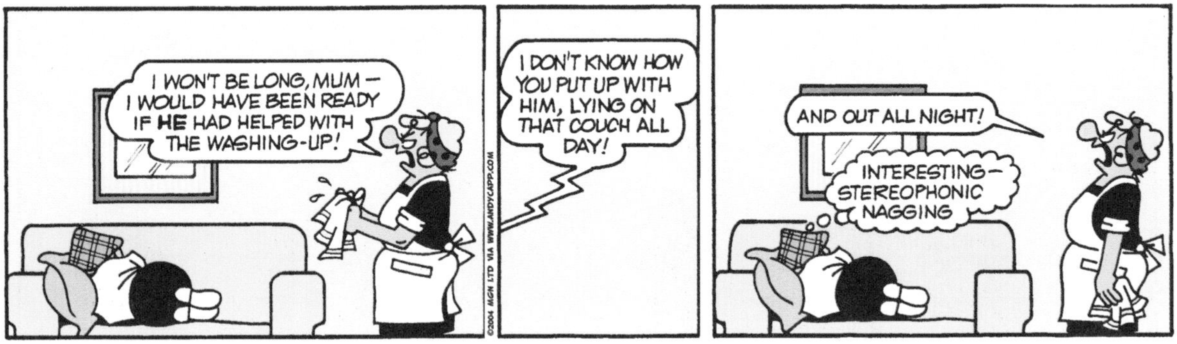
I WON'T BE LONG, MUM — I WOULD HAVE BEEN READY IF **HE** HAD HELPED WITH THE WASHING-UP!
©2004 MGN LTD VIA WWW.ANDYCAPP.COM
I DON'T KNOW HOW YOU PUT UP WITH HIM, LYING ON THAT COUCH ALL DAY!
AND OUT ALL NIGHT!
INTERESTING— STEREOPHONIC NAGGING

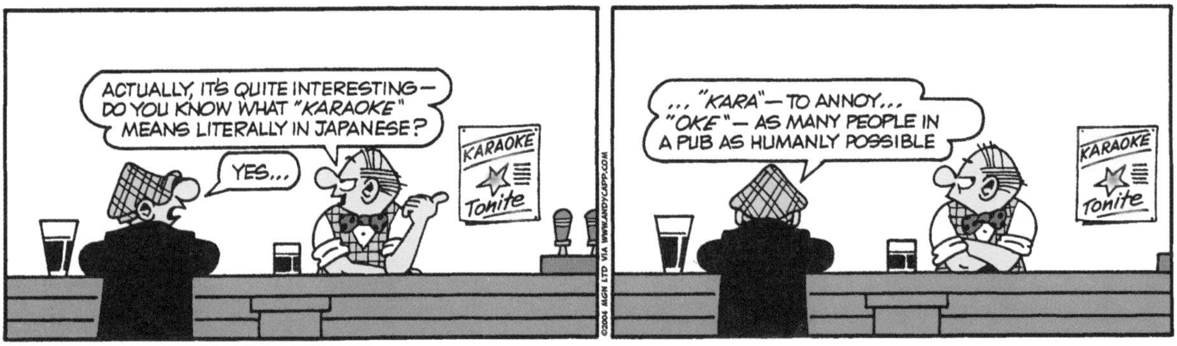
ACTUALLY, IT'S QUITE INTERESTING— DO YOU KNOW WHAT "KARAOKE" MEANS LITERALLY IN JAPANESE?
YES...
KARAOKE Tonite
©2004 MGN LTD VIA WWW.ANDYCAPP.COM
... "KARA"— TO ANNOY... "OKE"— AS MANY PEOPLE IN A PUB AS HUMANLY POSSIBLE
KARAOKE Tonite

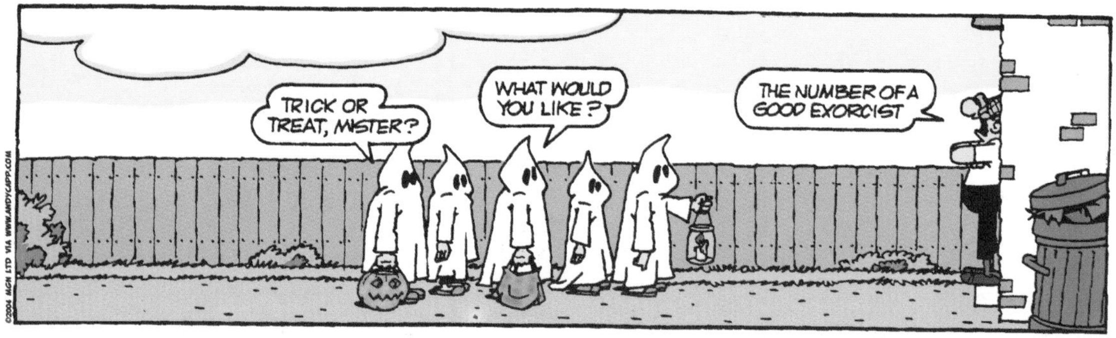
©2004 MGN LTD VIA WWW.ANDYCAPP.COM
TRICK OR TREAT, MISTER?
WHAT WOULD YOU LIKE?
THE NUMBER OF A GOOD EXORCIST

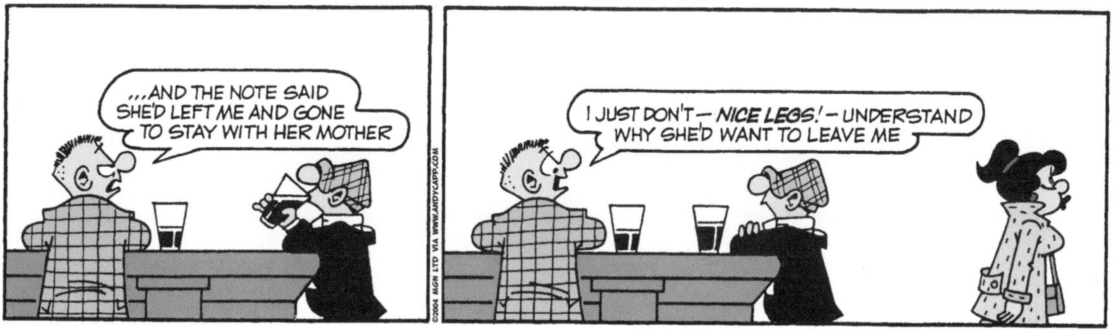
...AND THE NOTE SAID SHE'D LEFT ME AND GONE TO STAY WITH HER MOTHER
©2004 MGN LTD VIA WWW.ANDYCAPP.COM
I JUST DON'T — **NICE LEGS!** — UNDERSTAND WHY SHE'D WANT TO LEAVE ME

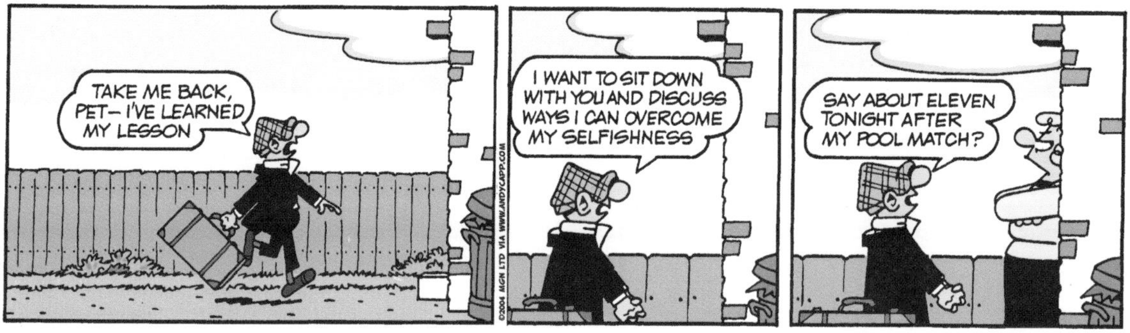
TAKE ME BACK, PET— I'VE LEARNED MY LESSON
©2004 MGN LTD VIA WWW.ANDYCAPP.COM
I WANT TO SIT DOWN WITH YOU AND DISCUSS WAYS I CAN OVERCOME MY SELFISHNESS
SAY ABOUT ELEVEN TONIGHT AFTER MY POOL MATCH?

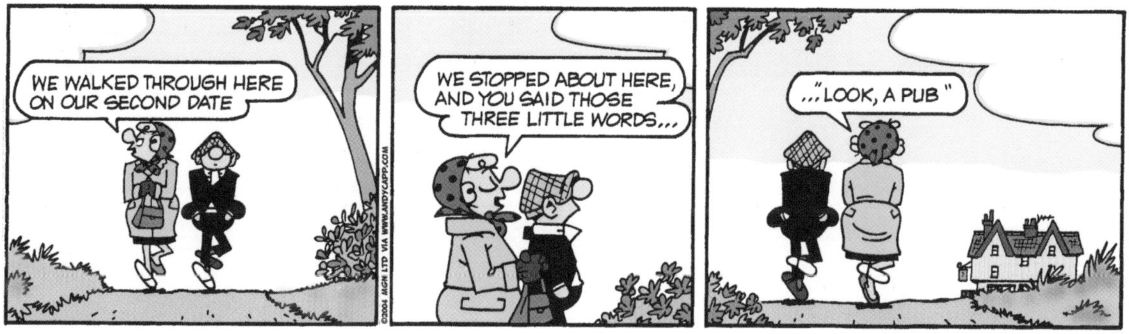
WE WALKED THROUGH HERE ON OUR SECOND DATE
©2004 MGN LTD VIA WWW.ANDYCAPP.COM
WE STOPPED ABOUT HERE, AND YOU SAID THOSE THREE LITTLE WORDS...
..."LOOK, A PUB"

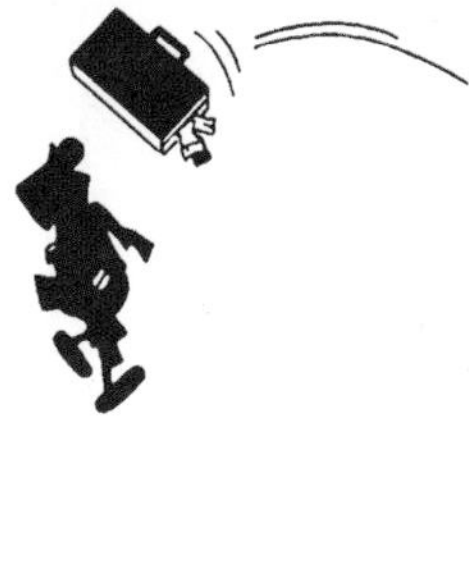

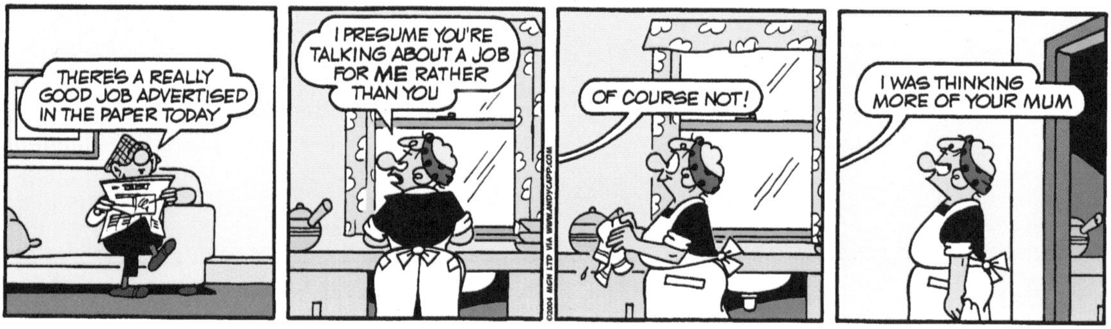
THERE'S A REALLY GOOD JOB ADVERTISED IN THE PAPER TODAY
I PRESUME YOU'RE TALKING ABOUT A JOB FOR ME RATHER THAN YOU
OF COURSE NOT!
I WAS THINKING MORE OF YOUR MUM
©2004 MGN LTD VIA WWW.ANDYCAPP.COM

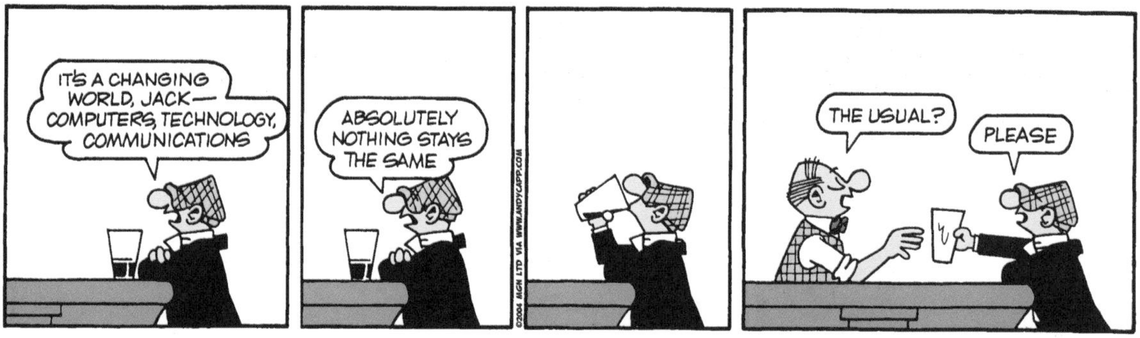
IT'S A CHANGING WORLD, JACK— COMPUTERS, TECHNOLOGY, COMMUNICATIONS
ABSOLUTELY NOTHING STAYS THE SAME
©2004 MGN LTD VIA WWW.ANDYCAPP.COM
THE USUAL?
PLEASE

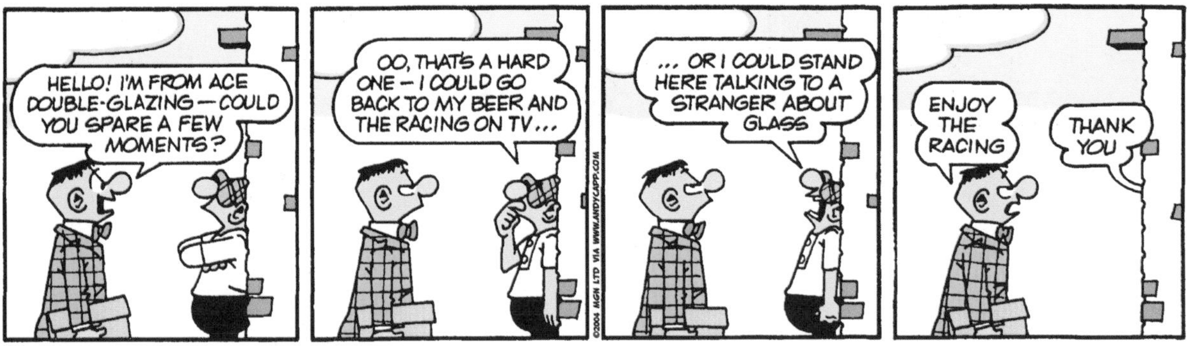
HELLO! I'M FROM ACE DOUBLE-GLAZING — COULD YOU SPARE A FEW MOMENTS?
OO, THAT'S A HARD ONE – I COULD GO BACK TO MY BEER AND THE RACING ON TV...
©2004 MGN LTD VIA WWW.ANDYCAPP.COM
... OR I COULD STAND HERE TALKING TO A STRANGER ABOUT GLASS
ENJOY THE RACING
THANK YOU

YOU SHOULD HAVE BEEN IN THE PUB TONIGHT, PET— IT WAS BRILLIANT!
THEY HAD NEW BEERMATS!
THERE SPEAKS A MAN IN SERIOUS NEED OF A LIFE
©2004 MGN LTD VIA WWW.ANDYCAPP.COM

NOW I KNOW WHY ALL JOGGERS WEAR EARPHONES
THEY'RE GETTING HELP FROM "STUPID CLOTHES ANONYMOUS"
©2004 MGN LTD VIA WWW.ANDYCAPP.COM

MARRIAGE GUIDANCE
THIS IS AN EXERCISE I GIVE TO A LOT OF COUPLES
I WANT YOU EACH TO WRITE DOWN THE TWO MOST IMPORTANT THINGS IN YOUR LIFE
MARRIAGE? LOVE? FAMILY? HEALTH?
DOES HORSE RACING HAVE A HYPHEN?
©2004 MGN LTD VIA WWW.ANDYCAPP.COM

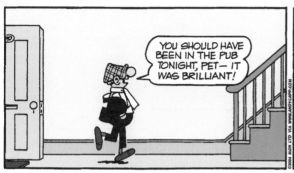

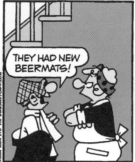

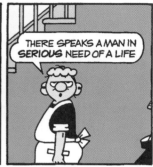

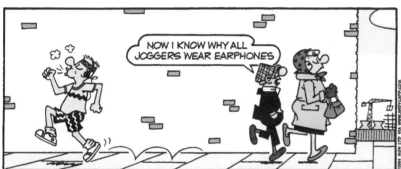

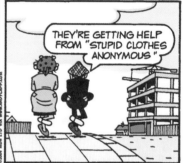

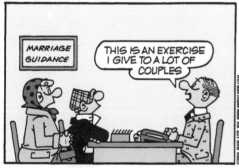

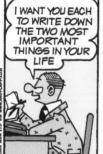

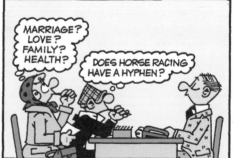

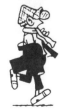

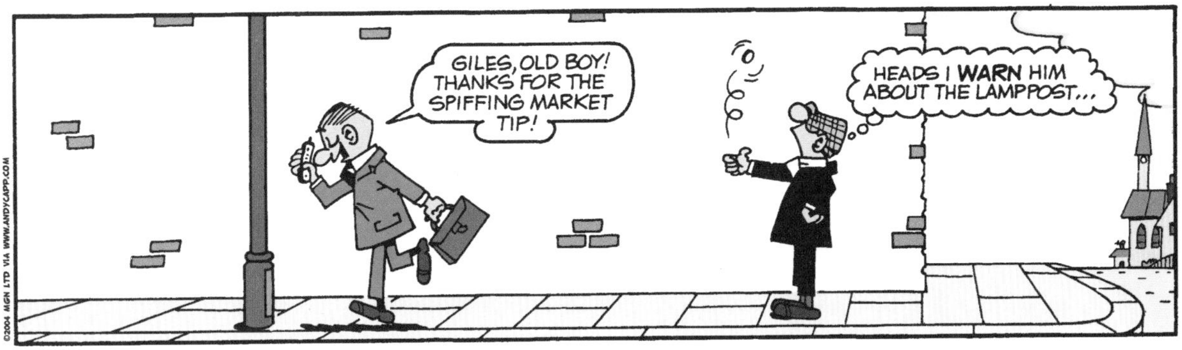
©2004 MGN LTD VIA WWW.ANDYCAPP.COM
GILES, OLD BOY! THANKS FOR THE SPIFFING MARKET TIP!
HEADS I **WARN** HIM ABOUT THE LAMPPOST...

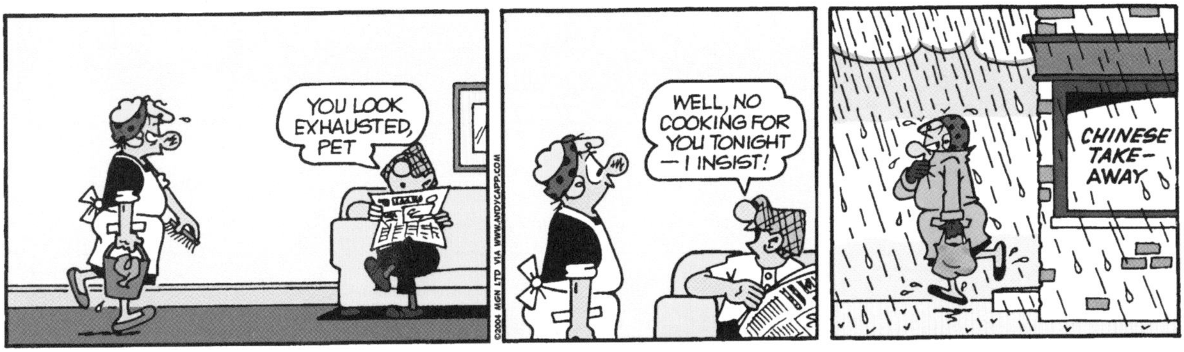
YOU LOOK EXHAUSTED, PET
©2004 MGN LTD VIA WWW.ANDYCAPP.COM
WELL, NO COOKING FOR YOU TONIGHT — I INSIST!
CHINESE TAKE-AWAY

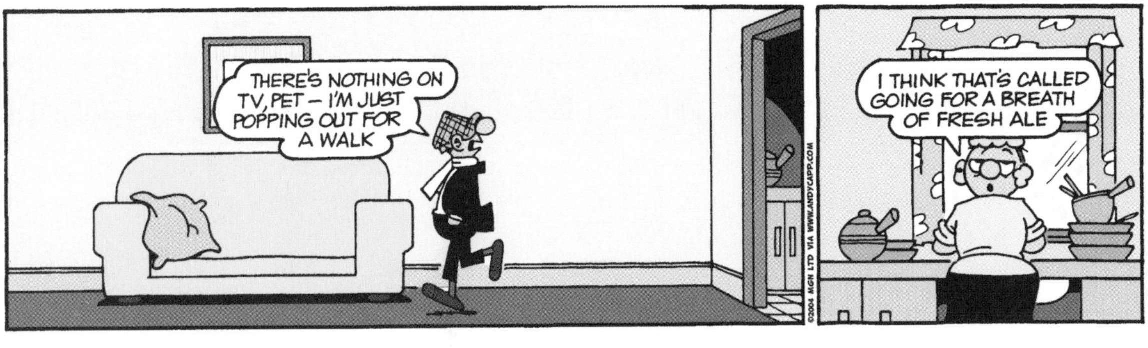
THERE'S NOTHING ON TV, PET — I'M JUST POPPING OUT FOR A WALK
©2004 MGN LTD VIA WWW.ANDYCAPP.COM
I THINK THAT'S CALLED GOING FOR A BREATH OF FRESH ALE

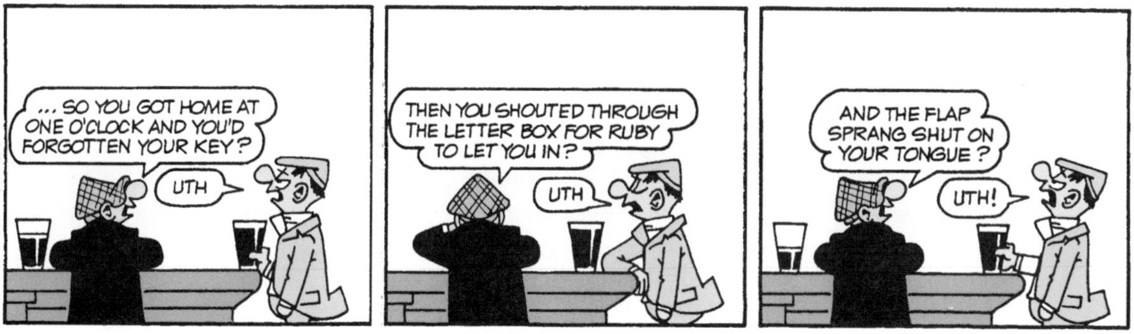
...SO YOU GOT HOME AT ONE O'CLOCK AND YOU'D FORGOTTEN YOUR KEY?
UTH
THEN YOU SHOUTED THROUGH THE LETTER BOX FOR RUBY TO LET YOU IN?
UTH
AND THE FLAP SPRANG SHUT ON YOUR TONGUE?
UTH!
©2004 MGN LTD VIA WWW.ANDYCAPP.COM

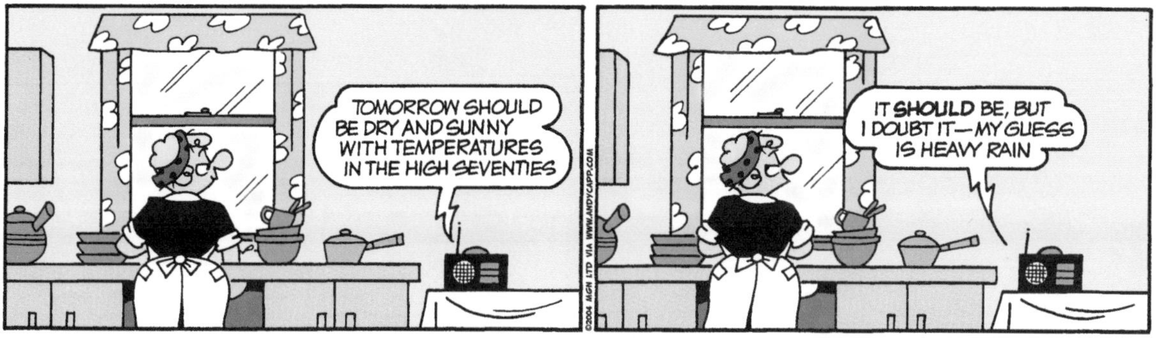
TOMORROW SHOULD BE DRY AND SUNNY WITH TEMPERATURES IN THE HIGH SEVENTIES
IT **SHOULD** BE, BUT I DOUBT IT—MY GUESS IS HEAVY RAIN
©2004 MGN LTD VIA WWW.ANDYCAPP.COM

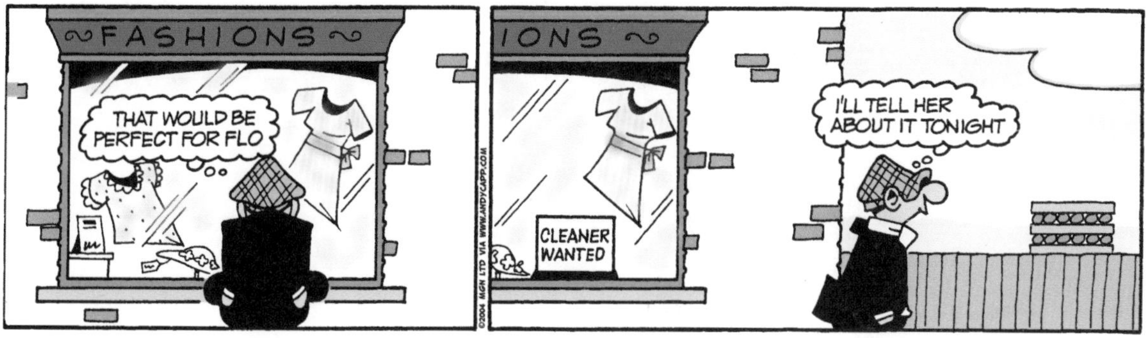
FASHIONS
THAT WOULD BE PERFECT FOR FLO
IONS
CLEANER WANTED
I'LL TELL HER ABOUT IT TONIGHT
©2004 MGN LTD VIA WWW.ANDYCAPP.COM

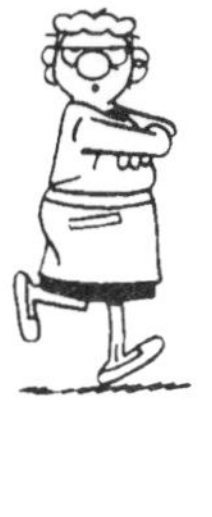

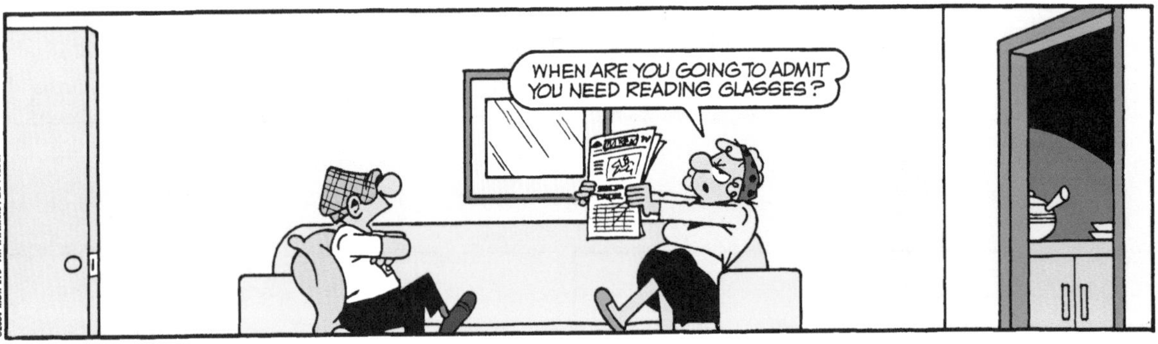
WHEN ARE YOU GOING TO ADMIT YOU NEED READING GLASSES?
©2004 MGN LTD VIA WWW.ANDYCAPP.COM

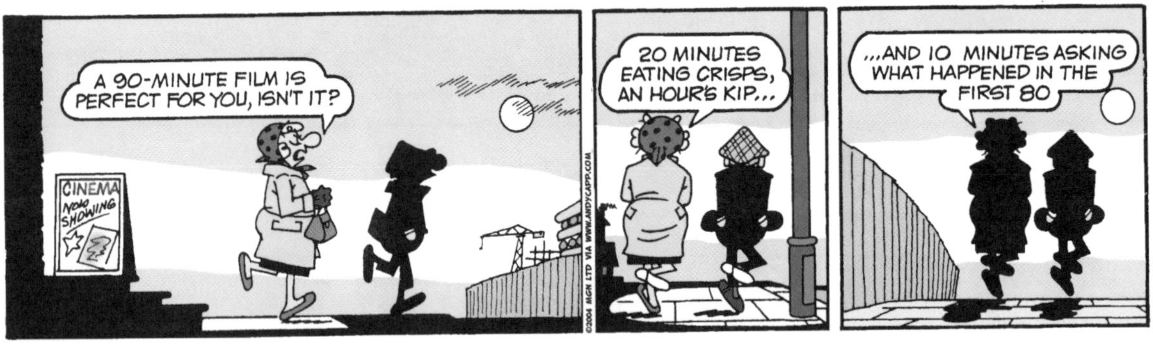
A 90-MINUTE FILM IS PERFECT FOR YOU, ISN'T IT?
CINEMA
NOW SHOWING
20 MINUTES EATING CRISPS, AN HOUR'S KIP...
...AND 10 MINUTES ASKING WHAT HAPPENED IN THE FIRST 80
©2004 MGN LTD VIA WWW.ANDYCAPP.COM

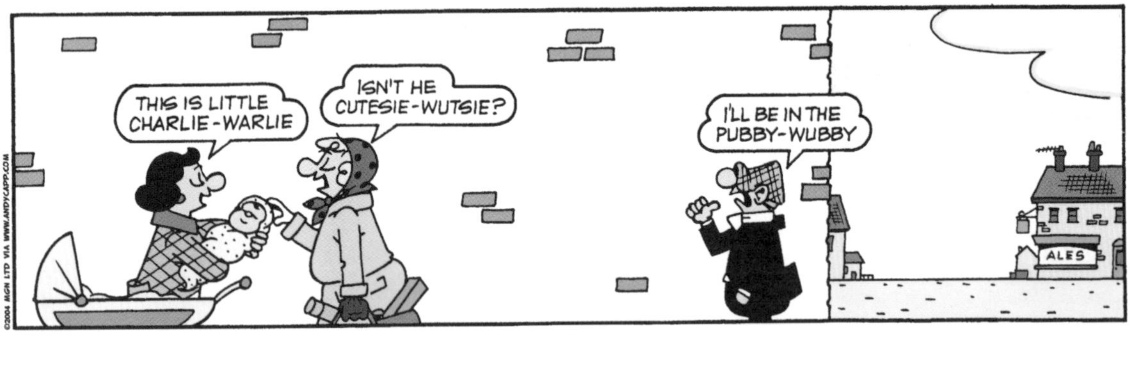
THIS IS LITTLE CHARLIE-WARLIE
ISN'T HE CUTESIE-WUTSIE?
I'LL BE IN THE PUBBY-WUBBY
ALES
©2004 MGN LTD VIA WWW.ANDYCAPP.COM

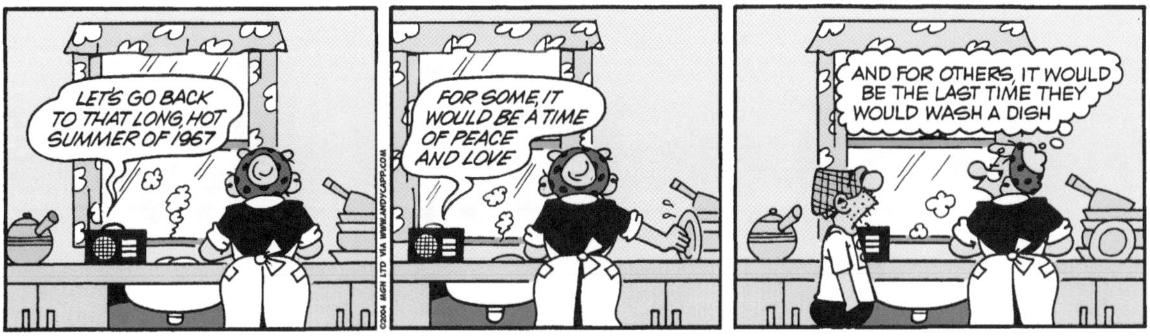
LET'S GO BACK TO THAT LONG, HOT SUMMER OF 1967
©2004 MGN LTD VIA WWW.ANDYCAPP.COM
FOR SOME, IT WOULD BE A TIME OF PEACE AND LOVE
AND FOR OTHERS, IT WOULD BE THE LAST TIME THEY WOULD WASH A DISH

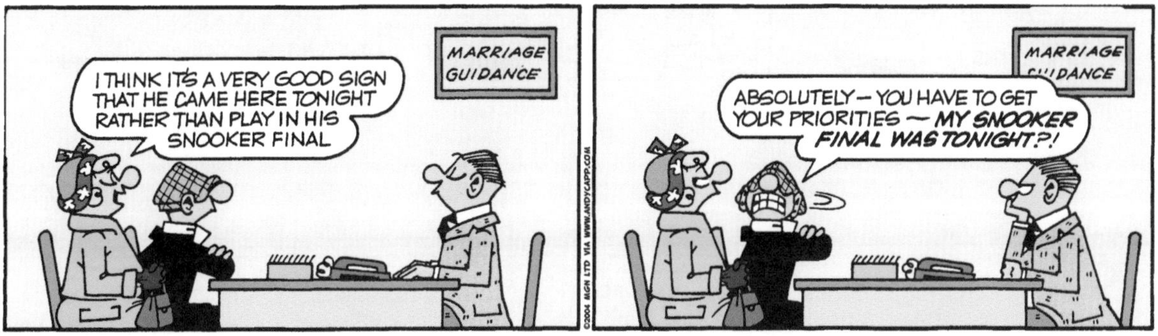
MARRIAGE GUIDANCE
I THINK IT'S A VERY GOOD SIGN THAT HE CAME HERE TONIGHT RATHER THAN PLAY IN HIS SNOOKER FINAL
©2004 MGN LTD VIA WWW.ANDYCAPP.COM
MARRIAGE GUIDANCE
ABSOLUTELY — YOU HAVE TO GET YOUR PRIORITIES — MY SNOOKER FINAL WAS TONIGHT?!

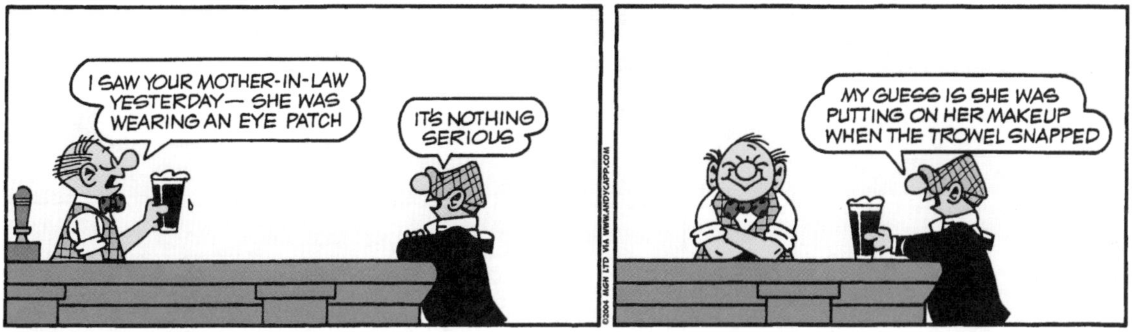
I SAW YOUR MOTHER-IN-LAW YESTERDAY — SHE WAS WEARING AN EYE PATCH
IT'S NOTHING SERIOUS
©2004 MGN LTD VIA WWW.ANDYCAPP.COM
MY GUESS IS SHE WAS PUTTING ON HER MAKEUP WHEN THE TROWEL SNAPPED

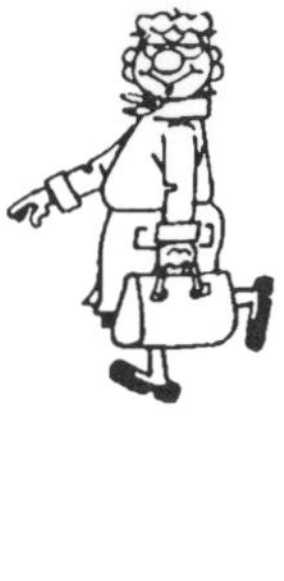

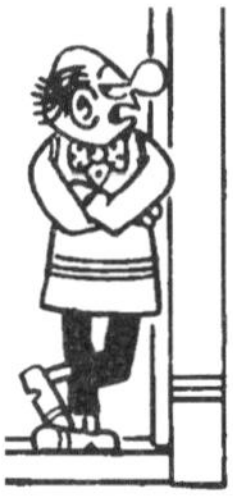

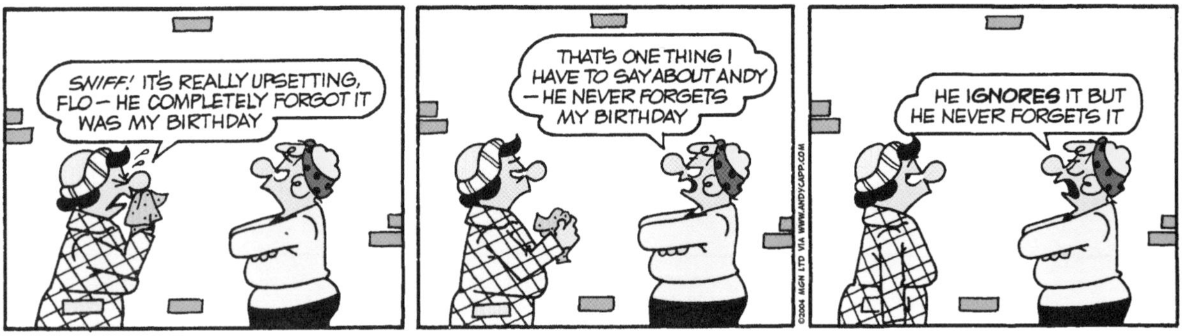
SNIFF! IT'S REALLY UPSETTING, FLO — HE COMPLETELY FORGOT IT WAS MY BIRTHDAY
THAT'S ONE THING I HAVE TO SAY ABOUT ANDY — HE NEVER FORGETS MY BIRTHDAY
©2004 MGN LTD VIA WWW.ANDYCAPP.COM
HE IGNORES IT BUT HE NEVER FORGETS IT

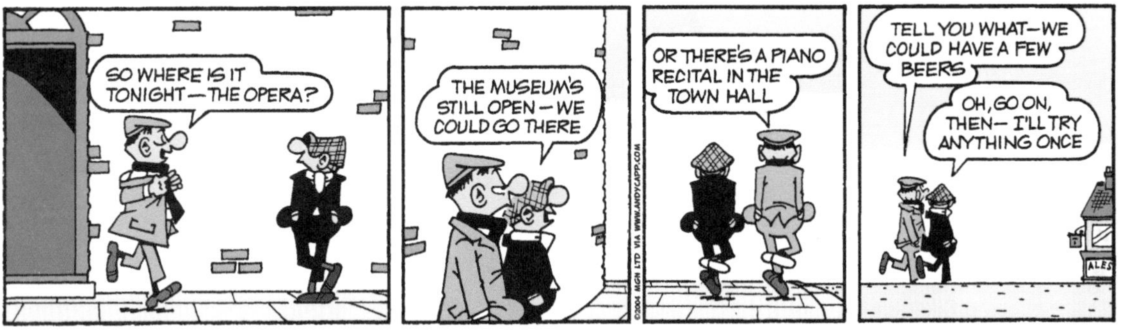
SO WHERE IS IT TONIGHT — THE OPERA?
THE MUSEUM'S STILL OPEN — WE COULD GO THERE
©2004 MGN LTD VIA WWW.ANDYCAPP.COM
OR THERE'S A PIANO RECITAL IN THE TOWN HALL
TELL YOU WHAT—WE COULD HAVE A FEW BEERS
OH, GO ON, THEN— I'LL TRY ANYTHING ONCE
ALES

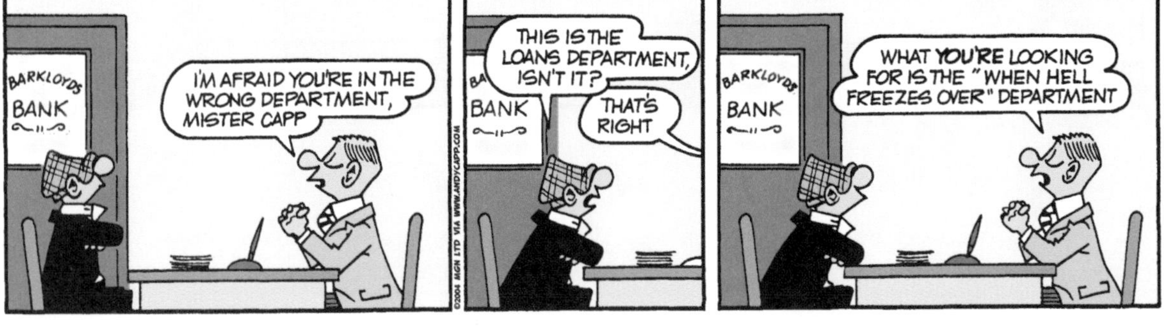
BARKLOYDS BANK
I'M AFRAID YOU'RE IN THE WRONG DEPARTMENT, MISTER CAPP
©2004 MGN LTD VIA WWW.ANDYCAPP.COM
BANK
THIS IS THE LOANS DEPARTMENT, ISN'T IT?
THAT'S RIGHT
BARKLOYDS BANK
WHAT YOU'RE LOOKING FOR IS THE "WHEN HELL FREEZES OVER" DEPARTMENT

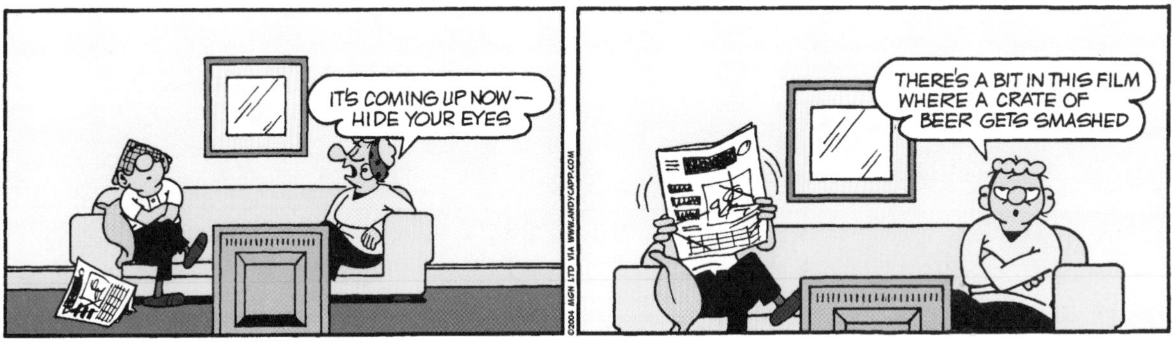
IT'S COMING UP NOW — HIDE YOUR EYES
©2004 MGN LTD VIA WWW.ANDYCAPP.COM
THERE'S A BIT IN THIS FILM WHERE A CRATE OF BEER GETS SMASHED

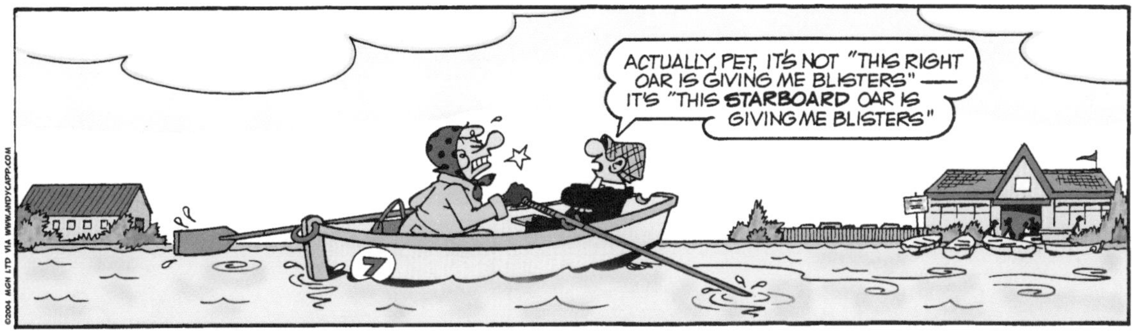
©2004 MGN LTD VIA WWW.ANDYCAPP.COM
ACTUALLY, PET, IT'S NOT "THIS RIGHT OAR IS GIVING ME BLISTERS" — IT'S "THIS **STARBOARD** OAR IS GIVING ME BLISTERS"

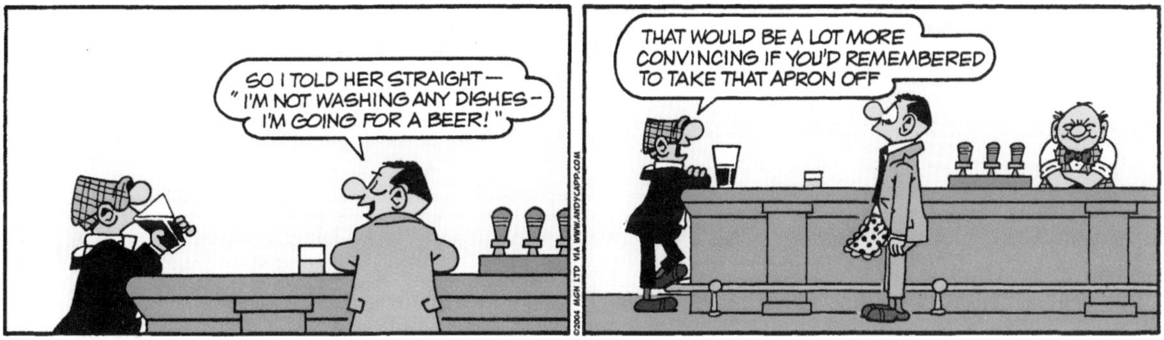
SO I TOLD HER STRAIGHT — " I'M NOT WASHING ANY DISHES - I'M GOING FOR A BEER! "
©2004 MGN LTD VIA WWW.ANDYCAPP.COM
THAT WOULD BE A LOT MORE CONVINCING IF YOU'D REMEMBERED TO TAKE THAT APRON OFF

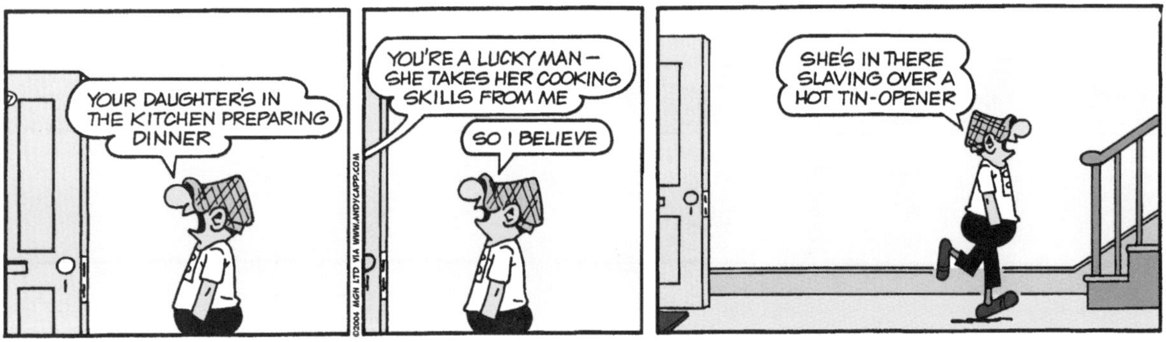
YOUR DAUGHTER'S IN THE KITCHEN PREPARING DINNER
YOU'RE A LUCKY MAN – SHE TAKES HER COOKING SKILLS FROM ME
SO I BELIEVE
SHE'S IN THERE SLAVING OVER A HOT TIN-OPENER
©2004 MGN LTD VIA WWW.ANDYCAPP.COM

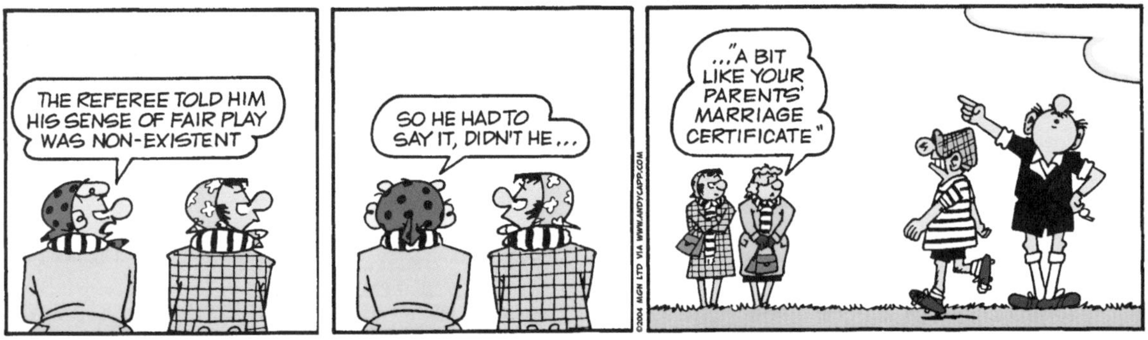
THE REFEREE TOLD HIM HIS SENSE OF FAIR PLAY WAS NON-EXISTENT
SO HE HAD TO SAY IT, DIDN'T HE...
..."A BIT LIKE YOUR PARENTS' MARRIAGE CERTIFICATE"
©2004 MGN LTD VIA WWW.ANDYCAPP.COM

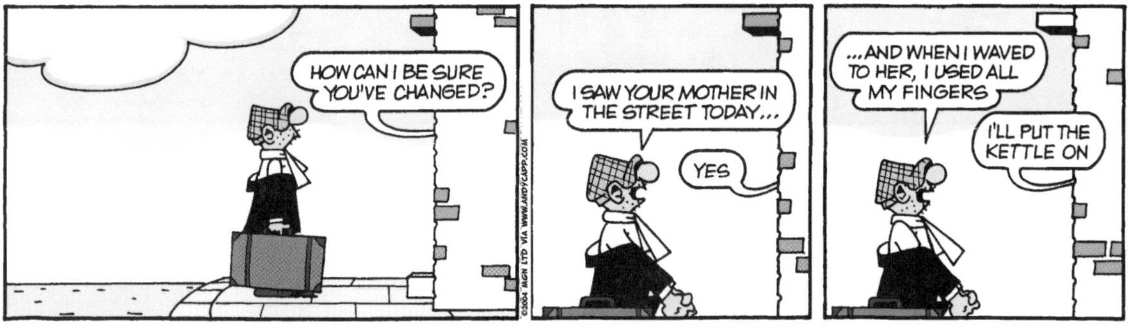
HOW CAN I BE SURE YOU'VE CHANGED?
I SAW YOUR MOTHER IN THE STREET TODAY...
YES
...AND WHEN I WAVED TO HER, I USED ALL MY FINGERS
I'LL PUT THE KETTLE ON
©2004 MGN LTD VIA WWW.ANDYCAPP.COM

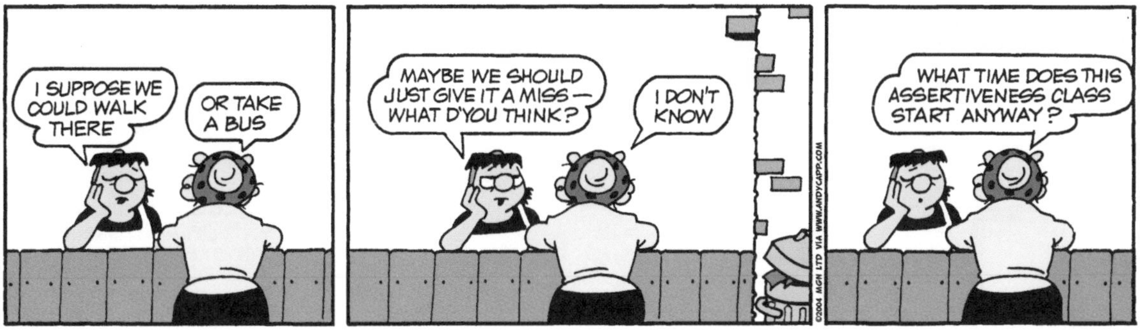
I SUPPOSE WE COULD WALK THERE
OR TAKE A BUS
MAYBE WE SHOULD JUST GIVE IT A MISS — WHAT D'YOU THINK?
I DON'T KNOW
WHAT TIME DOES THIS ASSERTIVENESS CLASS START ANYWAY?
©2004 MGN LTD VIA WWW.ANDYCAPP.COM

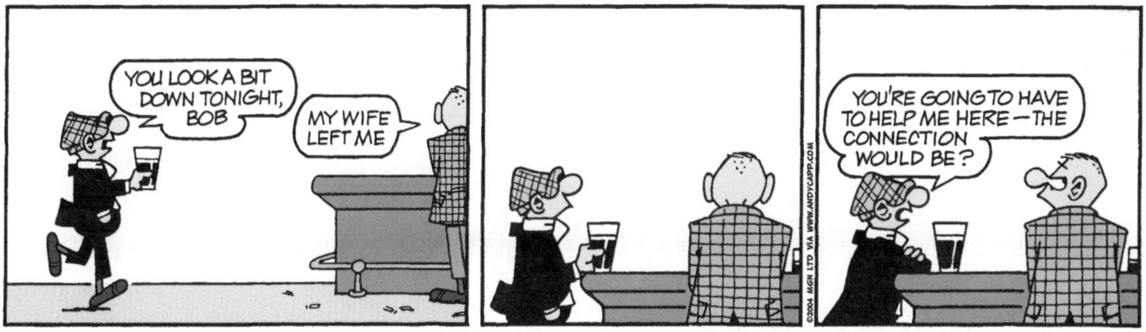
YOU LOOK A BIT DOWN TONIGHT, BOB
MY WIFE LEFT ME
YOU'RE GOING TO HAVE TO HELP ME HERE — THE CONNECTION WOULD BE?
©2004 MGN LTD VIA WWW.ANDYCAPP.COM

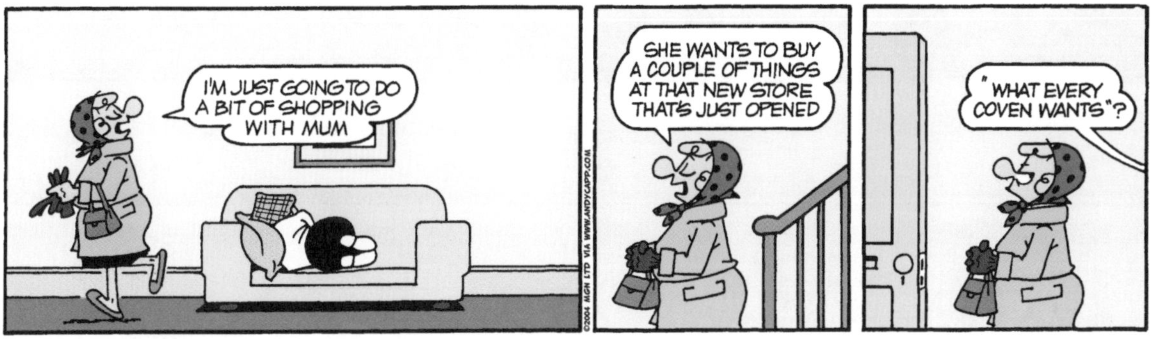
I'M JUST GOING TO DO A BIT OF SHOPPING WITH MUM
SHE WANTS TO BUY A COUPLE OF THINGS AT THAT NEW STORE THAT'S JUST OPENED
"WHAT EVERY COVEN WANTS"?
©2004 MGN LTD VIA WWW.ANDYCAPP.COM

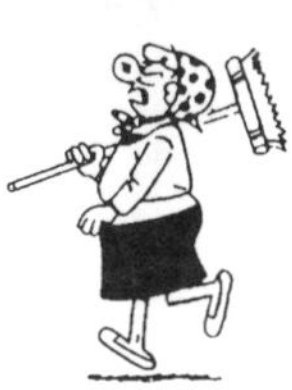

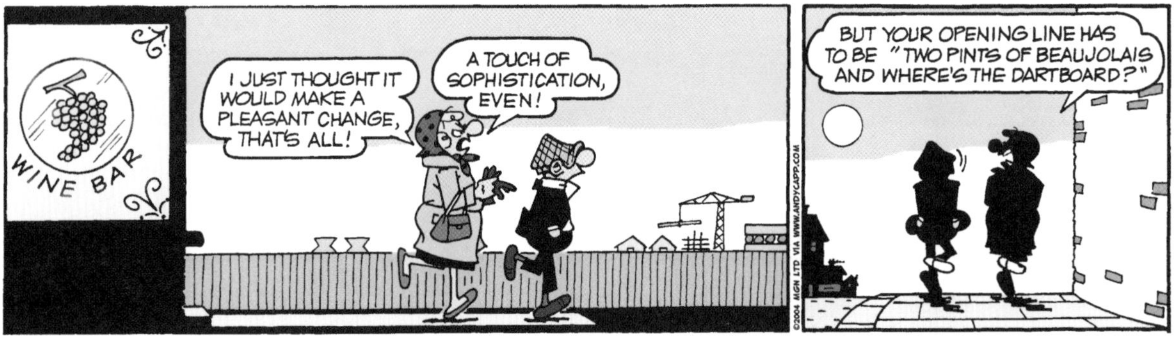
WINE BAR
I JUST THOUGHT IT WOULD MAKE A PLEASANT CHANGE, THAT'S ALL!
A TOUCH OF SOPHISTICATION, EVEN!
©2004 MGN LTD VIA WWW.ANDYCAPP.COM
BUT YOUR OPENING LINE HAS TO BE "TWO PINTS OF BEAUJOLAIS AND WHERE'S THE DARTBOARD?"

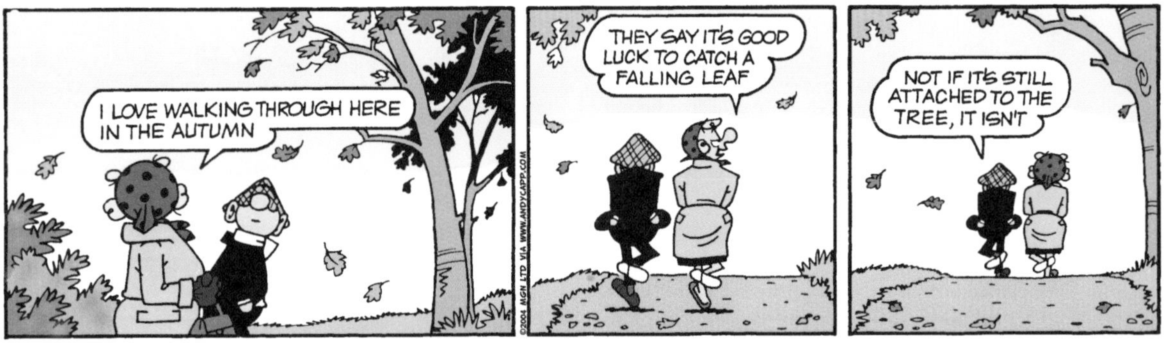
I LOVE WALKING THROUGH HERE IN THE AUTUMN
©2004 MGN LTD VIA WWW.ANDYCAPP.COM
THEY SAY IT'S GOOD LUCK TO CATCH A FALLING LEAF
NOT IF IT'S STILL ATTACHED TO THE TREE, IT ISN'T

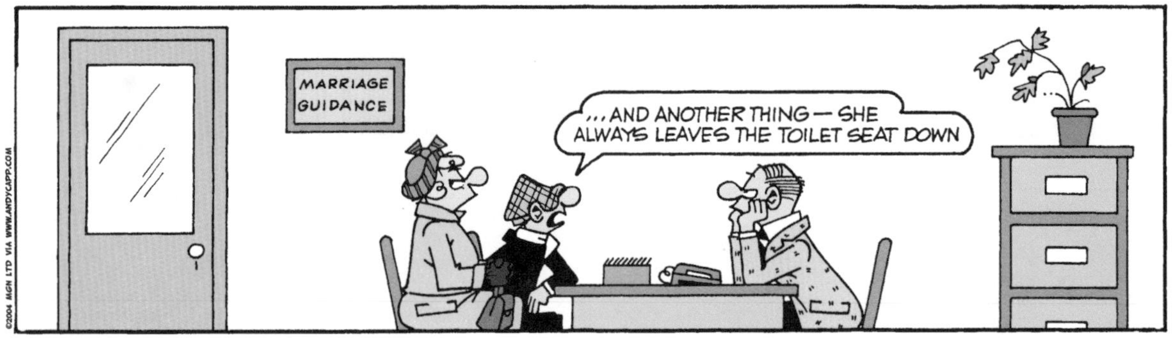
©2004 MGN LTD VIA WWW.ANDYCAPP.COM
MARRIAGE GUIDANCE
...AND ANOTHER THING — SHE ALWAYS LEAVES THE TOILET SEAT DOWN

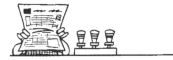

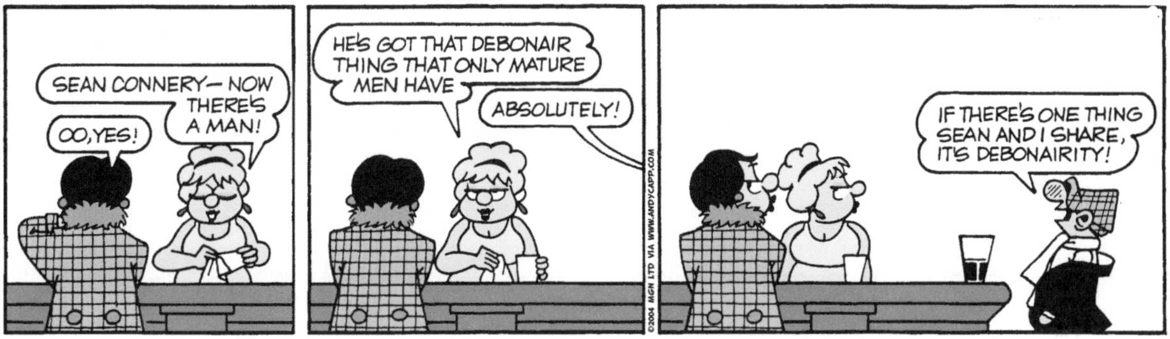
SEAN CONNERY— NOW THERE'S A MAN!
OO, YES!
HE'S GOT THAT DEBONAIR THING THAT ONLY MATURE MEN HAVE
ABSOLUTELY!
©2004 MGN LTD VIA WWW.ANDYCAPP.COM
IF THERE'S ONE THING SEAN AND I SHARE, IT'S DEBONAIRITY!

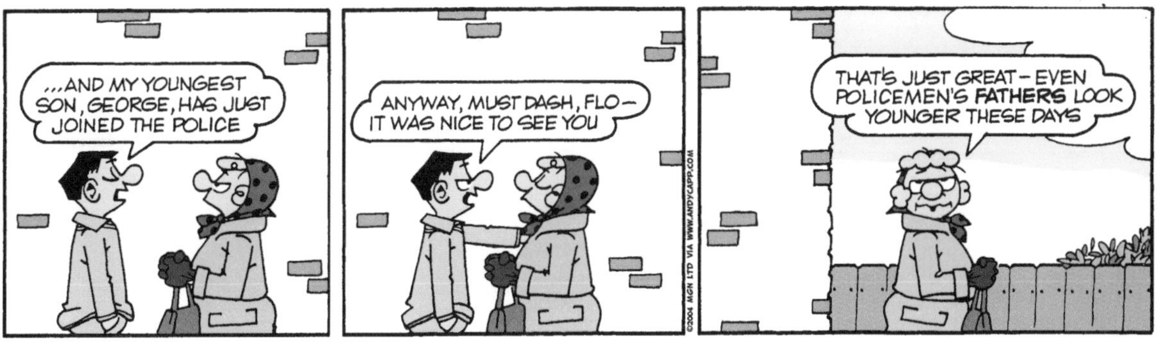
...AND MY YOUNGEST SON, GEORGE, HAS JUST JOINED THE POLICE
ANYWAY, MUST DASH, FLO— IT WAS NICE TO SEE YOU
©2004 MGN LTD VIA WWW.ANDYCAPP.COM
THAT'S JUST GREAT— EVEN POLICEMEN'S **FATHERS** LOOK YOUNGER THESE DAYS

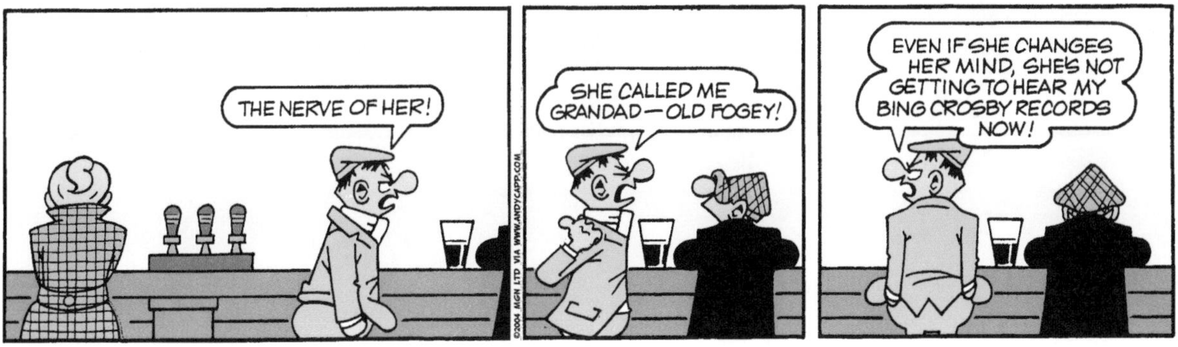
THE NERVE OF HER!
©2004 MGN LTD VIA WWW.ANDYCAPP.COM
SHE CALLED ME GRANDAD— OLD FOGEY!
EVEN IF SHE CHANGES HER MIND, SHE'S NOT GETTING TO HEAR MY BING CROSBY RECORDS NOW!

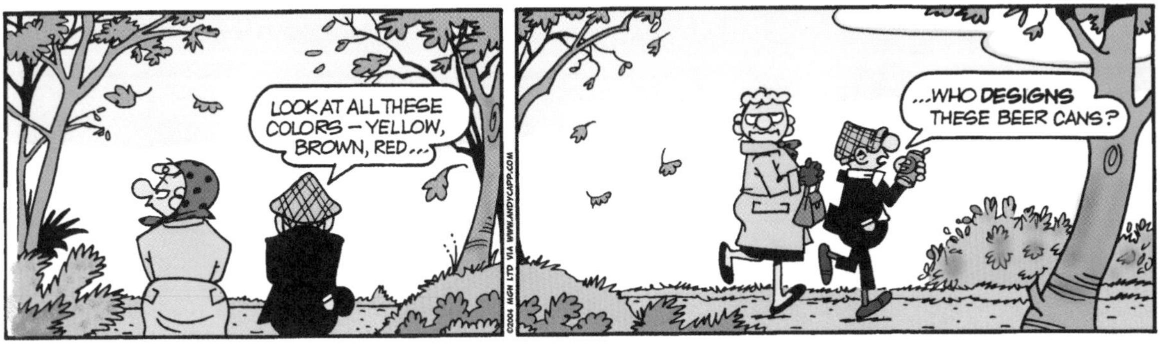
LOOK AT ALL THESE COLORS – YELLOW, BROWN, RED...
©2004 MGN LTD VIA WWW.ANDYCAPP.COM
...WHO **DESIGNS** THESE BEER CANS?

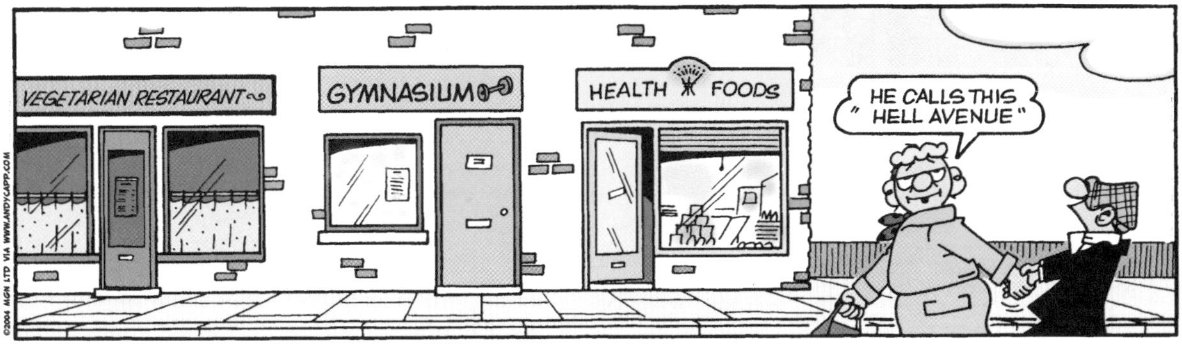
VEGETARIAN RESTAURANT
GYMNASIUM
HEALTH FOODS
©2004 MGN LTD VIA WWW.ANDYCAPP.COM
HE CALLS THIS " HELL AVENUE "

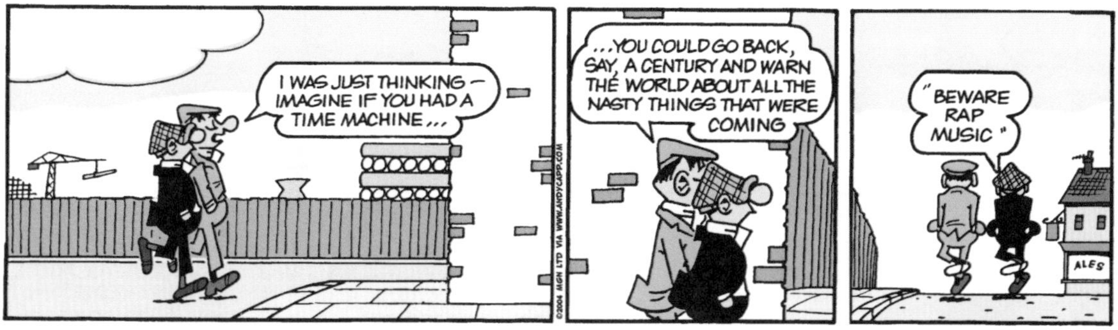
I WAS JUST THINKING – IMAGINE IF YOU HAD A TIME MACHINE...
©2004 MGN LTD VIA WWW.ANDYCAPP.COM
...YOU COULD GO BACK, SAY, A CENTURY AND WARN THE WORLD ABOUT ALL THE NASTY THINGS THAT WERE COMING
" BEWARE RAP MUSIC "
ALES

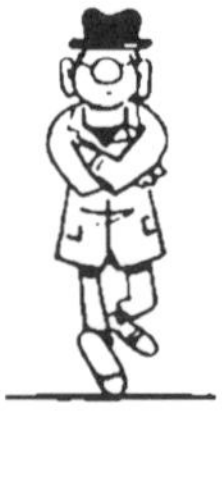

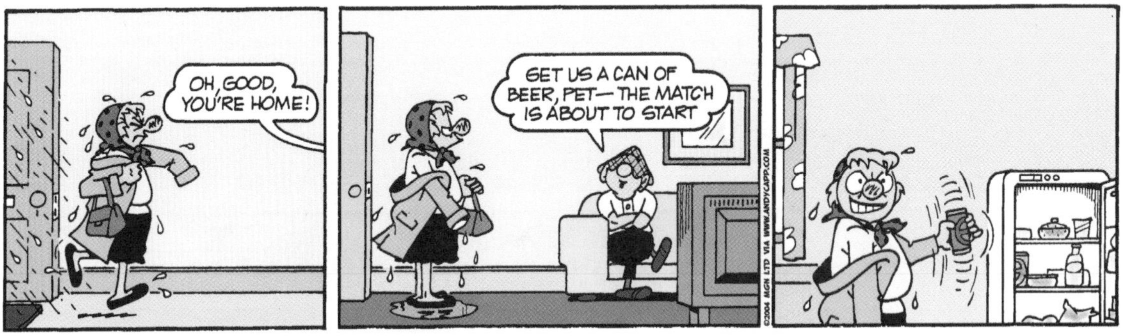
OH, GOOD, YOU'RE HOME!
GET US A CAN OF BEER, PET— THE MATCH IS ABOUT TO START
©2004 MGN LTD VIA WWW.ANDYCAPP.COM

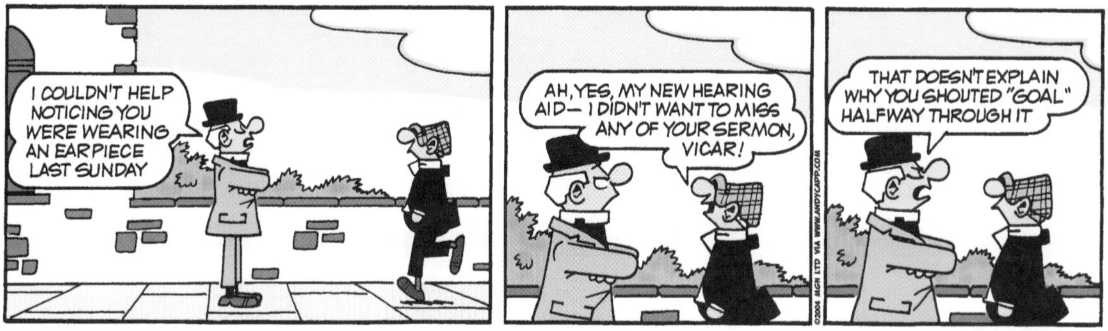
I COULDN'T HELP NOTICING YOU WERE WEARING AN EARPIECE LAST SUNDAY
AH, YES, MY NEW HEARING AID— I DIDN'T WANT TO MISS ANY OF YOUR SERMON, VICAR!
THAT DOESN'T EXPLAIN WHY YOU SHOUTED "GOAL" HALFWAY THROUGH IT
©2004 MGN LTD VIA WWW.ANDYCAPP.COM

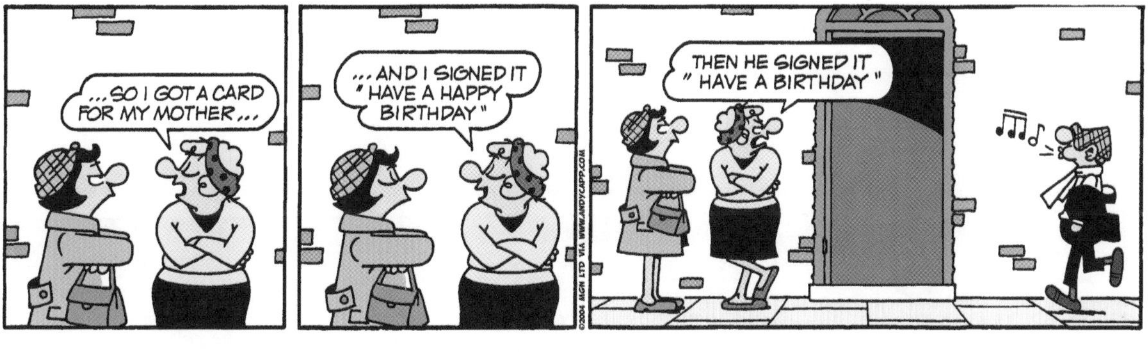
...SO I GOT A CARD FOR MY MOTHER...
...AND I SIGNED IT "HAVE A HAPPY BIRTHDAY"
THEN HE SIGNED IT "HAVE A BIRTHDAY"
©2004 MGN LTD VIA WWW.ANDYCAPP.COM

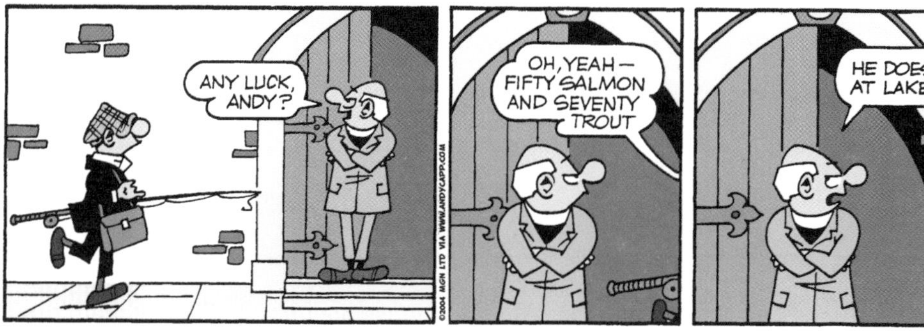
ANY LUCK, ANDY?
OH, YEAH — FIFTY SALMON AND SEVENTY TROUT
HE DOES HIS FISHING AT LAKE SARCASTIC
©2004 MGN LTD VIA WWW.ANDYCAPP.COM

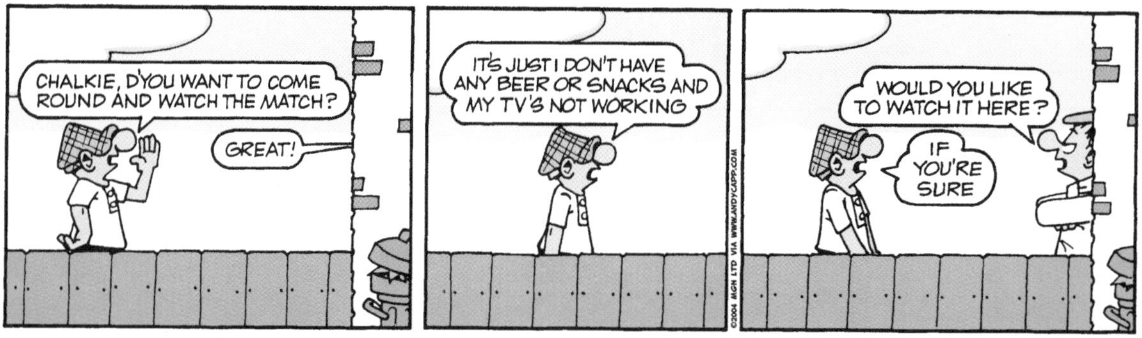
CHALKIE, D'YOU WANT TO COME ROUND AND WATCH THE MATCH?
GREAT!
IT'S JUST I DON'T HAVE ANY BEER OR SNACKS AND MY TV'S NOT WORKING
WOULD YOU LIKE TO WATCH IT HERE?
IF YOU'RE SURE
©2004 MGN LTD VIA WWW.ANDYCAPP.COM

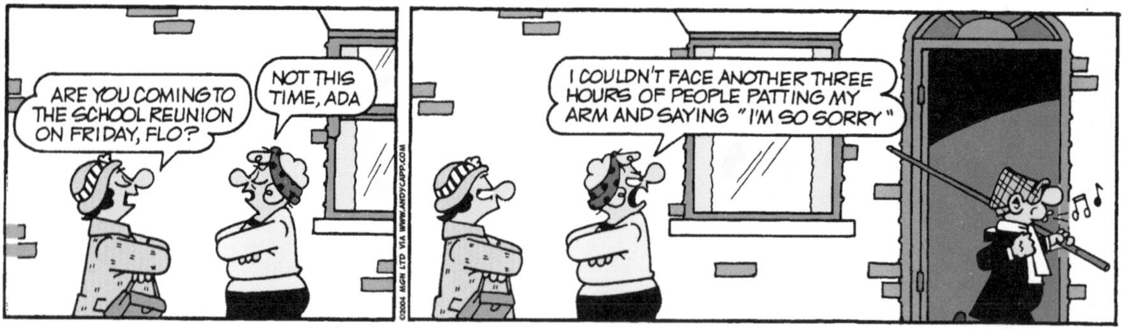
ARE YOU COMING TO THE SCHOOL REUNION ON FRIDAY, FLO?
NOT THIS TIME, ADA
I COULDN'T FACE ANOTHER THREE HOURS OF PEOPLE PATTING MY ARM AND SAYING "I'M SO SORRY"
©2004 MGN LTD VIA WWW.ANDYCAPP.COM

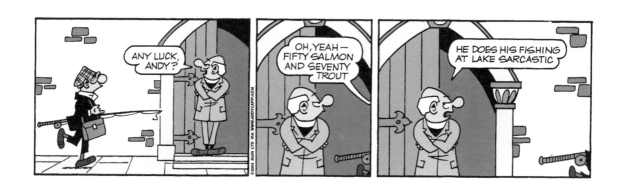

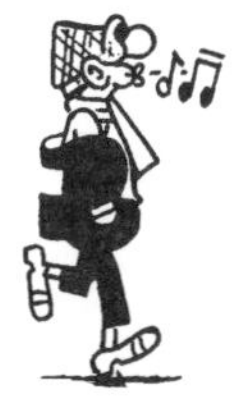

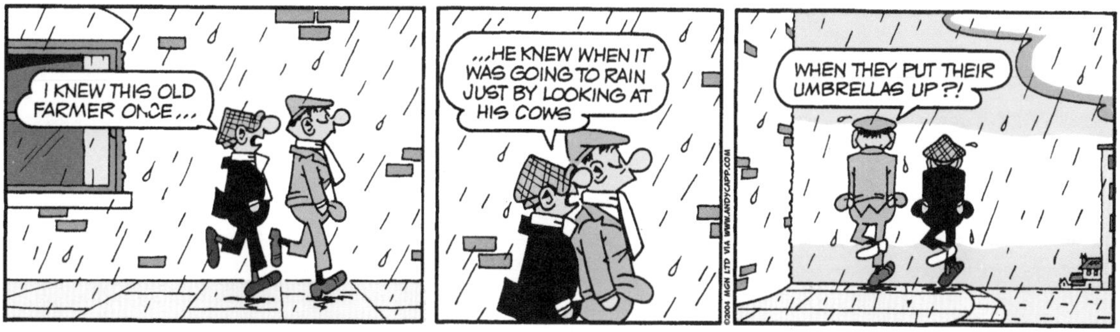

I KNEW THIS OLD FARMER ONCE...
...HE KNEW WHEN IT WAS GOING TO RAIN JUST BY LOOKING AT HIS COWS
©2004 MGN LTD VIA WWW.ANDYCAPP.COM
WHEN THEY PUT THEIR UMBRELLAS UP?!

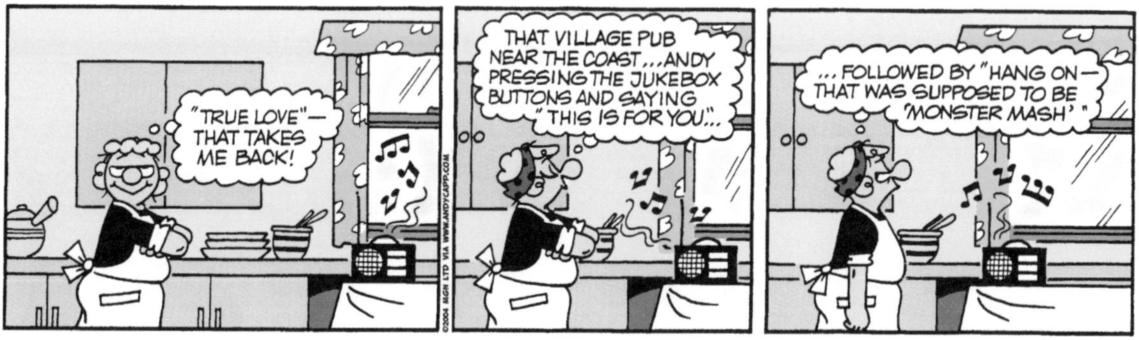

"TRUE LOVE"— THAT TAKES ME BACK!
©2004 MGN LTD VIA WWW.ANDYCAPP.COM
THAT VILLAGE PUB NEAR THE COAST...ANDY PRESSING THE JUKEBOX BUTTONS AND SAYING "THIS IS FOR YOU."...
...FOLLOWED BY "HANG ON— THAT WAS SUPPOSED TO BE 'MONSTER MASH' "

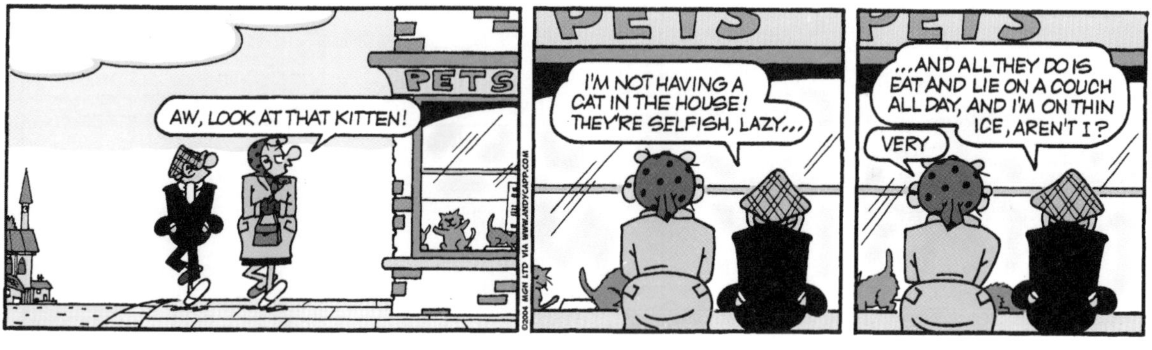

PETS
AW, LOOK AT THAT KITTEN!
©2004 MGN LTD VIA WWW.ANDYCAPP.COM
PETS
I'M NOT HAVING A CAT IN THE HOUSE! THEY'RE SELFISH, LAZY...
PETS
...AND ALL THEY DO IS EAT AND LIE ON A COUCH ALL DAY, AND I'M ON THIN ICE, AREN'T I?
VERY

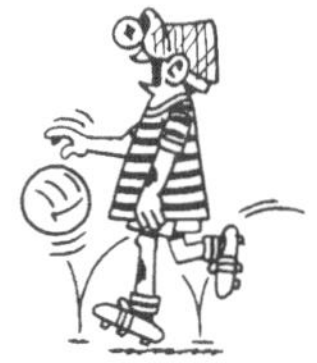

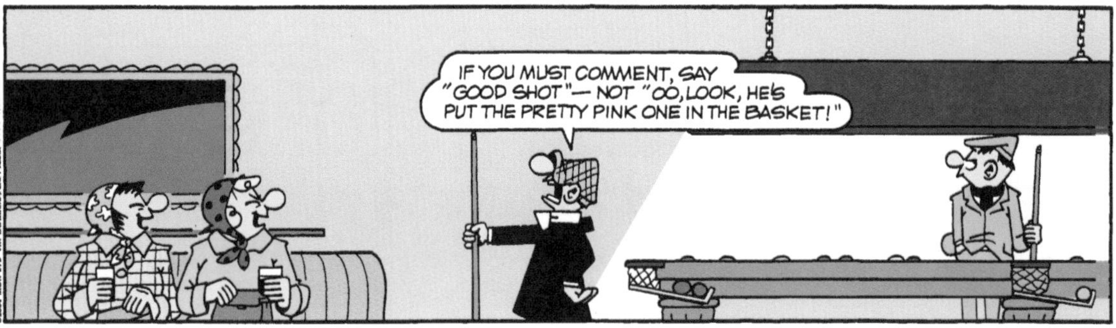
IF YOU MUST COMMENT, SAY "GOOD SHOT" — NOT "OO, LOOK, HE'S PUT THE PRETTY PINK ONE IN THE BASKET!"

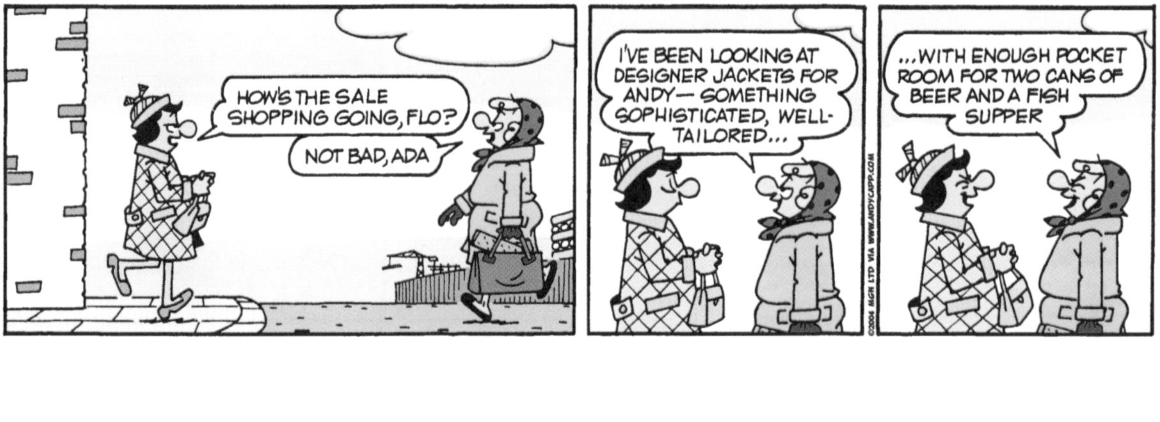
HOW'S THE SALE SHOPPING GOING, FLO?
NOT BAD, ADA
I'VE BEEN LOOKING AT DESIGNER JACKETS FOR ANDY— SOMETHING SOPHISTICATED, WELL-TAILORED...
...WITH ENOUGH POCKET ROOM FOR TWO CANS OF BEER AND A FISH SUPPER

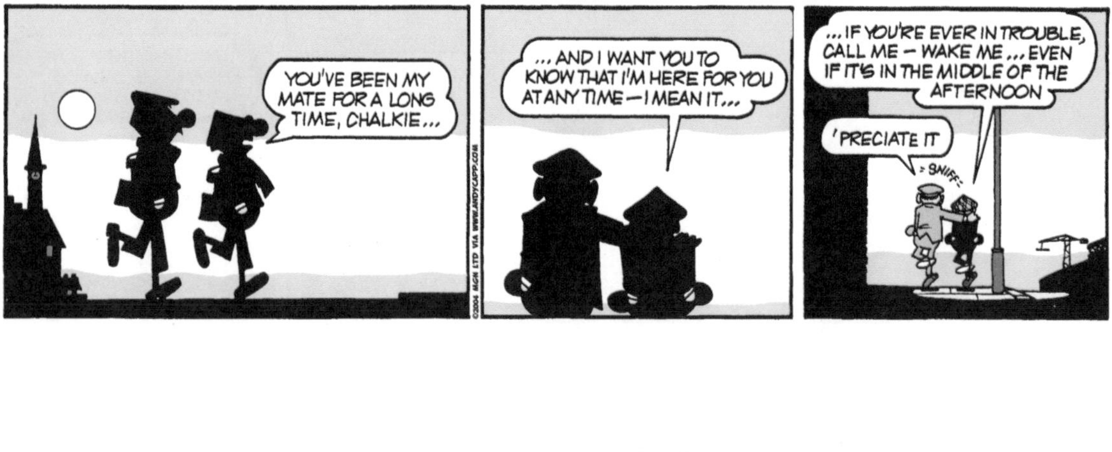
YOU'VE BEEN MY MATE FOR A LONG TIME, CHALKIE...
...AND I WANT YOU TO KNOW THAT I'M HERE FOR YOU AT ANY TIME — I MEAN IT...
...IF YOU'RE EVER IN TROUBLE, CALL ME – WAKE ME ... EVEN IF IT'S IN THE MIDDLE OF THE AFTERNOON
'PRECIATE IT
SNIFF

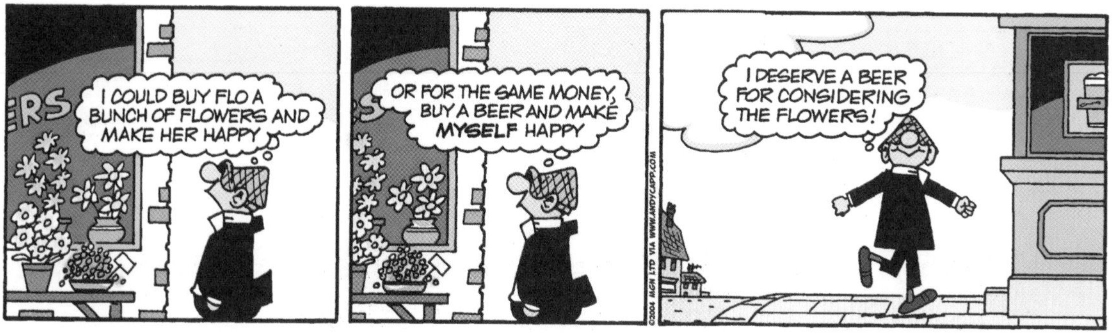
ERS
I COULD BUY FLO A BUNCH OF FLOWERS AND MAKE HER HAPPY
OR FOR THE SAME MONEY, BUY A BEER AND MAKE MYSELF HAPPY
©2004 MGN LTD VIA WWW.ANDYCAPP.COM
I DESERVE A BEER FOR CONSIDERING THE FLOWERS!

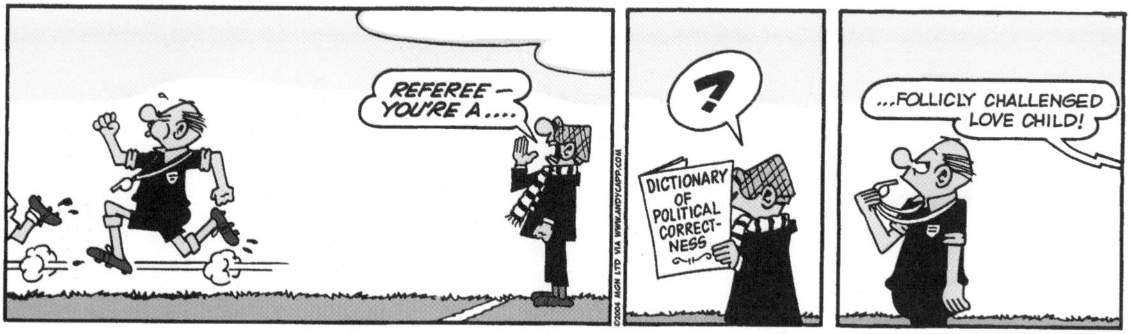
REFEREE – YOU'RE A....
©2004 MGN LTD VIA WWW.ANDYCAPP.COM
?
DICTIONARY OF POLITICAL CORRECT-NESS
...FOLLICLY CHALLENGED LOVE CHILD!

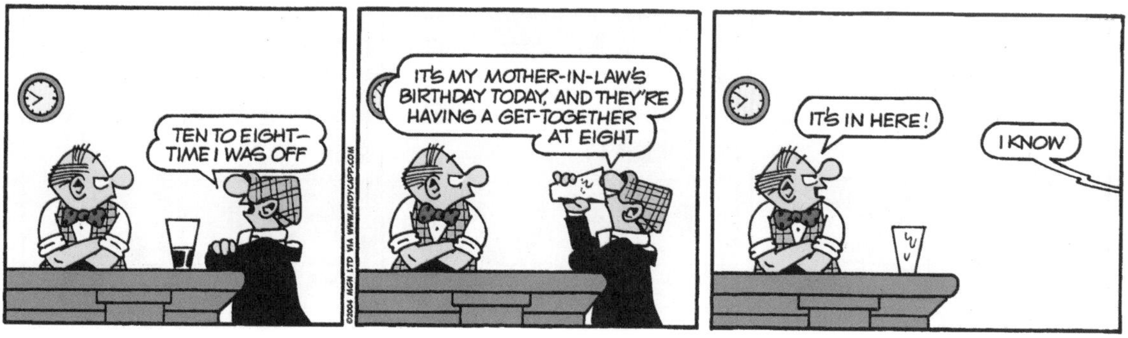
TEN TO EIGHT– TIME I WAS OFF
©2004 MGN LTD VIA WWW.ANDYCAPP.COM
IT'S MY MOTHER-IN-LAW'S BIRTHDAY TODAY, AND THEY'RE HAVING A GET-TOGETHER AT EIGHT
IT'S IN HERE!
I KNOW

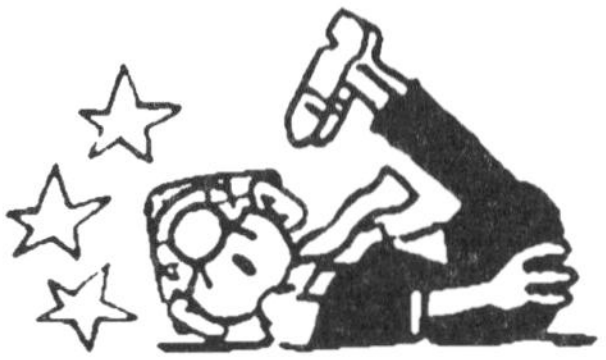

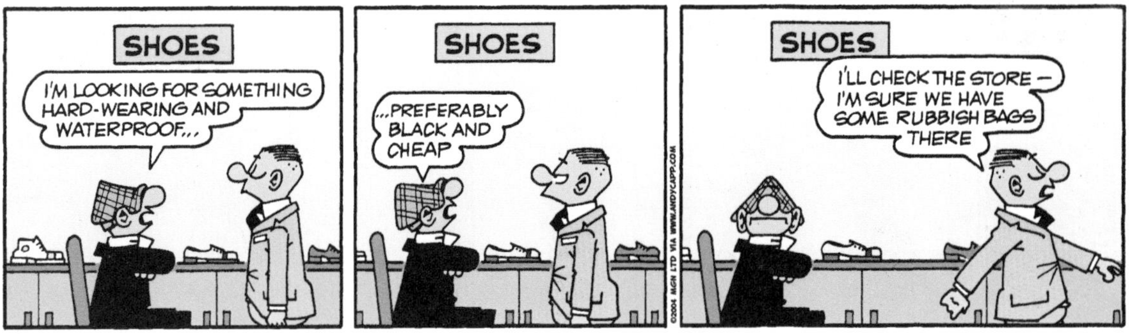
SHOES
I'M LOOKING FOR SOMETHING HARD-WEARING AND WATERPROOF,,,
SHOES
,,,PREFERABLY BLACK AND CHEAP
©2004 MGN LTD VIA WWW.ANDYCAPP.COM
SHOES
I'LL CHECK THE STORE — I'M SURE WE HAVE SOME RUBBISH BAGS THERE

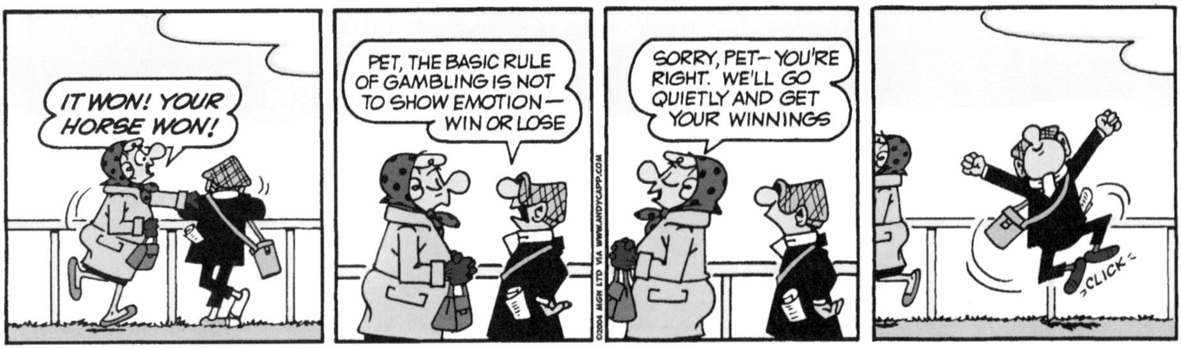
IT WON! YOUR HORSE WON!
PET, THE BASIC RULE OF GAMBLING IS NOT TO SHOW EMOTION — WIN OR LOSE
©2004 MGN LTD VIA WWW.ANDYCAPP.COM
SORRY, PET— YOU'RE RIGHT. WE'LL GO QUIETLY AND GET YOUR WINNINGS
CLICK

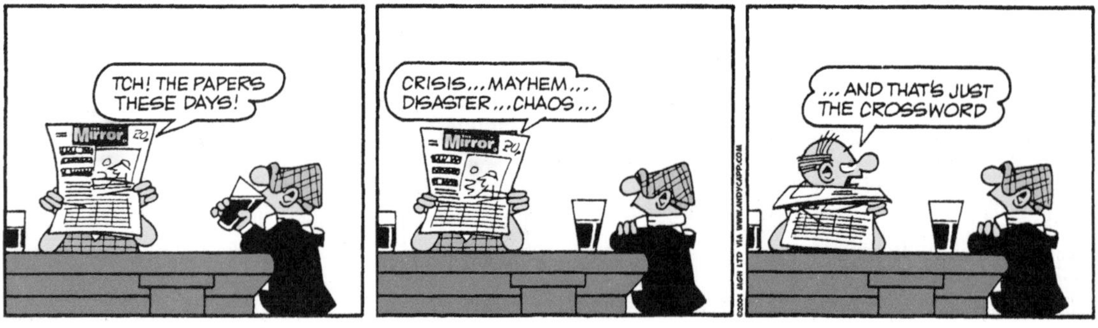
TCH! THE PAPERS THESE DAYS!
Mirror
CRISIS,,, MAYHEM,,, DISASTER,,, CHAOS,,,
Mirror
©2004 MGN LTD VIA WWW.ANDYCAPP.COM
,,, AND THAT'S JUST THE CROSSWORD

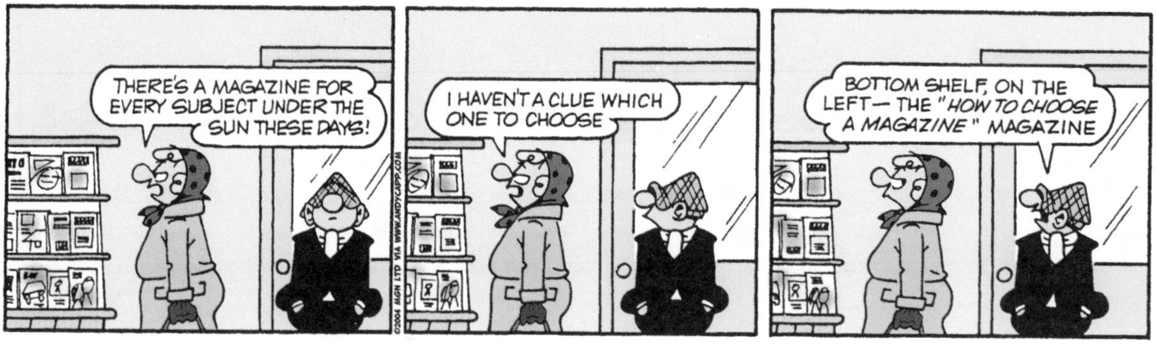
THERE'S A MAGAZINE FOR EVERY SUBJECT UNDER THE SUN THESE DAYS!
I HAVEN'T A CLUE WHICH ONE TO CHOOSE
BOTTOM SHELF, ON THE LEFT— THE "HOW TO CHOOSE A MAGAZINE" MAGAZINE
©2004 MGN LTD VIA WWW.ANDYCAPP.COM

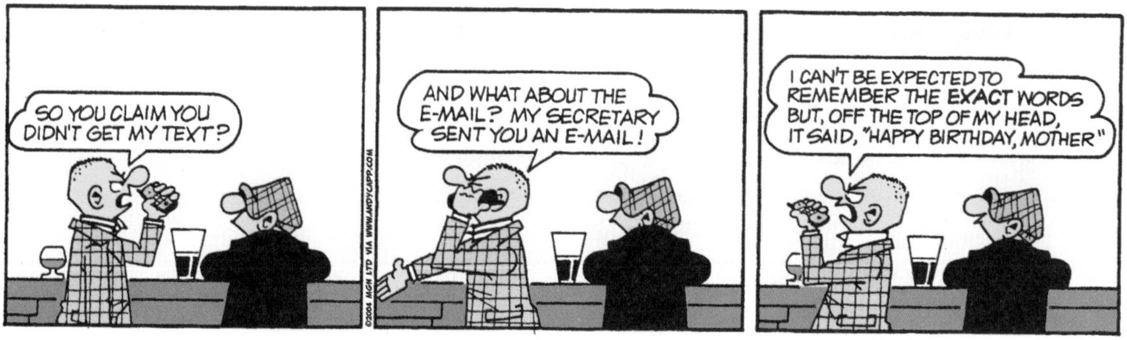
SO YOU CLAIM YOU DIDN'T GET MY TEXT?
AND WHAT ABOUT THE E-MAIL? MY SECRETARY SENT YOU AN E-MAIL!
I CAN'T BE EXPECTED TO REMEMBER THE EXACT WORDS BUT, OFF THE TOP OF MY HEAD, IT SAID, "HAPPY BIRTHDAY, MOTHER"
©2004 MGN LTD VIA WWW.ANDYCAPP.COM

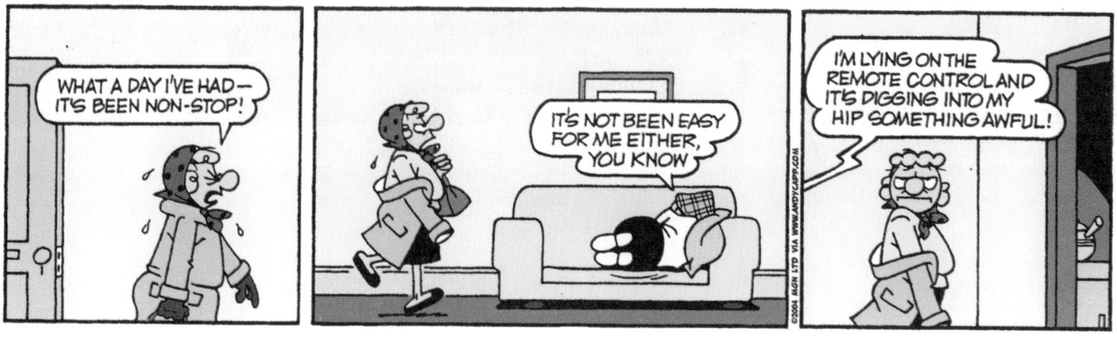
WHAT A DAY I'VE HAD— IT'S BEEN NON-STOP!
IT'S NOT BEEN EASY FOR ME EITHER, YOU KNOW
I'M LYING ON THE REMOTE CONTROL AND IT'S DIGGING INTO MY HIP SOMETHING AWFUL!
©2004 MGN LTD VIA WWW.ANDYCAPP.COM

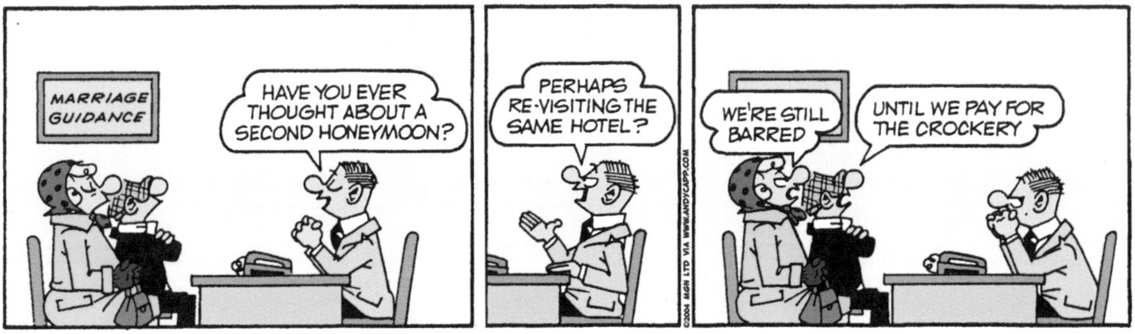
MARRIAGE GUIDANCE
HAVE YOU EVER THOUGHT ABOUT A SECOND HONEYMOON?
PERHAPS RE-VISITING THE SAME HOTEL?
©2004 MGN LTD VIA WWW.ANDYCAPP.COM
WE'RE STILL BARRED
UNTIL WE PAY FOR THE CROCKERY

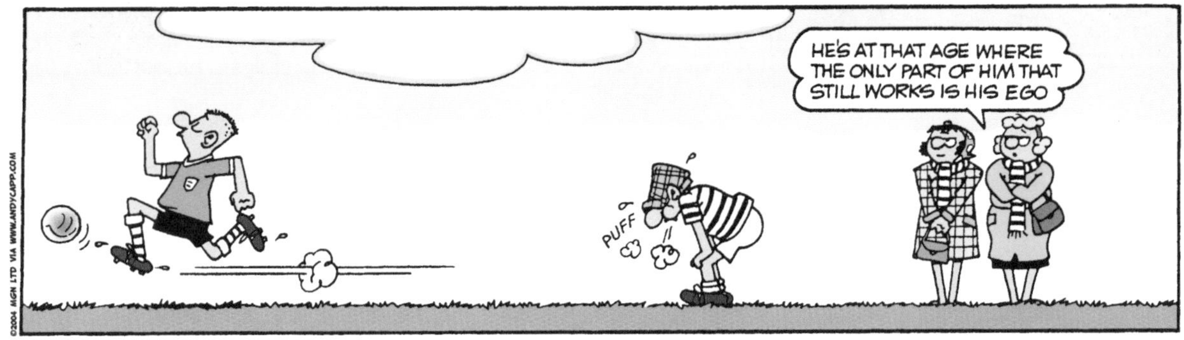
©2004 MGN LTD VIA WWW.ANDYCAPP.COM
PUFF
HE'S AT THAT AGE WHERE THE ONLY PART OF HIM THAT STILL WORKS IS HIS EGO

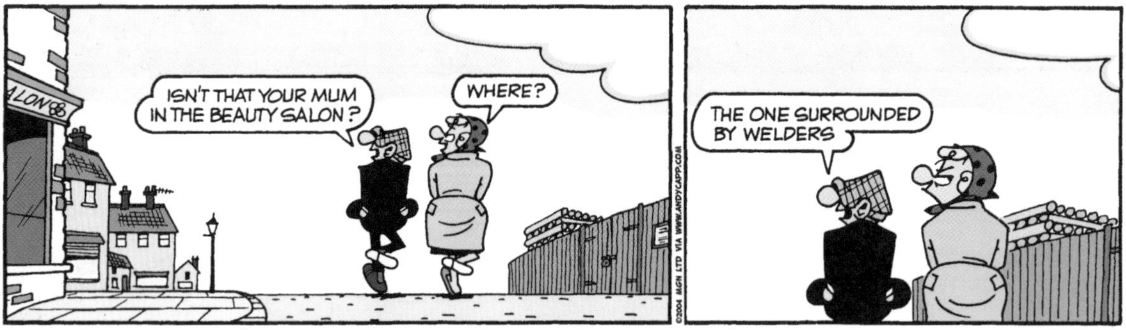
ISN'T THAT YOUR MUM IN THE BEAUTY SALON?
WHERE?
©2004 MGN LTD VIA WWW.ANDYCAPP.COM
THE ONE SURROUNDED BY WELDERS

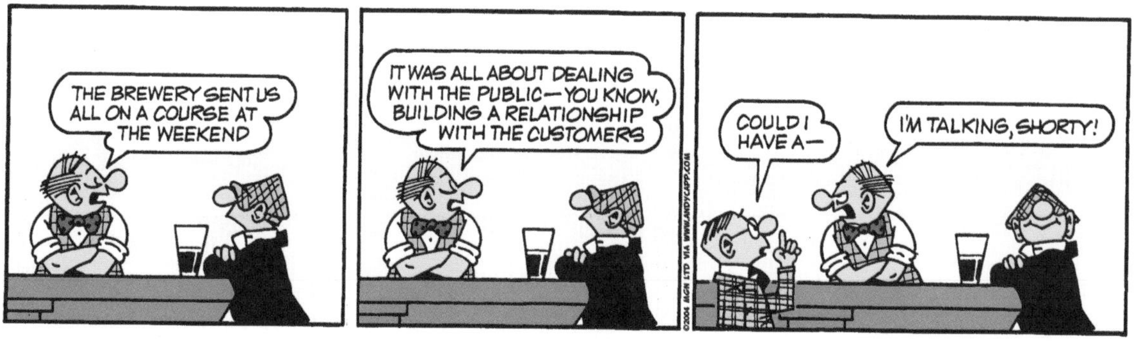
THE BREWERY SENT US ALL ON A COURSE AT THE WEEKEND
IT WAS ALL ABOUT DEALING WITH THE PUBLIC—YOU KNOW, BUILDING A RELATIONSHIP WITH THE CUSTOMERS
COULD I HAVE A—
I'M TALKING, SHORTY!

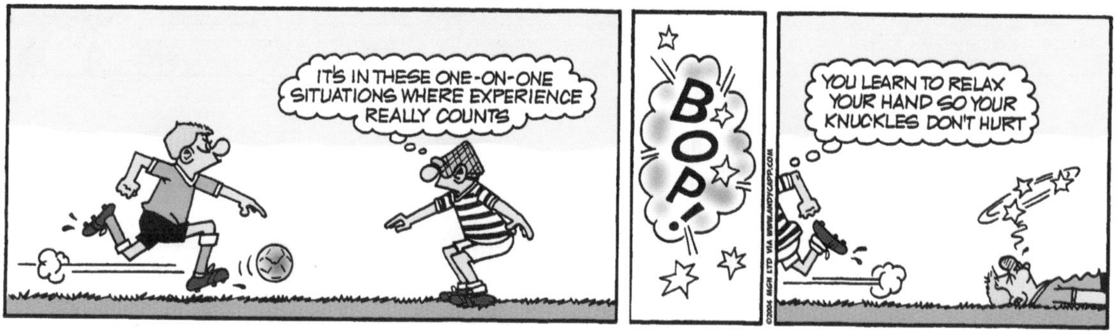
IT'S IN THESE ONE-ON-ONE SITUATIONS WHERE EXPERIENCE REALLY COUNTS
BOP!
YOU LEARN TO RELAX YOUR HAND SO YOUR KNUCKLES DON'T HURT

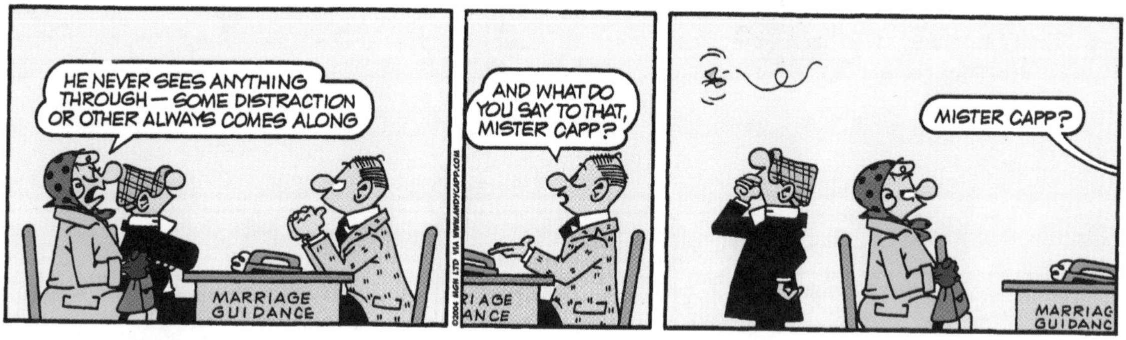
HE NEVER SEES ANYTHING THROUGH — SOME DISTRACTION OR OTHER ALWAYS COMES ALONG
MARRIAGE GUIDANCE
AND WHAT DO YOU SAY TO THAT, MISTER CAPP?
MISTER CAPP?

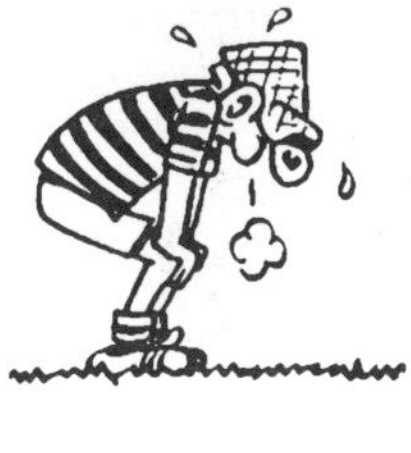

DID YOU SEE THIS BIG ADVERT IN THE PAPER, PET?
Mirror
THE ONE ABOUT DISHWASHERS
YES!
WELL, JUST BELOW THAT, THERE'S ONE FOR A POOL TABLE — WHAT DO YOU THINK?

D F.C.
THE CLASSIC GAME OF TWO HALVES — WE WERE POOR IN THE FIRST HALF...
... AND *!!@*!! AWFUL IN THE SECOND

APPARENTLY, THAT MISSED PUTT HAS JUST COST THAT GUY HALF A MILLION DOLLARS
YOU SEE? THAT'S WHY GOLF IS SUCH A GENTLEMANLY SPORT
HE SHOOK HANDS WITH HIS CADDY BEFORE THROWING HIM IN THE LAKE

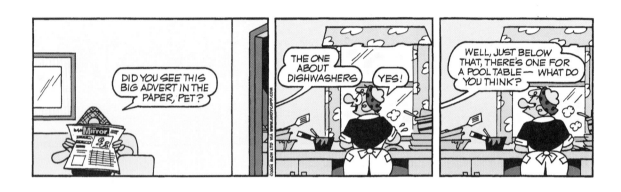

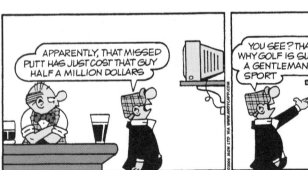

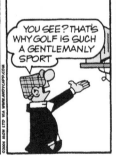

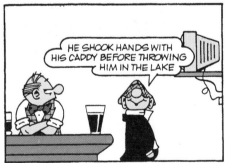

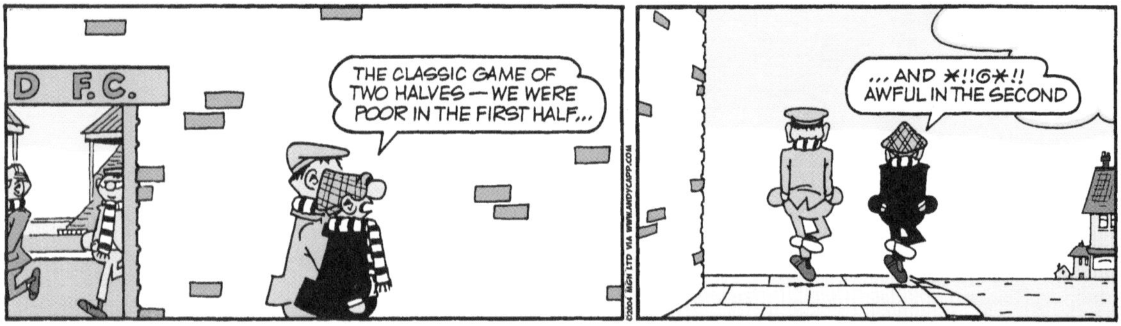

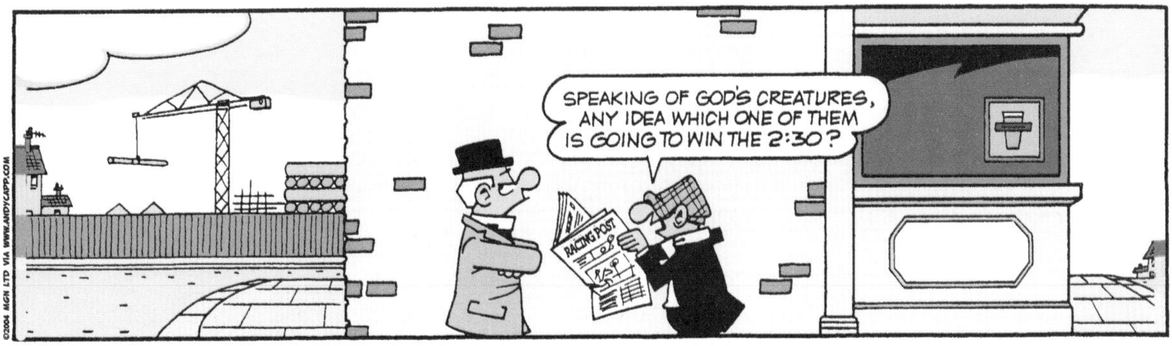
SPEAKING OF GOD'S CREATURES, ANY IDEA WHICH ONE OF THEM IS GOING TO WIN THE 2:30?
RACING POST
©2004 MGN LTD VIA WWW.ANDYCAPP.COM

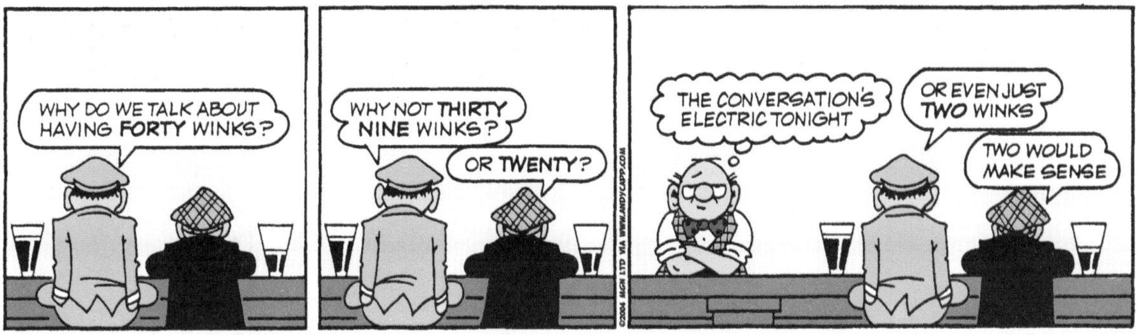
WHY DO WE TALK ABOUT HAVING FORTY WINKS?
WHY NOT THIRTY NINE WINKS?
OR TWENTY?
THE CONVERSATION'S ELECTRIC TONIGHT
OR EVEN JUST TWO WINKS
TWO WOULD MAKE SENSE
©2004 MGN LTD VIA WWW.ANDYCAPP.COM

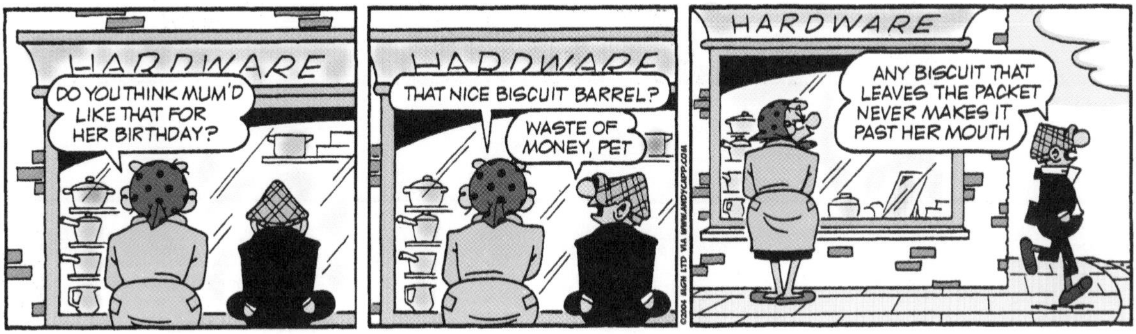
HARDWARE
DO YOU THINK MUM'D LIKE THAT FOR HER BIRTHDAY?
THAT NICE BISCUIT BARREL?
WASTE OF MONEY, PET
ANY BISCUIT THAT LEAVES THE PACKET NEVER MAKES IT PAST HER MOUTH
©2004 MGN LTD VIA WWW.ANDYCAPP.COM

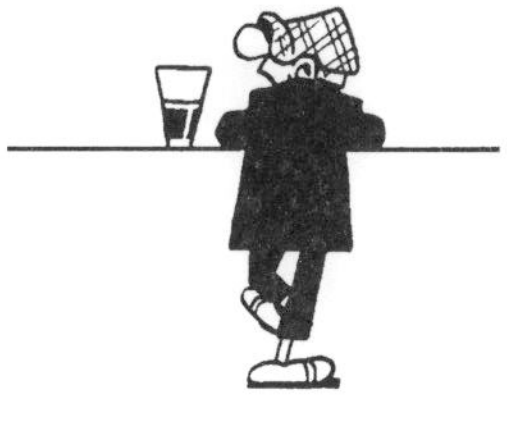

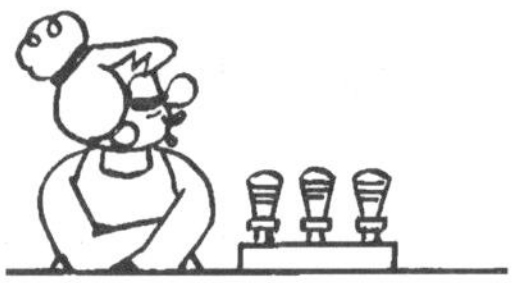

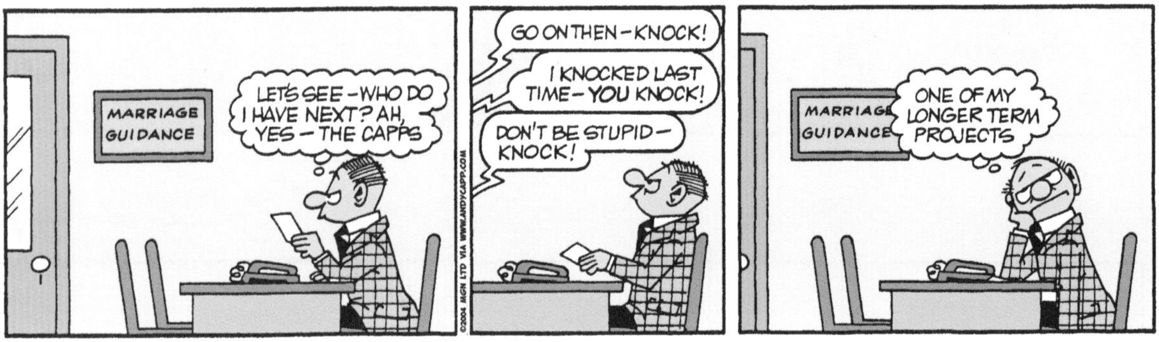
MARRIAGE GUIDANCE
LET'S SEE - WHO DO I HAVE NEXT? AH, YES - THE CAPPS
©2004 MGN LTD VIA WWW.ANDYCAPP.COM
GO ON THEN - KNOCK!
I KNOCKED LAST TIME - YOU KNOCK!
DON'T BE STUPID - KNOCK!
MARRIAGE GUIDANCE
ONE OF MY LONGER TERM PROJECTS

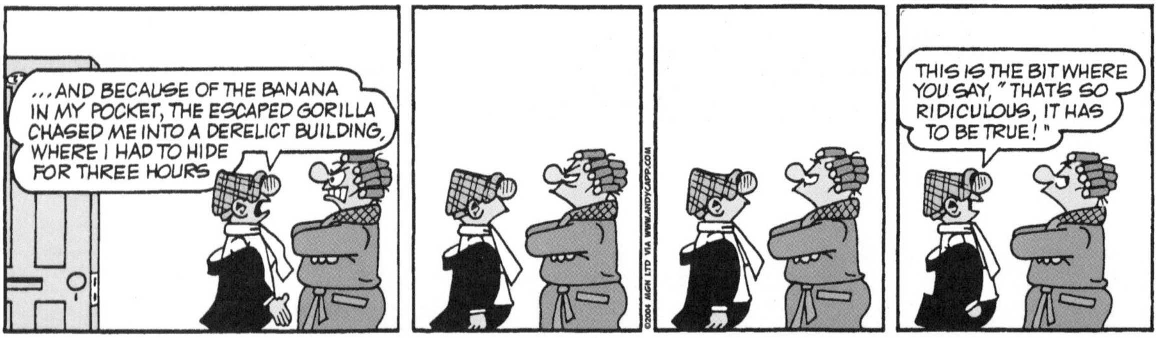
...AND BECAUSE OF THE BANANA IN MY POCKET, THE ESCAPED GORILLA CHASED ME INTO A DERELICT BUILDING, WHERE I HAD TO HIDE FOR THREE HOURS
©2004 MGN LTD VIA WWW.ANDYCAPP.COM
THIS IS THE BIT WHERE YOU SAY, "THAT'S SO RIDICULOUS, IT HAS TO BE TRUE!"

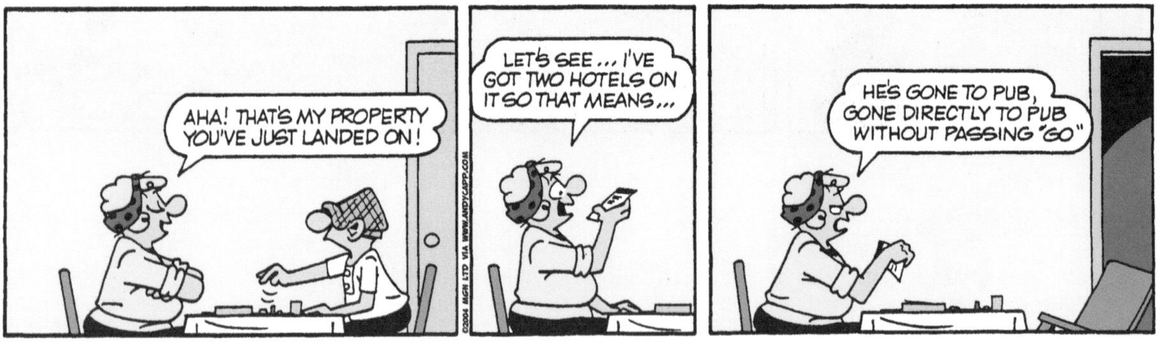
AHA! THAT'S MY PROPERTY YOU'VE JUST LANDED ON!
©2004 MGN LTD VIA WWW.ANDYCAPP.COM
LET'S SEE... I'VE GOT TWO HOTELS ON IT SO THAT MEANS,...
HE'S GONE TO PUB, GONE DIRECTLY TO PUB WITHOUT PASSING "GO"

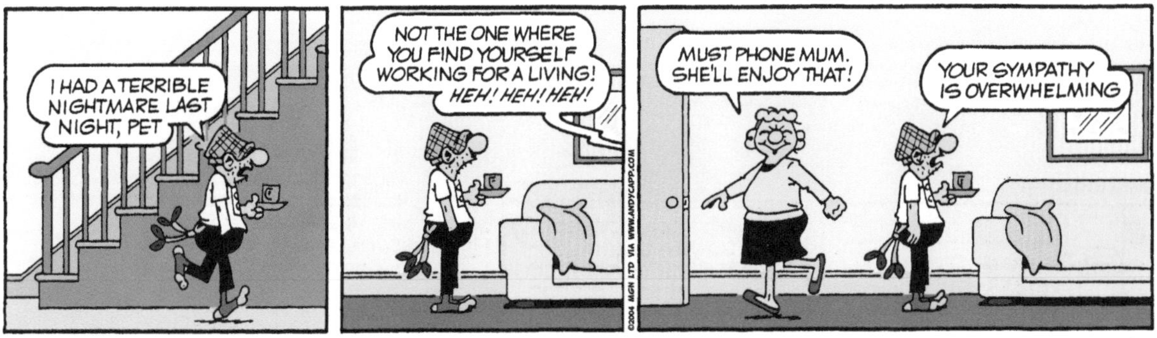
I HAD A TERRIBLE NIGHTMARE LAST NIGHT, PET
NOT THE ONE WHERE YOU FIND YOURSELF WORKING FOR A LIVING! HEH! HEH! HEH!
©2004 MGN LTD VIA WWW.ANDYCAPP.COM
MUST PHONE MUM. SHE'LL ENJOY THAT!
YOUR SYMPATHY IS OVERWHELMING

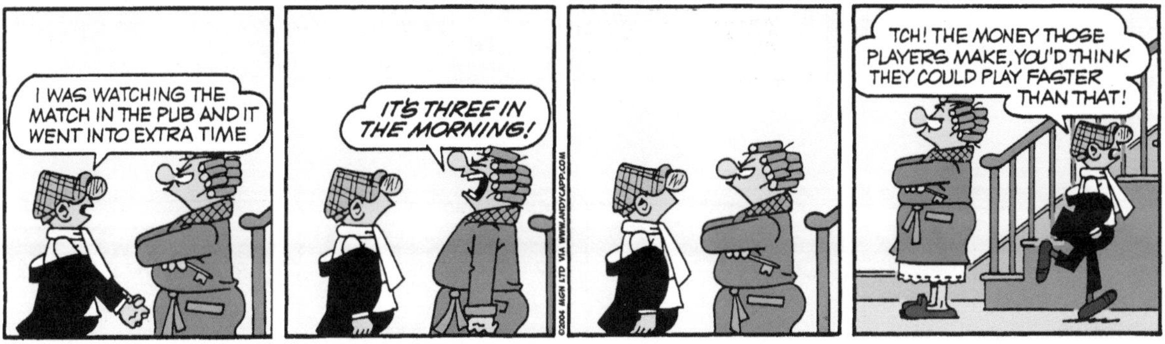
I WAS WATCHING THE MATCH IN THE PUB AND IT WENT INTO EXTRA TIME
IT'S THREE IN THE MORNING!
©2004 MGN LTD VIA WWW.ANDYCAPP.COM
TCH! THE MONEY THOSE PLAYERS MAKE, YOU'D THINK THEY COULD PLAY FASTER THAN THAT!

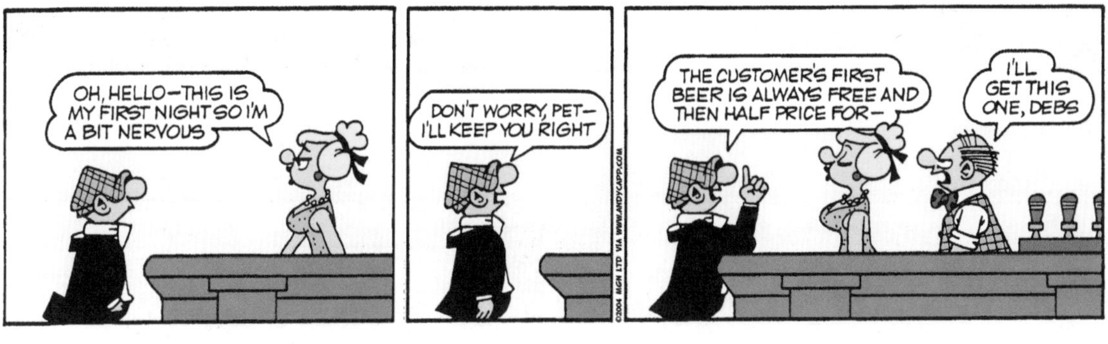
OH, HELLO—THIS IS MY FIRST NIGHT SO I'M A BIT NERVOUS
DON'T WORRY, PET—I'LL KEEP YOU RIGHT
©2004 MGN LTD VIA WWW.ANDYCAPP.COM
THE CUSTOMER'S FIRST BEER IS ALWAYS FREE AND THEN HALF PRICE FOR—
I'LL GET THIS ONE, DEBS

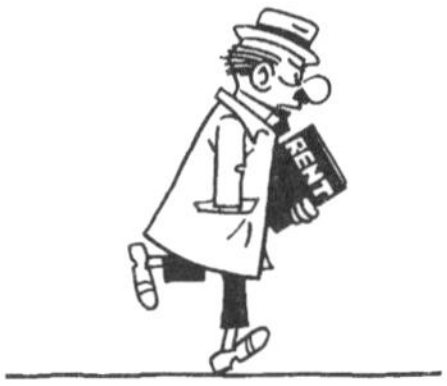
RENT

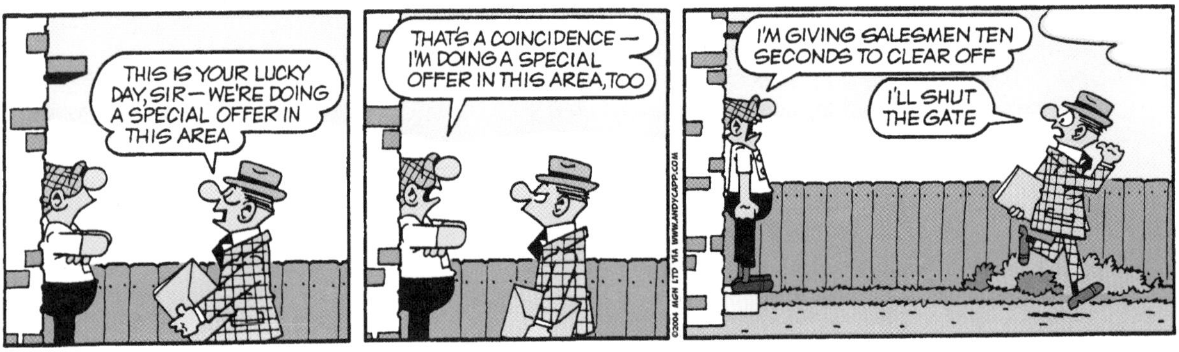
THIS IS YOUR LUCKY DAY, SIR—WE'RE DOING A SPECIAL OFFER IN THIS AREA
THAT'S A COINCIDENCE— I'M DOING A SPECIAL OFFER IN THIS AREA, TOO
©2004 MGN LTD VIA WWW.ANDYCAPP.COM
I'M GIVING SALESMEN TEN SECONDS TO CLEAR OFF
I'LL SHUT THE GATE

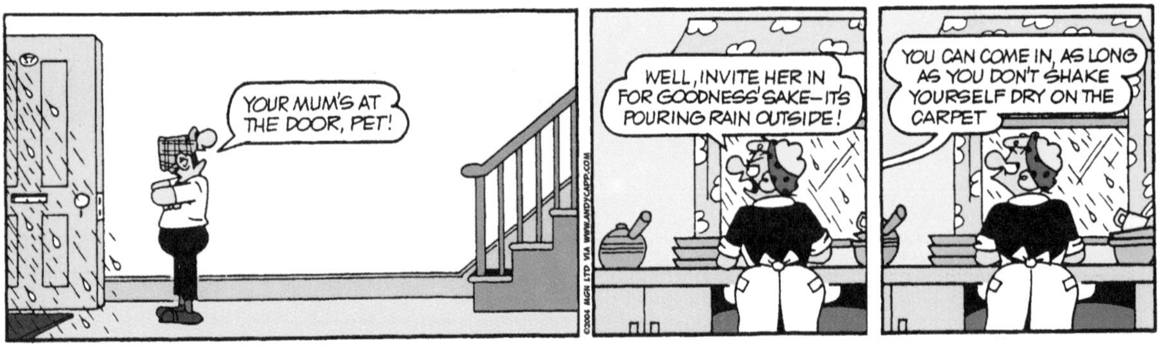
YOUR MUM'S AT THE DOOR, PET!
©2004 MGN LTD VIA WWW.ANDYCAPP.COM
WELL, INVITE HER IN FOR GOODNESS' SAKE—IT'S POURING RAIN OUTSIDE!
YOU CAN COME IN, AS LONG AS YOU DON'T SHAKE YOURSELF DRY ON THE CARPET

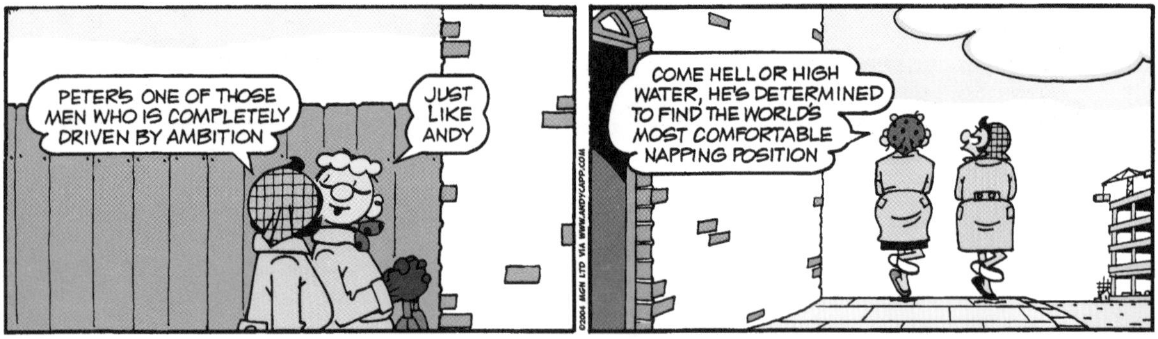
PETER'S ONE OF THOSE MEN WHO IS COMPLETELY DRIVEN BY AMBITION
JUST LIKE ANDY
©2004 MGN LTD VIA WWW.ANDYCAPP.COM
COME HELL OR HIGH WATER, HE'S DETERMINED TO FIND THE WORLD'S MOST COMFORTABLE NAPPING POSITION

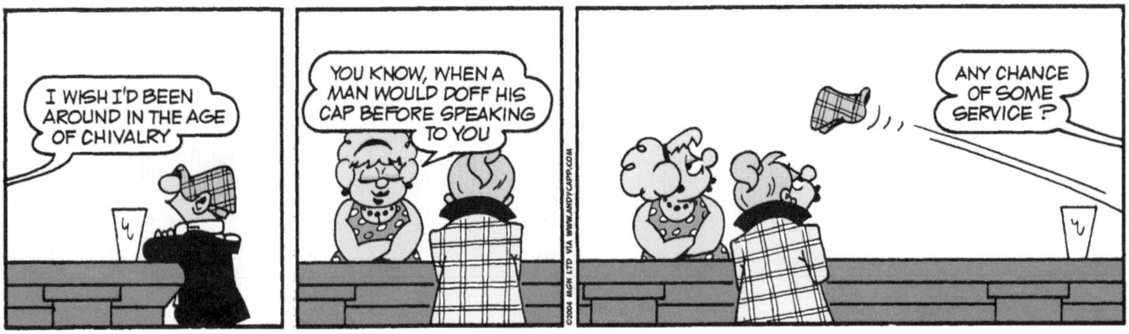

I WISH I'D BEEN AROUND IN THE AGE OF CHIVALRY
YOU KNOW, WHEN A MAN WOULD DOFF HIS CAP BEFORE SPEAKING TO YOU
ANY CHANCE OF SOME SERVICE ?
©2004 MGN LTD VIA WWW.ANDYCAPP.COM

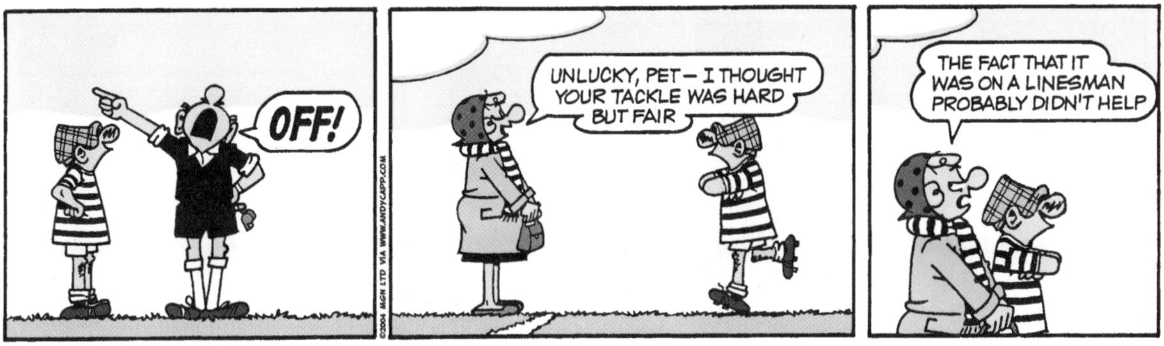

OFF!
©2004 MGN LTD VIA WWW.ANDYCAPP.COM
UNLUCKY, PET – I THOUGHT YOUR TACKLE WAS HARD BUT FAIR
THE FACT THAT IT WAS ON A LINESMAN PROBABLY DIDN'T HELP

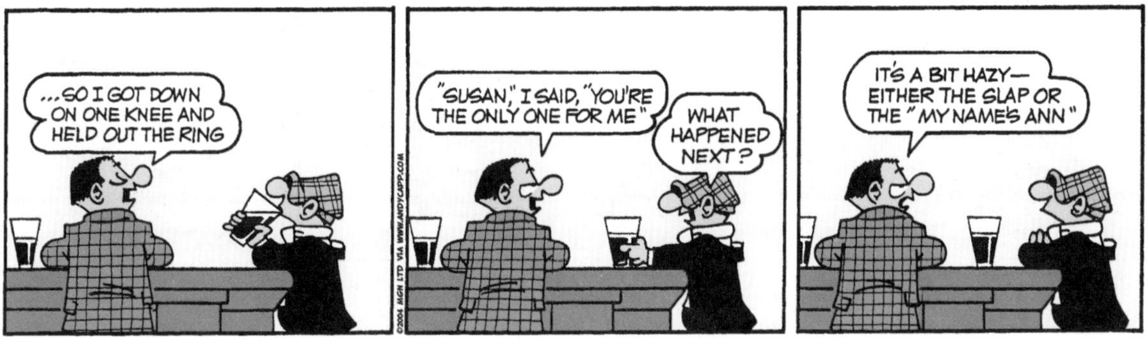

...SO I GOT DOWN ON ONE KNEE AND HELD OUT THE RING
©2004 MGN LTD VIA WWW.ANDYCAPP.COM
"SUSAN," I SAID, "YOU'RE THE ONLY ONE FOR ME"
WHAT HAPPENED NEXT ?
IT'S A BIT HAZY— EITHER THE SLAP OR THE "MY NAME'S ANN"

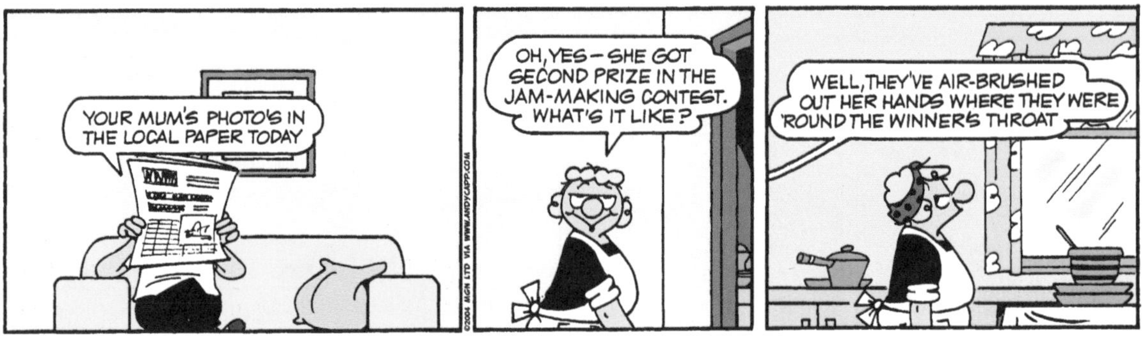
YOUR MUM'S PHOTO'S IN THE LOCAL PAPER TODAY
OH, YES – SHE GOT SECOND PRIZE IN THE JAM-MAKING CONTEST. WHAT'S IT LIKE?
WELL, THEY'VE AIR-BRUSHED OUT HER HANDS WHERE THEY WERE 'ROUND THE WINNER'S THROAT
©2004 MGN LTD VIA WWW.ANDYCAPP.COM

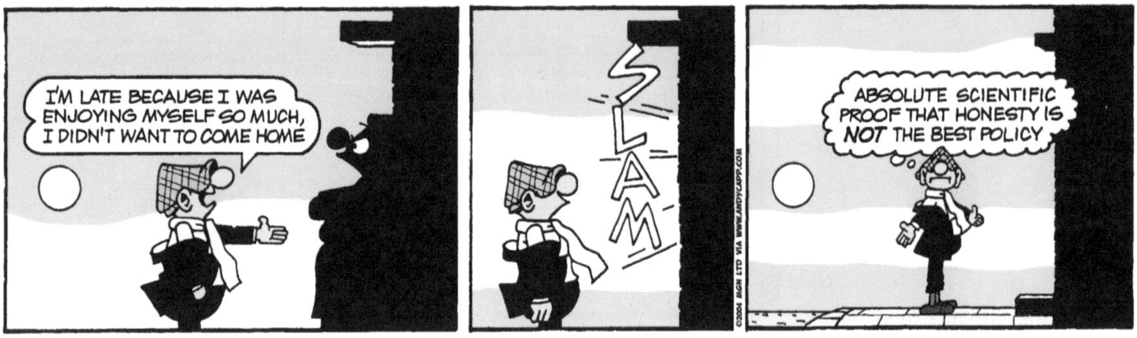
I'M LATE BECAUSE I WAS ENJOYING MYSELF SO MUCH, I DIDN'T WANT TO COME HOME
SLAM
ABSOLUTE SCIENTIFIC PROOF THAT HONESTY IS *NOT* THE BEST POLICY
©2004 MGN LTD VIA WWW.ANDYCAPP.COM

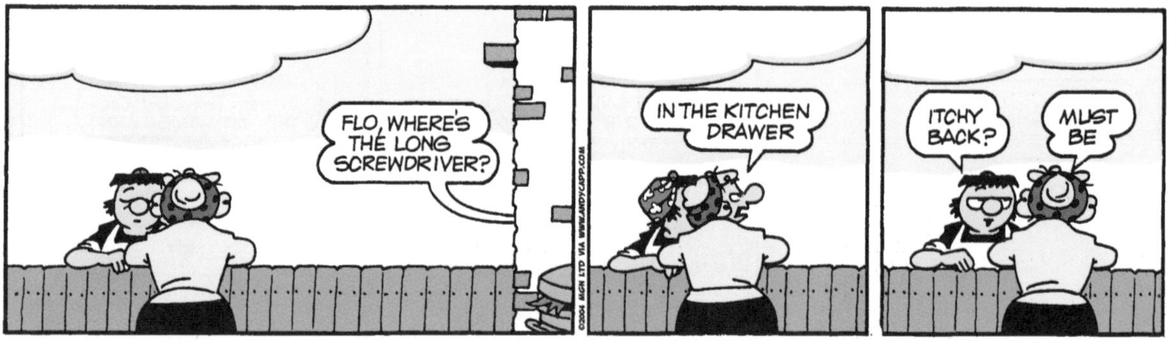
FLO, WHERE'S THE LONG SCREWDRIVER?
IN THE KITCHEN DRAWER
ITCHY BACK?
MUST BE
©2004 MGN LTD VIA WWW.ANDYCAPP.COM

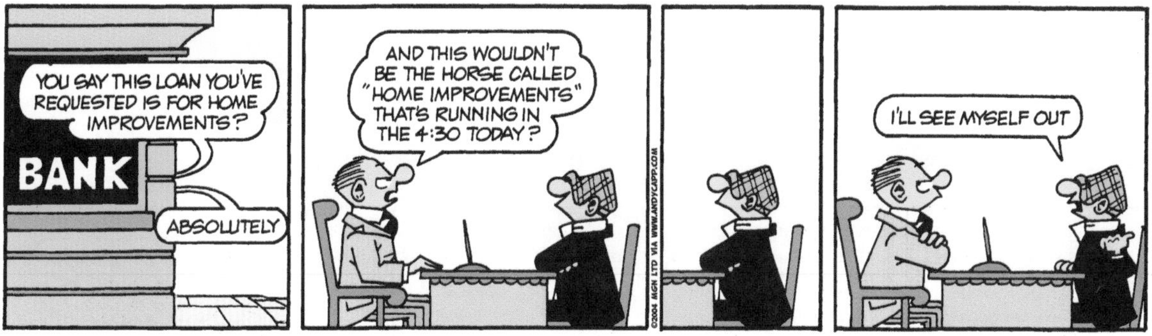
YOU SAY THIS LOAN YOU'VE REQUESTED IS FOR HOME IMPROVEMENTS?
BANK
ABSOLUTELY
AND THIS WOULDN'T BE THE HORSE CALLED "HOME IMPROVEMENTS" THAT'S RUNNING IN THE 4:30 TODAY?
©2004 MGN LTD VIA WWW.ANDYCAPP.COM
I'LL SEE MYSELF OUT

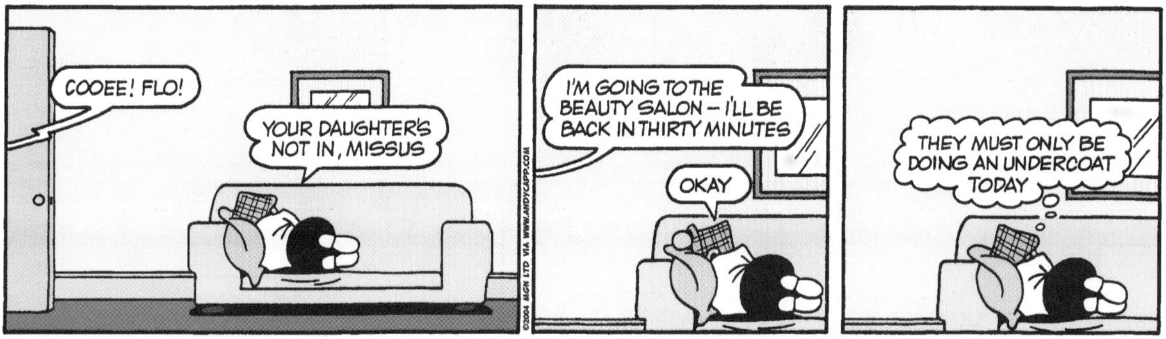
COOEE! FLO!
YOUR DAUGHTER'S NOT IN, MISSUS
©2004 MGN LTD VIA WWW.ANDYCAPP.COM
I'M GOING TO THE BEAUTY SALON – I'LL BE BACK IN THIRTY MINUTES
OKAY
THEY MUST ONLY BE DOING AN UNDERCOAT TODAY

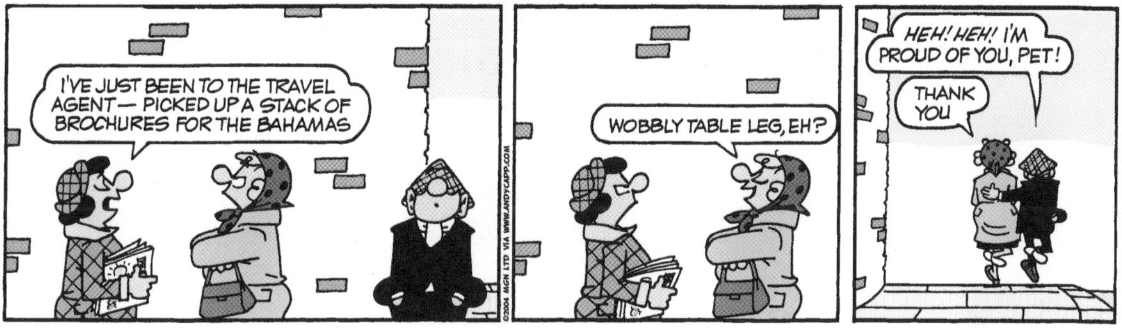
I'VE JUST BEEN TO THE TRAVEL AGENT— PICKED UP A STACK OF BROCHURES FOR THE BAHAMAS
©2004 MGN LTD VIA WWW.ANDYCAPP.COM
WOBBLY TABLE LEG, EH?
HEH! HEH! I'M PROUD OF YOU, PET!
THANK YOU

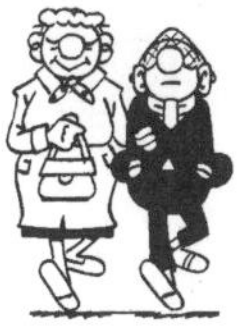

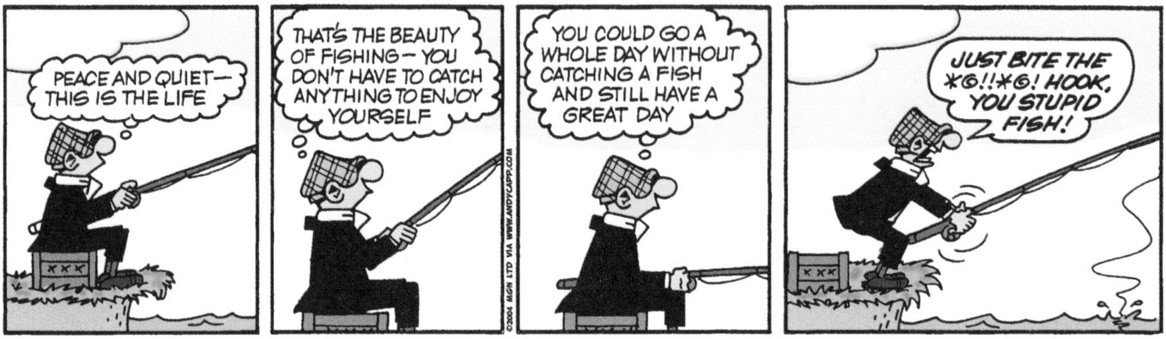
PEACE AND QUIET— THIS IS THE LIFE
THAT'S THE BEAUTY OF FISHING— YOU DON'T HAVE TO CATCH ANYTHING TO ENJOY YOURSELF
©2004 MGN LTD VIA WWW.ANDYCAPP.COM
YOU COULD GO A WHOLE DAY WITHOUT CATCHING A FISH AND STILL HAVE A GREAT DAY
JUST BITE THE *@!!*@! HOOK, YOU STUPID FISH!

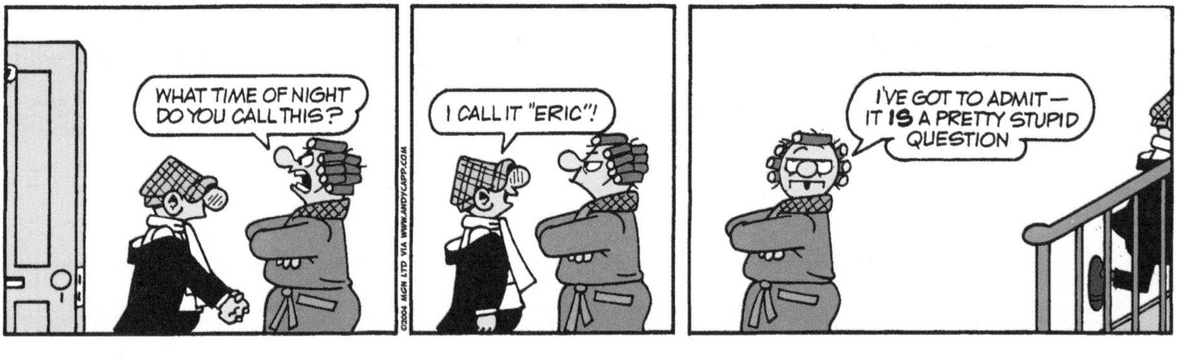
WHAT TIME OF NIGHT DO YOU CALL THIS?
©2004 MGN LTD VIA WWW.ANDYCAPP.COM
I CALL IT "ERIC"!
I'VE GOT TO ADMIT— IT **IS** A PRETTY STUPID QUESTION

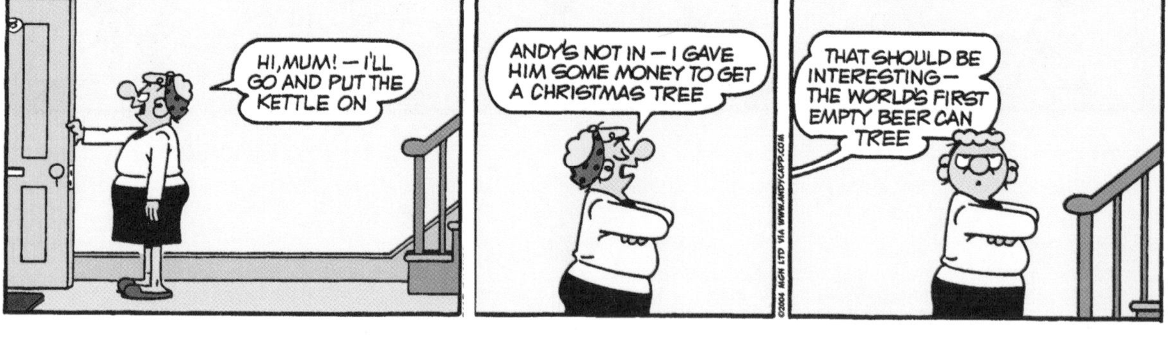
HI, MUM! — I'LL GO AND PUT THE KETTLE ON
ANDY'S NOT IN — I GAVE HIM SOME MONEY TO GET A CHRISTMAS TREE
©2004 MGN LTD VIA WWW.ANDYCAPP.COM
THAT SHOULD BE INTERESTING— THE WORLD'S FIRST EMPTY BEER CAN TREE

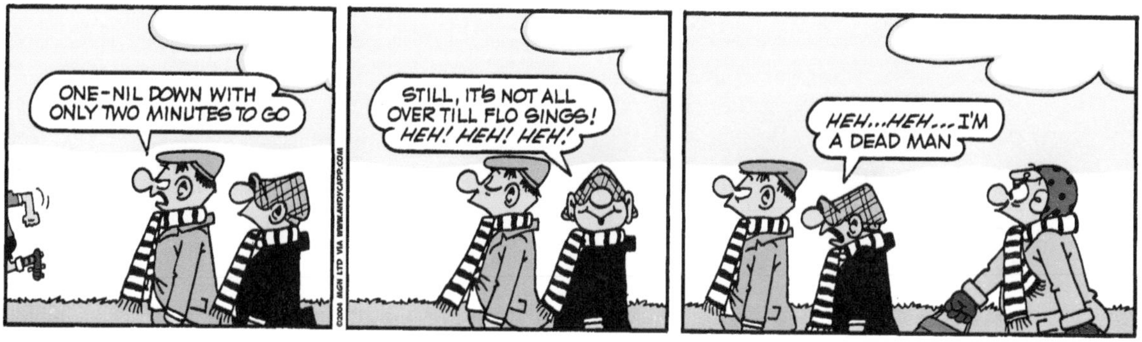
ONE-NIL DOWN WITH ONLY TWO MINUTES TO GO
©2004 MGN LTD VIA WWW.ANDYCAPP.COM
STILL, IT'S NOT ALL OVER TILL FLO SINGS! *HEH! HEH! HEH!*
HEH...HEH... I'M A DEAD MAN

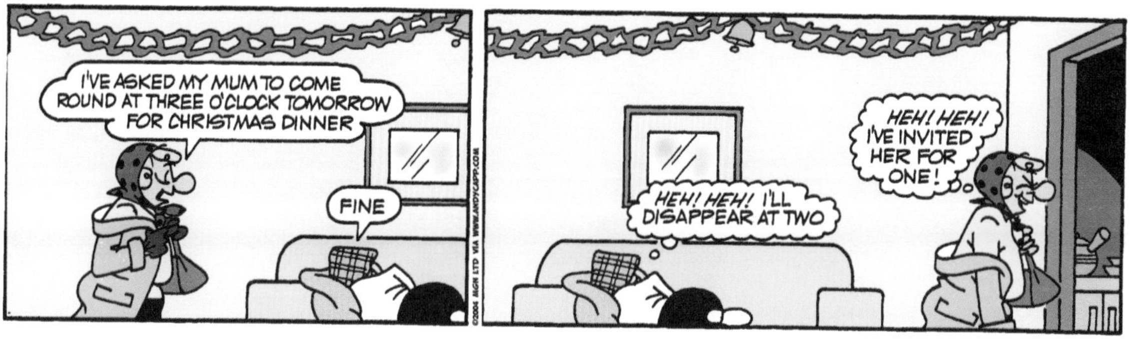
I'VE ASKED MY MUM TO COME ROUND AT THREE O'CLOCK TOMORROW FOR CHRISTMAS DINNER
FINE
©2004 MGN LTD VIA WWW.ANDYCAPP.COM
HEH! HEH! I'LL DISAPPEAR AT TWO
HEH! HEH! I'VE INVITED HER FOR ONE!

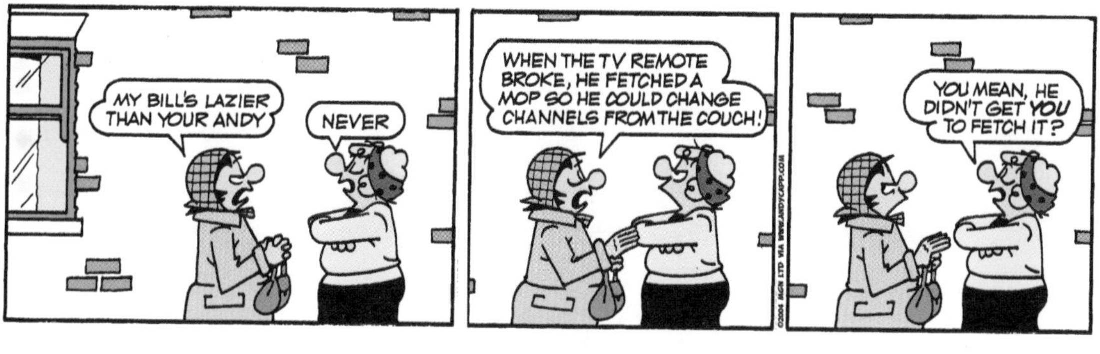
MY BILL'S LAZIER THAN YOUR ANDY
NEVER
WHEN THE TV REMOTE BROKE, HE FETCHED A MOP SO HE COULD CHANGE CHANNELS FROM THE COUCH!
©2004 MGN LTD VIA WWW.ANDYCAPP.COM
YOU MEAN, HE DIDN'T GET ***YOU*** TO FETCH IT?

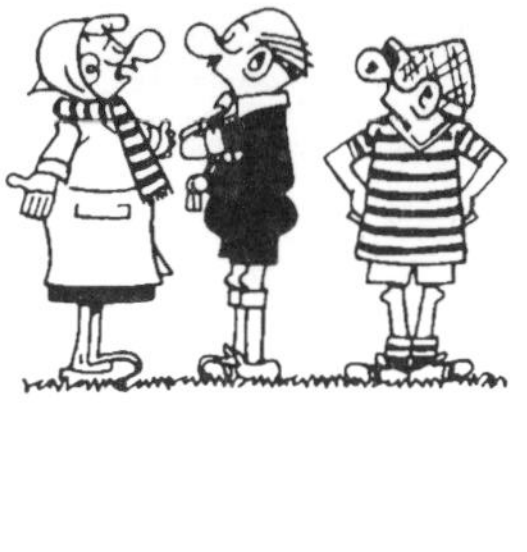